A Political History of Immigration in France

GLOBAL FRENCH HISTORIES

The *Global French Histories* series is an open-ended series of books that address the histories of modern France and the Francophone world in terms of key global themes since the mid-seventeenth century. Carefully situating French histories within global history frameworks, the series will foreground connections and networks across time and space, comparisons with other contexts and interdisciplinary approaches.

Forthcoming:
Roads out of French Empire: Resisting Imperialism in the 20th Century, Sarah C. Dunstan

A Political History of Immigration in France

From Colonial to Global, and Back

ANGÉLINE ESCAFRÉ-DUBLET

BLOOMSBURY ACADEMIC

LONDON · NEW YORK · OXFORD · NEW DELHI · SYDNEY

BLOOMSBURY ACADEMIC
Bloomsbury Publishing Plc, 50 Bedford Square, London, WC1B 3DP, UK
Bloomsbury Publishing Inc, 1359 Broadway, New York, NY 10018, USA
Bloomsbury Publishing Ireland, 29 Earlsfort Terrace, Dublin 2, D02 AY28, Ireland

BLOOMSBURY, BLOOMSBURY ACADEMIC and the Diana logo are trademarks of
Bloomsbury Publishing Plc

First published in Great Britain 2026

A catalogue record for this book is available from the British Library.

A catalog record for this book is available from the Library of Congress.

ISBN: HB: 978-1-3504-0772-5
PB: 978-1-3504-0771-8
ePDF: 978-1-3504-0773-2
eBook: 978-1-3504-0774-9

Typeset by Amnet
Printed and bound in Great Britain

Series: Global French Histories

For product safety related questions contact productsafety@bloomsbury.com.

To find out more about our authors and books visit www.bloomsbury.com
and sign up for our newsletters.

Contents

Preface

It is our pleasure to introduce Angéline Escafré-Dublet's *A Political History of Immigration in France*, accompanied by an afterword by Hana Qugana. This book is the first in our new Bloomsbury Global French History series, launched to showcase work that foregrounds global themes in histories of modern France and the Francophone world from the mid-seventeenth century. Carefully situating French and Francophone histories within global history frameworks, the series illuminates connections and networks across time and space, comparisons with other historical contexts and interdisciplinary approaches.

A rationale for the series

The series' starting point is the concept of new directions in interpretation, historiography and archival research. Chronologically, the series begins in the mid-seventeenth century with the 1648 Peace of Westphalia. Although not obvious at the time, this moment opened the way to French political and cultural dominance in mainland Europe and the wider world during the second half of the seventeenth century, as France replaced Spain as the major continental power.

At the same time, the settlement embodied within the Treaty of Westphalia contained a set of tensions around the national and the colonial that would come to be definitive in the modern world. This is because 1648 is central to the emergence and consolidation of the idea of national sovereignty and the political equality of states within Western and Central Europe. In the first instance, it brought to an end the Thirty Years War between Protestant and Catholic powers on the Continent by assigning each state exclusive authority within its territorial boundaries. Over the subsequent centuries, however, European states did not just exercise their sovereignty within the territorial boundaries of the national state. They also exerted power and violence over territories and populations elsewhere. Sovereignty was respected only in relation to other European powers and was not considered significant in encounters with peoples and lands beyond Europe. Indeed, as the legal scholar Antony Anghie argues, the doctrine of sovereignty was itself explicitly only a statement of the relation among European powers; one that saw the exercise of rule over non-European others as a continued expression of that sovereignty.[1]

Significantly, by adopting this much longer periodization, this series eschews more familiar chronological starting points (1789, 1815, 1871) to rethink and reorientate French and Francophone histories. By breaking down the divide between the early modern and the modern period, the series will, it is hoped, open up new understandings and connections across time regarding continuities, ruptures and changing contexts.

Moreover, this chronology resolutely locates French histories within this longer global and imperial moment, analysing them not in terms of a centralized French state expanding outwards across the globe, but as a complex part of a global conjuncture that was multi-directional, multi-layered and multi-polar. The French Empire and the Francophone world, therefore, will not be understood as extensions of France. Rather, they will be analysed as spaces that have been key to defining and redefining multiple, often conflicting histories in both the colonial and postcolonial eras. Throughout the series, we will consider French, French Empire, Francophone histories within a globally connected context, that is, how these histories were profoundly shaped and reshaped by much broader processes at the level of economics, culture and politics which transcended imperial and national boundaries. Consequently, the series underlines the importance of comparative histories, which deepen our understanding of France and the Francophone world by opening up complex questions of commonality and difference with other contexts since 1648.

Five key historical themes animate the series:

- changes across time and space, in other words, how and what particular shapes complex transformations took place across these histories;

- causation, that is, the short-term, medium-term and long-term reasons why transformations took place;

- connections between the cultural, social, intellectual, economic, gender, environmental, and political histories since 1648;

- power relations and how they operated at the level of culture, economics, politics, and society;

- representations and the changing role of communication and media.

---

[1] Antony Anghie, 'The Evolution of International Law: Colonial and Postcolonial Realities', *Third World Quarterly*, 27, no. 5, (2006): 739–53.

In considering these five themes, the series foregrounds an interdisciplinary approach that aims to cross disciplinary boundaries and reflect upon the ways that history engages with research in anthropology, art history, criminology, geography, international relations, literary studies, politics and sociology. Crucially, the series is also comparative. Each volume, therefore, will contain an afterword from another global historian focusing on a different geographical area, in which they will further reflect on the volume's key arguments, assessing similarities and differences across space.

Angéline Escafré-Dublet's *A Political History of Immigration in France*

Given this approach to our series, as editors, we are very pleased that this first volume by Angéline Escafré-Dublet focuses upon immigration in France and, indeed, begins in the seventeenth century with the Treaty of Westphalia. Within France and the wider contemporary world, immigration is a key subject, perhaps even the key contemporary subject, intimately connected to questions of global movement, global human rights and the assertion of national borders. The French political discourse around immigration has, as Escafré-Dublet so incisively puts it, since the 1980s become 'a catch-all phrase to discuss issues ranging from race-relations, secularism and the French model of citizenship' (p. 3).

The history of the French Museum of the History of Immigration in eastern Paris exemplifies the acute political sensitivities surrounding this immigration debate. Established by President Jacques Chirac during his second presidential mandate between 2002 and 2007, he envisaged the project as the French equivalent to New York's Ellis Island National Museum of Immigration. It was a means through which to celebrate immigration as a foundation stone of the country's history. It was believed that telling a positive story of French immigration history through the museum would promote inclusion, cohesion and anti-racism. As such, it would offer a powerful retort to the contemporary anti-immigrant discourse disseminated by Jean-Marie Le Pen and his supporters.

Tellingly, the whole initiative was shunned by Chirac's successor, President Nicolas Sarkozy. He refused to officially inaugurate the museum as a national institution because its message of migrant contribution did not appeal to the Le Pen voters he was assiduously trying to win over. Indeed, Sarkozy oversaw the establishment of the Ministry of Immigration and National Identity in 2007. This body, as Escafré-Dublet makes clear, institutionalized the process of 'making citizenship acquisition a means to regulate immigration' (p. 159). The announcement of the new ministry prompted all the academics involved in planning the museum to resign. They feared that it embedded the stigmatization of immigrants into ideas of French national identity, referring back to the rise of xenophobia in the 1930s that 'paved the way for the fall of democracy and the advent of the authoritarian Vichy regime (1940–1944)' (p. 159). The museum still opened in 2007, but the formal inauguration had to wait until December 2014, two and a half years after Socialist President François Hollande defeated Sarkozy in the May 2012 presidential elections.

President Hollande's election softened the tone of immigration rhetoric in France, but it did not usher in a sea change, politically or culturally. The rise, once more, of far-right and anti-immigrant discourse in French and European politics more broadly prompted the curators at the Museum of the History of Immigration to redesign its permanent exhibition. This process began with a specially commissioned report by the historians Romain Bertrand and Patrick Boucheron in conjunction with a forty-strong multidisciplinary team. Significantly, their final new vision was not only much more global in perspective but also attuned to the concept of the long view, one that foregrounded immigration and movement as a common historical thread, perhaps even the common historical thread, which has woven together in French society since the seventeenth century.[2] The realization of this vision was then handed over to a special committee, made up of Sébastien Gökalp, then director of the museum and four specially appointed experts in the field of immigration history – Marianne Amar, Emmanuel Blanchard, Delphine Diaz and Camille Schmoll.

On this basis, the exhibition reopened in June 2023 with a slate of publicity posters designed around the slogan 'It is incredible how many foreigners have made French history'. In the permanent exhibition's new schema, France is cast as a country of immigration, with a history punctuated by movement and mobility. It begins with the 1685 revocation of the Edict of Nantes, which had granted Protestants protected status in France, and the promulgation of the 'Black Code', which regulated enslaved people's lives, deaths, purchases, religion and treatment by their masters in the French Empire. It encompasses the arrival of Italian and Polish communities in the nineteenth century and Portuguese and Spanish-speaking communities in the twentieth, placing them amongst many other such arrivals and departures. Through the presentation of almost six hundred archival documents, sculptures, paintings and personal belongings, this portrait of over three hundred years of movement to, in and

---

[2]On the rationale and process behind the redesign, see 'Le musée de l'immigration revisité – entretien avec Delphine Diaz', *L'Histoire*, 16 June 2023, lhistoire.fr/entretien/le-musée-de -l'immigration-revisité.

around France allows visitors to see both the broad brush strokes of group migration as well as come to know the individual stories of the real people who make up this history. So, for example, in July 2024, in the midst of a snap general election where the immigration question was once again central, the Paris Mayor Anne Hidalgo entrusted the original copy of her French nationality certificate to the Museum. In an accompanying Instagram post, she then succinctly set out just exactly what this document meant to her in emotional terms, given her Spanish heritage: 'Like many children of immigrants, I've always feared losing and parting with this administrative act that proves my nationality'.[3]

In tandem with such primary sources, the permanent exhibition also carefully positions the work of thematically relevant artists held by the Museum at strategic points, including Algerian-French artists Zineb Sedira and Kader Attia, and Cameroonian artist Barthelemy Toguo, amongst many others, in order to pose questions about fragile status, citizenship and belonging, thereby opening up conversations between historical evidence and how these artists connect this evidence with their own personal histories. In so doing, it pushes back against the racialized fictions that have so defined French political discourse in the last seventy years: namely, that immigration to France is relatively new and synonymous with the arrival of people from Africa, Asia and the Caribbean.

Hana Qugana's evocative afterword to this book likewise emphasizes the human nature of migration, using the frame of Kidlat Tahimik's 1977 film *Perfumed Nightmare* to insist on the significance of understanding this movement through individual stories. Qugana is a historian of the oceanic South, focusing on Southeast Asia, the Pacific and the Philippines in the nineteenth and twentieth centuries. Using the film's central story of Kidlat – a Filipino jeepney driver – and his unlikely friendship with Lola, an elderly Parisian vendor, Qugana reflects on themes of solidarity, displacement and cultural hybridity during France's post-war period of decolonization and immigration. She reminds us that the categories of 'citizen', 'migrant' and 'native' do no justice to the reality of the communities that form in the process of migration, nor to their influence in shaping the Francophone world.

Qugana's essay is the perfect foil to Escafré-Dublet's book, offering a sample of 'micro-personal' migratory experiences to illustrate the 'macro-political context' so expertly laid out in *A Political History of Immigration in France*. Read together, the two works remind us of the importance of understanding immigration history as a dynamic interplay of personal stories and structural

---

[3]Anne Hidalgo cited by Roxana Azimi, 'Un an après sa réouverture, le Musée national de l'histoire de l'immigration fait le plein de visiteurs à Paris', *Le Monde*, 14 July 2024.

forces, where solidarity and exclusion coexist amid shifting global and local contexts. It puts us in mind of Frantz Fanon's declaration in his 1952 work, *Black Skin, White Masks*: 'In the world through which I travel, I am endlessly creating myself. I am a part of Being to the degree that I go beyond it'.[4]

---

[4]Frantz Fanon, *Black Skin, White Masks*, Trans. Charles Lam Markmann (Pluto Press, 1986 [Reprint, Seuils, 192]), 229.

Acknowledgements

Writing a synthesis of the subject of immigration in France has made me indebted to many historians who laid the foundations for what is now a key topic of study in the twenty-first century. Their works are referenced throughout the book, but I would like to thank in particular Marie-Claude Blanc-Chaléard, who first set out to write a synthesis of the subject more than twenty years ago. Our discussions have always inspired my own writing.

Historians do not hold a monopoly on the research on immigration in France. This book is the product of cross-disciplinary work and discussions, which have created a stimulating environment for my reflections over the years: teaching political science in Université Lumière Lyon 2; working with sociologists and demographers in the National Institute for Demographic Studies (INED); and sharing the task of coordinating scientific activities in the Institut Convergences Migrations (ICM). Across these different research sites, I am particularly indebted to Solène Brun, Florent Chossière, François Héran, Lionel Kesztenbaum, Narguesse Keyhani and Patrick Simon.

It was a humbling task to attempt to explain the history of immigration in France to English-speaking readers. I would like to thank Martin Evans for his generous invitation to contribute to the series on the Francophone world, and my colleagues outside France for showing their interest in the project. In particular, I would like to thank Emile Chabal for inviting me to join the project, 'A New Democratic (Dis)Order' on race, identity, and political mobilization in France and the UK, funded under the British Academy Knowledge Frontier scheme. Together with Rachida Brahim, Daniel Gordon, Alexander Hensby, Liam Liburd, Tim Peace, Camilla Schofield, Emilie Wiedemann and Virginie Guiraudon, they gave me the comparative perspective that is so useful for this subject.

Finally, I want to express my infinite gratitude to my family and close friends, for their time, understanding and support – all this would have never been possible without them.

Introduction

The politics of immigration history

The history of immigration in France is inextricably linked to the politics of immigration, as most French historiography of immigration began in the 1980s, as opposed to the demographic fact of immigration, which began in the mid-nineteenth century. In fact, as early as 1850, the country experienced slow population growth and low rates of population mobility.[1] As a result, the French economy could only meet the labour needs of the Industrial Revolution by relying on labour migration. Immigrants from neighbouring countries such as Belgium, Italy and Spain arrived and settled in France, making it Europe's oldest country of immigration.

The beginning of the twentieth century saw Europeans departing from Germany, the United Kingdom, Italy and the Scandinavian countries, to reach foreign shores, particularly those located along the American continent. France, however, was an exception. The total population of the country already included a significant number of foreigners (2.86 per cent in 1914). Moreover, when the United States government passed the Immigration Act of 1924, which set immigration quotas, the migratory flows from Eastern and Southern Europe shifted to France, so much so that, in the interwar period, the proportion of foreign-born residents in France was 6.6 per cent in 1931, and in the United States in 1940 it was 8.8 per cent. However, by contrast with American historians, who began to publish on the contribution of immigrants to the country as early as 1952,[2] French historians only began investigating immigration issues at the beginning of the 1980s.[3]

---

[1] Nancy L. Green, 'Filling the Void: Immigration to France, Before World War I', in *Labor Migration in the Atlantic Economies: The European and North American Working Classes During the Period of Industrialization*, ed. Dirk Hoerder (Westport, CT: Greenwood Press, 1985), 143–61.

[2] Oscar Handlin, *The Uprooted: The Epic Story of the Great Migrations That Made the American People*, 2nd ed. (Philadelphia: University of Pennsylvania Press, 1952).

[3] Philippe Rygiel, 'Archives et historiographie de l'immigration', *Migrances*, no. 33 (2009): 50–9.

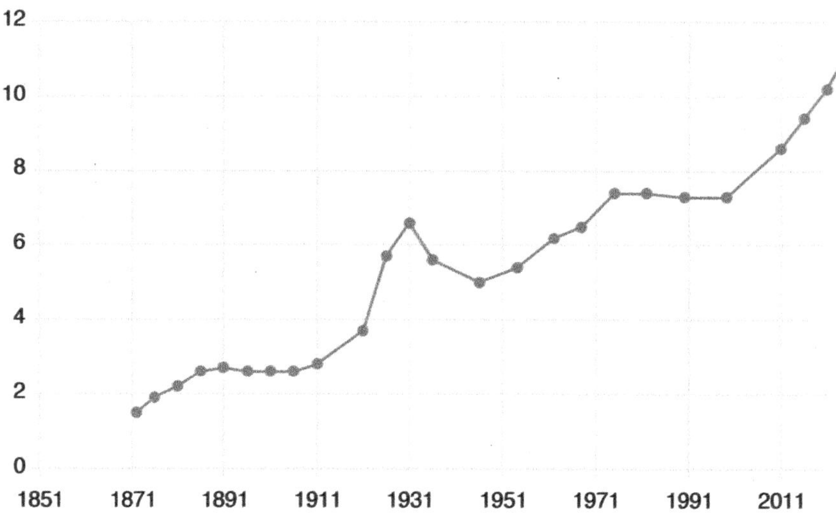

GRAPH 1 *Evolution of the proportion of immigrants in the French population (in per cent).*[4]

France's late start in the history of immigration comes from the way in which the topic of immigration has been politicized. In the 1980s, far-right politicians such as the leader of the National Front, Jean-Marie Le Pen, used anti-immigration rhetoric to attract more votes. As a result, mainstream politicians who wanted to stay in the race began systematically addressing immigration during their electoral campaigns. As a case in point, right-wing leader Jacques Chirac called for a reform of the nationality code in the run-up to the legislative election of 1986.[5] Once in office, he tasked the justice minister to come up with a bill that would reassess the automatic naturalization of immigrant children born in France. The bill was not passed amid protests against the reforms undertaken by the Chirac government. Nevertheless, the presentation of the nationality code reform as a response to issues of immigration and the settlement of immigrants in France was indicative of a shift in context. It was from that point on – and only from that point on – that the issue of immigration was inextricably intertwined with that of national identity and that immigration became a matter of national concern.[6]

The politicization of immigration in the 1980s resulted in a disconnect between the history of immigration as the movement of people to the

---

[4] There was no record of nationality in the 1856, 1861 and 1866 censuses.

[5] Patrick Weil, *La France et ses étrangers: L'aventure d'une politique de l'immigration de 1938 à nos jours* (Paris: Gallimard, 1991).

[6] Adrian Favell, *Philosophies of Integration: Immigration and the Idea of Citizenship in France and Britain*, 2nd ed. (New York: Palgrave Macmillan, 1998).

country and the topic of immigration, which is now one of the main issues affecting the public debate in France.[7] This book aims to reconnect these two developments and explain how immigration became a catch-all term for issues ranging from race relations, secularism and the French model of citizenship. It seeks to address the following questions: Why did it take so long for the French to realize that France was a country of immigration? And why, in the twenty-first century, do people self-identify according to their immigrant origin, rather than in terms of race or ethnicity? What role did colonization and decolonization play in the process? And how does that set France apart from other countries?

To answer these questions, the book focuses on the political dimension of immigration history in France. The central argument is that the politics of immigration redefined the country in the second half of the twentieth century. France has indeed gone from being a colonial empire, with territorial possessions progressively conquered on every continent, governing millions of people of different faiths and ethnicities, to whom different statuses applied, to a country of immigration, confined within its hexagonal borders, populated by individuals of diverse ethnic origins and where a single status applied: French citizenship.

To highlight the continuity and discontinuity before and after decolonization, the book adopts a long historical arch going back to the mid-seventeenth century. This is because the 1648 Peace of Westphalia, which put an end to years of conflicts in central Europe, also marked the beginning of a new world order. France replaced Spain as the new continental power, conquering and exerting authority over new territories and populations outside Europe. In doing so, the Kingdom of France initiated the first regulations that organized the relations between individuals based on status and skin colour: a set of regulations put together in 1685 and later labelled the Black Code.[8] Aimed at ensuring economic prosperity, in particular sugarcane production, the first attempts at policing the colonies are key to understanding the conditions under which the encounter with peoples and lands beyond Europe took place. As such, the book departs from usual chronological accounts of French political history in 1789. To be clear, the foundational moment of the French Revolution is part of the story, as it marked the definition of the French citizen. However, it is even more important to highlight the way citizenship was defined apart from any consideration regarding race and gender in 1789 – hence the necessity to eschew more familiar chronological starting points, such as 1789, and take the topic of immigration history as a way to disrupt the conventional timeline of French history.

---

[7] Emile Chabal, *France* (Oxford: Wiley, 2020).

[8] Frédéric Régent, 'Du préjugé de couleur au préjugé de race, le cas des Antilles françaises', *Revue d'histoire moderne & contemporaine* 68-3, no. 3 (2021): 64–90, https://doi.org/10.3917/rhmc.683.0066.

The book frames immigration as the movement of people to the country and their subsequent settlement into society. It examines the forced displacement of people from Africa during the transatlantic slave trade as part of the movement of people during the premodern era. However, it does not consider enslaved people as immigrants and only includes them as part of a discussion on the colonial encounter with non-European peoples. It also outlines the movement of people who left or settled in the French kingdom, even though they were not yet referred to as immigrants, because it helps to understand the origin of the naturalization process. The term immigration only appeared in the nineteenth century, at the time of the emergence of the nation-state. It refers to the action of coming to live in another country, where people do not possess a nationality. Moreover, the book includes the movement of people within the boundaries of the empire, such as colonial migrants and repatriates at the time of decolonization, because they challenge the boundaries of who is considered a citizen.

The organization of the book is chronological in order to show the changing nature of what immigration meant in a changing political landscape. A detailed focus on the post-war period explains why and how the French government responded to immigration: the (failed) attempts at immigrant selection, the management of colonial migrants and general attitudes towards immigrant reception. The Algerian War of Independence from 1954 to 1962 serves as a backdrop to a pivotal moment in immigration history: the unexpected surge in migration from the former colony and the challenge of the immigrants' reception. However, the concern for their reception and adaptation to French society later gave way to an economic one, in the wake of the 1973 oil shock. A deep dive into the politics of protest, in the wake of May '68, helps understand how activism contributed to the politics of immigration and immigrant claim-making in France.

The book takes a political perspective yet does not confine itself to a history of top-down immigration politics. It is interested in the circulation of ideas, how policymakers make decisions and how politics affect people's lives. It takes a social approach to political history, one that is interested not only in governmental actions and administrative officials but also in what drives people's political behaviours. It is based on first-hand research in the archives of the French administration (labour, social affairs and foreign affairs ministries) and on oral interviews with governmental and non-governmental actors. It portrays a variety of historical actors: politicians, administrative officials, social workers, activists, artists and citizens, who all inform the understanding of immigration issues today.

The broad framing of immigration reflects the language in use in France. The French national census defines immigrants as foreign-born who may or may not have acquired citizenship. As for their children born and raised in France, they are French citizens but are often referred to according to their immigrant background. They are also part of this story. The broad framing of immigration does not aim to flatten the heterogeneity of situations and experiences pertaining to immigration. On the contrary, the book contrasts the different experiences of immigrants born abroad, or in the French colonies; French people born in France of immigrant parents; and French people from the overseas departments of Guadalupe, Guyana, Martinique and Reunion. It seeks to explain why the French refer to immigrant origin – or even sometimes use the term 'origin' alone – rather than race or ethnicity to describe identities.

A broad understanding of the topic of immigration allows us to connect the history of immigration to that of racial formation and the consequences of decolonization in France. It highlights a series of debates and reactions to political events that may seem remote from immigration policy as such but that end up being linked to the topic of immigration, in practice. This is the case of the first headscarf affair of 1989 and the subsequent political and media debate on French secularism (*laïcité*). It is also apparent when considering the 2005 urban riots and the difficulty of mobilizing against discrimination in the French colour-blind context. As such, the book seeks to provide the necessary tools to envision several issues in French politics from the perspective of immigration history.

Finally, the choice to end the long chronological arch on the 2015 attacks aims to highlight the specificity of the French response to the global threat of terrorism. In particular, the governmental decision to articulate a discourse on Republican values. The book explains this decision in terms of the country's historical and political trajectory. In doing so, it lays to rest the notion of French exceptionalism and traces the origins of Republican ideas and how they came to be established.

This chapter presents the origins of French immigration historiography and argues that the ways in which French historians took an interest in immigration are revealing of the politicization of immigration in France. It was when the settlement of immigrants and their families began to attract media and political scrutiny that the first historical accounts appeared. Historians have sought to demonstrate the long-standing tradition of immigration and integration. However, this scholarship could not fully account for persistent xenophobia and racism. Another stream of research developed on the colonial dimension of immigration history and the consequences of decolonization on the state's response to immigrant permanent settlement. The development of immigration history in France did not operate in a vacuum. In particular, the outsiders call for a more global perspective on the history of France, which played a crucial role in the development of research on immigration in France.[9]

---

[9]Ann Laura Stoler, Frederick Cooper and Christian Jeanmougin, *Repenser le colonialisme* (Paris: Payot, 2013).

However, it is the development of French historiography from the inside that reveals what can be called the politics of immigration history in France. It is presented in the following two sections. A third section provides a brief overview of subsequent chapters.

The origins of French immigration historiography

The first book to take immigration history as its central topic is Gérard Noiriel's *The French Crucible* (*Le Creuset français*).[10] The author had completed a PhD dissertation on workers in the mining industry of northern France, under the supervision of labour historian Madeleine Rebérioux. He then published a book on the history of immigration in France, as a follow-up to some of the perspectives he had initiated during his doctoral research. It is not to say that labour historians had not already mentioned immigration, or more precisely, immigrant workers in their work.[11] However, it was not until the publication of *The French Crucible* that immigration featured as a key element of French society and history in a monograph.

In the title of the book, the term 'crucible' is a reference to the process of newcomers *melting* into a common national population and identity.[12] The ambition of such a title is twofold. First, it is a call for historians to place immigrants in the nation's memory and understand the history of France as that of a country of immigration. Second, it is a way to demonstrate that the making of foreigners into Frenchmen – to paraphrase Eugene Weber's Peasants into Frenchmen – had always happened, and would eventually take place, in the face of anti-immigrant rhetoric of the mid-1980s.[13]

---

[10]Gérard Noiriel, *Le Creuset français: Histoire de l'immigration XIXe-XXe siècle* (Paris: Seuil, 1988).
[11]Michelle Perrot, 'Les rapports des ouvriers français et des ouvriers étrangers, 1871–1893', *Bulletin de la Société d'Histoire Moderne*, 12, 1960; Yves Lequin, *Les ouvriers de la région lyonnaise (1848–1914)* (Lyon: University of Lyon Press, 1977).
[12]A translation of the book into English was published in 1996 and entitled *The French Melting Pot: Immigration, Citizenship, and National Identity*, for a more explicit reference to that process in the English language. For an investigation into the varying understanding of the phrase *melting pot* across the United States and France, see Nancy L. Green, 'Le Melting-Pot: Made in America, Produced in France', *Journal of American History* 86, no. 3 (1999): 1188–208.
[13]Eugen Weber, *Peasants into Frenchmen: The Modernization of Rural France, 1870–1914* (Stanford, CA: Stanford University Press, 1976).

The same can be said of Yves Lequin's history of foreigners, published the same year.[14] The labour historian who edited the volume – a series of chapters authored by various historians from the Roman Empire to twentieth century France – chose the title *The French Mosaïc* (La Mosaïque France) and began the foreword with the following sentence: 'Raising the issue of foreigners in France at the end of the twentieth century should come as no surprise: it occupies the written word, the speeches and the minds of many people, probably far too much so'.[15] The accusation of presentism – the tendency to approach issues from the past with the concern of the present – is a strong impediment for historians. In this case, however, the rise of anti-immigrant rhetoric justified overcoming this obstacle and initiating a new field of research.[16] Along these lines, historian Ralph Schor published an analysis of French public opinion on foreigners, from 1919 to 1939, that aimed at putting in perspective rising racism and political feuds of the 1980s.[17]

Most of the historiography on immigration that developed in the 1980s and the 1990s followed a common pattern: highlighting the central role of immigration in the making of the nation and demonstrating the integration of immigrants into French society. Several historians researched the history of a group of immigrants of the same origin, in the same location, sometimes even in the same profession: Janine Ponty wrote a history of Polish immigrants who signed contracts to come and work in agriculture and mining industry in northern France; Nancy Green compared Jewish garment workers who came and settled in Paris and in New York; Marie-Claude Blanch-Chaléard investigated the integration of Italian immigrants into the Parisian urban fabric and Geneviève Dreyfus-Armand researched Spanish Republicans exiles in France.[18] Most of this initial work focused on European migration waves of the interwar period, when the number of foreigners living in France reached a peak.[19] Their research demonstrated that foreigners did assimilate and become

---

[14]Yves Lequin, *La Mosaïque France: histoire des étrangers et de l'immigration* (Paris: Larousse, 1988).

[15]Lequin, *La Mosaïque France*, 5.

[16]Gérard Noiriel, 'Histoire de l'immigration en France. État des lieux, perspectives d'avenir', *Hommes & migrations* 1255, no. 1 (2005): 38–48.

[17]Ralph Schor, *L'opinion française et les étrangers en France, 1919–1939* (Paris: Sorbonne, 1985).

[18]Janine Ponty, *Polonais méconnus: Histoire des travailleurs immigrés en France dans l'entre-deux-guerres, Polonais méconnus: Histoire des travailleurs immigrés en France dans l'entre-deux-guerres,* Internationale (Paris: Sorbonne, 1988); Nancy L. Green, 'La mode en production: la confection et les immigrés, Paris-New York, 1880–1980' (doctoral thesis, Paris 7, 1996); Marie-Claude Blanc-Chaléard, 'Les Italiens dans l'Est parisien des années 1880 aux années 1960: une histoire d'intégration' (doctoral thesis, Paris, Institut d'études politiques, 1995); Geneviève Dreyfus-Armand, *L'exil des républicains espagnols en France. De la guerre civile à la mort de franco* (Paris: Albin Michel, 1999).

[19]Philippe Rygiel, 'Mais où sont les immigrés d'antan?: trajectoires sociogéographiques des membres des familles issues de l'immigration européenne implantées dans le Cher durant l'entre-deux-guerres' (doctoral thesis, Besançon, 1996).

French in the interwar period, when they resided in France in comparable proportions (6.6 per cent in 1931 and 6.8 per cent in 1982).

However, evidence of the assimilationist power of the French melting pot could not dissipate concerns about immigration issues, nor could it fully explain the persistence of xenophobia and racism in society – another stream of research developed in the 1990s. Scholars set about exploring the consequences of decolonization and the state's response to immigration after the end of the Second World War.

The colonial dimension of immigration in France

Historians and social scientists conducted research on the politics of immigration, including Algerian immigration in the post-war period. For instance, Patrick Weil established a historical account of French immigration policy since 1938.[20] Vincent Viet, a historian of social affairs, traced the way the French administration governed immigration from 1914 onwards and demonstrated how Algerian immigration impacted this process.[21]

Algerians were indeed the second largest group of immigrants after Portuguese immigrants in 1975; and in 2022, one out of three immigrants was born in North Africa.[22] Yet it is too often assumed that policymakers sought to 'tap the reservoir of colonial labour' and to appeal to colonial migrants to fill the need in the labour force of the post-war period.[23] In fact, Algerians exercised their right to enter France freely as citizens of a French Overseas Department from 1947 to 1962. As a result, the French administration had no other choice than to govern these newcomers as its own citizens, which prompted a series of adjustments in the structure of the administration.

To be sure, France was not the only country to experience an increase in colonial migrants in the post-war period. The United Kingdom also created the Citizenship of the United Kingdom and the Colonies in 1948. As a result, British citizens from the New Commonwealth also exercised their right to enter Great Britain freely. Between 1955 and 1962, 200,000 colonial migrants

---

[20]Weil, *La France et ses étrangers.*
[21]Vincent Viet, *La France immigrée: Construction d'une politique 1914–1997* (Paris: Fayard, 1998).
[22]In 1975, 711,000 Algerians and 759,000 Portuguese lived in France; in 2022, 29 per cent of immigrants living in France were born in North Africa. Source: INSEE.
[23]Randall Hansen, 'Migration to Europe since 1945: Its History and Its Lessons', *Political Quarterly* 74, no. s1 (2003): 25–38.

(mainly from the West Indies: Jamaica, Trinidad and Barbados; and Asia: India and Pakistan) settled in the United Kingdom. Similarly, between 1954 and 1962, the French census indicated that the number of Algerians rose from 212,000 to 354,000.

However, the conversion of administrative structures to colonial migration regimes is a distinctive feature of the French administration. Its analysis is crucial in understanding immigration governance in post-war France. In particular, it explains why the period has been at the core of numerous historical inquiries into the governance of immigrant housing, labour regimes, social aid, policing, naturalization or cultural adaptation.[24] They all show how the governance of Algerian immigration served as a template for the decades that followed and how the analysis of decolonization is central to the understanding of immigration policies afterwards.

Moreover, the history of French immigration is closely related to that of the colonial empire. Immigrants who arrived in France in the 1960s and 1970s came from countries that had formerly been part of the French Empire in North Africa (Algeria, Morocco and Tunisia), Africa (Senegal and Mali) or Asia (Vietnam, Laos and Cambodia). Moreover, it has been argued that how immigration has been framed as an issue and immigrants as problematic parallels the way colonial administrators distanced themselves from colonial subjects.[25]

However, legislative decisions often stir debates over how to approach the colonial dimension of immigration in France. 2001 saw the passing of the Taubira law that established slavery and the slave trade as a crime against humanity. In the following years, a political and media debate emerged over the project to reform the school curriculum. A group of elected representatives in the National Assembly advocated for the addition of a provision to emphasize, what they called, 'positive aspects' of colonialism.[26] The provision was later

---

[24]Marc Bernardot, *Loger les immigrés: La Sonacotra 1956–2006* (Bellecombe-en-Bauges: Croquant, 2008); Choukri Hmed, 'Loger les étrangers "isolés" en France: socio-histoire d'une institution d'État: la Sonacotra (1956–2006)' (doctoral thesis, Paris 1, 2006); Laure Pitti, 'Ouvriers algériens à Renault-Billancourt, de la guerre d'Algérie aux grèves d'OS des années 1970: contribution à l'histoire sociale et politique des ouvriers étrangers en France' (doctoral thesis, Paris 8, 2002); Françoise de Barros, 'L'état au prisme des municipalités: Une comparaison historique des catégorisations des étrangers en France (1919–1984)' (doctoral thesis, Paris 1, 2004); Amelia H. Lyons, *The Civilizing Mission in the Metropole: Algerian Families and the French Welfare State during Decolonization* (Stanford, CA: Stanford University Press, 2013); Emmanuel Blanchard, *La police parisienne et les Algériens* (Paris: Nouveau Monde, 2011); Alexis Spire, *Etrangers à la carte* (Paris: Grasset, 2005); Angéline Escafré-Dublet, *Culture et immigration. De la question sociale à l'enjeu politique, 1958–2007* (Rennes: University of Rennes Press, 2014).

[25]Sylvain Laurens and Choukri Hmed, *L'invention de l'immigration*, Agone. Histoire, politique et sociologie 40 (Marseille: Agone, 2008).

[26]Stiina Loytomaki, *Law and the Politics of Memory: Confronting the Past* (London: Routledge, 2014).

repealed. However, it demonstrated the enduring presence of an uncritical perspective on colonization among politicians.[27]

The debate in the National Assembly prompted reactions in academia. Several historians and social scientists have argued for the need to acknowledge a deep 'colonial divide' in French society and widespread colonial mindset on issues such as urban segregation, religious diversity or the construction of national identity.[28] However, other scholars have called the appeal to decolonize institutions 'premature' and pointed out the necessity to demonstrate the continuity of institutional practices in the administration of immigrants to begin with.[29]

Finally, immigration from Southern European countries, particularly Portugal, has continued well into the 1960s and 1970s, so much so that focusing only on postcolonial migration does not capture the full picture of French immigration history in the second half of the twentieth century. As such, the comparative perspective between Portuguese and Algerian immigrants in the 1960s and 1970s provides insight into the better treatment European immigrants received, compared to non-Europeans.[30] As a result, the political history of immigration in France includes a colonial perspective but is not limited to it.

Finally, the first decade of the twenty-first century has seen a rise in calls for greater inclusion of the category of race in understanding the pervasive structure of inequality in France.[31] Despite the French universalist principle that all individuals are equal regardless of race, origin or religion, the analysis of socioeconomic inequalities requires consideration of race, or as it is often phrased in French, the racial issue (*la question raciale*).[32]

The word 'race' itself carries a strong stigma in France.[33] It comes from the period after the Second World War, when the suppression of the word race seemed the preferred option to combat racism and the principle of hierarchy between individuals based on biological differences.[34] In contrast to what has

---

[27]Eric Savarese, *L'ordre Colonial et Sa Légitimation en France Métropolitaine* (Paris: L'Harmattan, 1998).

[28]Pascal Blanchard, Nicolas Bancel and Sandrine Lemaire, *La fracture coloniale: La société française au prisme de l'héritage colonial* (Paris: La Découverte, 2006).

[29]'La colonie rapatriée', *Politix* 76, no. 4 (2006): 3–7. https://doi.org/10.3917/pox.076.0003.

[30]Victor Pereira, 'Une migration favorisée. Les représentations et pratiques étatiques vis-à-vis de la migration Portugaise en France (1945–1974)', in *L'étranger en questions du moyen âge à l'an 2000*, ed. Marie-Claude Blanc-Chaléard, Stéphane Dufoix and Patrick Weil (*Paris, Le Manuscrit*, 2005).

[31]Tyler Stovall, 'Universalisme, différence et invisibilité. Essai sur la notion de race dans l'histoire de la France contemporaine', trad. Maurice Genty, *Cahiers d'histoire. Revue d'histoire critique*, no. 96–7 (2005): 63–90, https://doi.org/10.4000/chrhc.956.

[32]Didier Fassin and Eric Fassin, *De la question sociale à la question raciale?* (Paris: La Découverte, 2009).

[33]Solène Brun and Claire Cosquer, *Sociologie de la race* (Malakoff: Armand Colin, 2022).

[34]Alana Lentin, *Racism and Anti-Racism in Europe* (London: Pluto, 2004).

happened in American and British academia, therefore, race has not been used to refer to the social construction of difference in much of the scholarship produced on migration-related issues, not least in the history of immigration.[35]

However, historians have called for greater inclusion of the category of race to better understand power dynamics and their change over time.[36] Historians working on France from abroad have already resorted to that type of categorization to refer to the racialization of Islam in twentieth-century France, for instance.[37] Race, therefore, appears as an operational category that is now used to refer to the official construction of difference in the French context, even though the term did not appear in official discourse at the time.[38]

Chapters overview

The book explores immigration in France from the early modern period onwards. Its central argument is that the politics of immigration redefined the nation, transforming it from a colonial empire to a country of immigration. It shows that this can only be understood by going back to some founding moments in French history when immigration was not a political issue. As such, chapters one and two cover a period during which most of the movement of people resulted from the push and pull of the economy (1648–1945).

Chapter 1 introduces the question of movement in French history within a global perspective (1648–1870). It situates the French Empire as a space of circulation in and out of its evolving boundaries and considers the push and pull of economic migration flows in this period. It distinguishes the early modern period, when the status of foreigners in the Kingdom of France was understood in relation to the king, from the modern period after 1789, when it was defined in terms of citizenship and belonging to the nation-state. The chapter also discusses the largest movement of people, which was the displacement of one million enslaved people from the American continent to the French West Indies. It highlights the necessity of engaging with the larger

---

[35]Erik Bleich, *Race Politics in Britain and France: Ideas and Policymaking Since the 1960s* (Cambridge: Cambridge University Press, 2003).

[36]Jean-Frédéric Schaub and Silvia Sebastiani, *Race et histoire dans les sociétés occidentales (XV-XVIIIe siècle)* (Paris: Albin Michel, 2021).

[37]Naomi Davidson, *Only Muslim: Embodying Islam in Twentieth-Century France* (Ithaca, NY: Cornell University Press, 2012).

[38]Laure Pitti, *Algériens au travail, une histoire (post)coloniale: Enquête sur les travailleurs immigrés de l'industrie automobile dans la France des 'Trente Glorieuses'* (Rennes: University of Rennes Press, 2025).

questions posed by global history and changing our perspective on the history of immigration in France, in relation to the history of the French Empire. In particular, the chapter discusses how citizenship was defined apart from any consideration of race, despite the continued presence of Black people on French soil since the eighteenth century.

Chapter 2 highlights the gap between the establishment of the republic in France and the pursuit of the colonial conquest (1870–1940). It sets out the history of the movement of people to the country against other developments, such as colonization and the establishment of the French Republic, as they later contributed to shaping the politicization of immigration. The chapter offers some explanations as to how democratization could harbour such a paradox as the pursuit of the colonial conquest. In particular, it explains how Republicans developed a colonial empire to maintain France's position in a Europe ruled by emperors (e.g. Queen Victoria, German Emperor Wilhelm I, Tsar Alexander II of Russia and Emperor Franz Joseph of Austria). Moreover, the empire proved essential during the First and Second World Wars, for it provided France with more troops and resources to fight its enemies. However, common narratives do not always give full credit to the contribution of foreigners and colonials to the victory, which explains the dynamics of exclusion that later shook French political life.

After the end of the Second World War, immigration flows intensified, and so did political regulations. Chapters 3 to 6 analyse the emergence of immigration policies: the definition of migration regimes, the management of immigrant reception and the beginning of immigration restrictions, in a context of political protests (1945–88).

Chapter 3 locates France in the turmoil of the post-war period (1945–54), with people on the move, economies in disarray and a change in political regimes. It shows how the need to regulate migration led French policymakers to decide and define the migrants they wanted and, in doing so, to outline a new narrative of what Frenchmen and Frenchwomen should be. One distinctive feature of the post-war period was the new relevance of national and international political dynamics in shaping population flows as opposed to the push and pull of the economy, until then. The chapter examines the post-war definition of three types of migration regimes: labour, colonial and refugee migration regimes. Moreover, the chapter analyses the influx of colonial subjects to the Metropole and their reception in French society.

Chapter 4 looks at the dismantling of the French Empire and analyses how the decolonization period contributed to shaping a general narrative of immigration in France as a necessary, yet temporary phase (1954–68). It shows how this resulted in the exclusion of postcolonial immigrants from national identity. The chapter starts with the Algerian War and how the Fourth Republic (1944–58) thought to oversee the colonial migrant population in

France. It highlights the differential treatment adopted towards European (mainly Italian, Spanish and Portuguese) versus postcolonial (mainly Algerian, but also Moroccan, Tunisian and sub-Saharan African) migrants. To illustrate this difference in treatment, the chapter analyses the views of the authorities, experts and organizations involved in managing the reception of immigrants in France. It shows how the colonial regime of racial distinction turned into an immigration regime of racial preference for European migrants after the end of the Algerian War in 1962. It highlights the redefinition of the civilizing mission of the French Empire into the need to assimilate immigrants in the Fifth Republic, which began in 1958.

Chapter 5 is set in the wake of May '68, amid political contestation and the emergence of new social movements (1968–81). It shows how the 1970s were a decade of political turmoil and also when the politicization of immigration really began. The participation of immigrants in the French social movement and their progression towards an autonomous movement is connected to global turmoil in and out of Europe. Between pan-Africanism and leftist ideologies, the emergence of a movement for the defence of migrants' rights is key to understanding the transformation of French political life at the time. Moreover, in a context of European immigration restrictions (France, but also Germany, and the United Kingdom stopped free economic migration, following the 1973 oil crisis), political protest and state restrictions paved the way for the rearticulation of the link between immigration and national identity.

Chapter 6 examines the political change of 1981 when Socialist Mitterrand became president (1981–9). It analyses the brief moment of the *differentialist* turn in France and how it changed immigrants' lives. The moment was short-lived, however, as discrimination and racist attacks did not stop. In this respect, the organization of the 1983 March for Equality and Against Racism was a moment of political empowerment for many descendants of immigrants. Yet, the National Front reversed the rhetoric of the Right to Difference to an exclusive one. The chapter shows how anti-immigrant rhetoric began to be a winning ticket to power for both far-right and right-wing candidates. It explains why the left-wing government ultimately chose not to deal with difference, relegating antiracist politics to the realm of protest and resistance.

In 1989, France entered the global age of migration, with an intensification of migration flows, of its population diversity and of the global threat of terrorism. Chapters 7 and 8 examine the general social politicization of immigration in response to these issues (1989–2015).

Chapter 7 analyses how France entered the global age of migration, standing by its national values of universalism and secularism (1989–2004). It starts with the first headscarf affair of 1989 and situates France in the larger context of rising extremism in the world. It analyses the media and political debate, the passing of new legislation, and the reactions of citizens and political protest. The chapter locates the French case among its European counterparts to expose the common challenges versus the specific national responses of countries of immigration. It highlights a common feature of immigration countries at the turn of the twenty-first century: the attempt to define a commonness in the face of the demographic fact of superdiversity. In France, it took the shape of reaffirming French secularism and defining 'integration' as central to national identity.

Chapter 8 analyses how French citizenship was profoundly challenged in its egalitarian and universal foundations (2005–15). It begins with the 2005 riots and how they led to greater recognition of the discrimination faced by the descendants of immigrants from North and sub-Saharan Africa. However, the intense politicization of immigration that followed the creation of a ministry of immigration and national identity in 2007 has not helped to solve the problem. On the contrary, political decisions on immigration, the control of migration flows and religious diversity ended up increasing the polarization of public opinion on the issue. When the terrorist attacks of 2015 took place, the inclusive and universalist discourse of the then left-wing government did little to prevent an increase in anti-Muslim attacks.

Finally, the conclusion highlights some of the key developments underpinning the politics of immigration in France and connects the political history of immigration to personal histories. Based on oral history interviews, it argues that the politics of immigration is as central to political debate as it is to social interactions. Reference to immigration as a background or an origin is crucial to self-identification and self-presentation. Moreover, research interviews reveal a desire to locate one's family history in a larger narrative. However, there are contrasting responses to the issue of immigration, which is plagued by intense politicization and negative framing.

1

Europeans on the move, 1648–1870

In the early modern period, the Kingdom of France was characterized by three different types of population movements of varying proportions: the settlement of foreigners for economic reasons (tens of thousands); the departure of Protestants fleeing religious persecutions (several hundred thousand) and the displacement of captives from the African continent to the French West Indies (one million). These different types of population movement resulted from different processes: the push and pull of the economy – as most Europeans, people moved to acquire new land or seek agricultural work across the countryside;[1] the government of newly conquered territories in the West Indies, Africa and Asia; the end of absolutist monarchy in 1789 and the military conquests of Napoleon Bonaparte, King Louis-Philippe and Napoleon III.

This chapter shows that from 1648 to 1870, France was a space of circulation, even though immigration was not a topic of political interest, nor even a word in use at the time. However, it was a crucial period during which major political decisions were made regarding the status of foreigners, the definition of citizenship and the status of enslaved people in the French West Indies. They determined long-lasting patterns in how race and religion shape the politics of immigration in France.

The chapter first deals with the early modern period, when religious conflict forced the departure of hundreds of thousands of French Protestants and the Kingdom of France engaged in the slave trade. It then turns to the French Revolution, during which political citizenship was introduced without much consideration for non-European populations in the French colony. It finally explains the modifications in the definition of French citizenship, amid successive regime changes and ongoing colonial expansion.

---

[1]Leslie Page Moch, *Moving Europeans: Migration in Western Europe Since 1650*, 2nd ed., Interdisciplinary Studies in History (Bloomington: Indiana University Press, 2003).

Religious conflict, economic migration and the slave trade, 1648–1789

The 1648 Peace of Westphalia established a new system of political order based on the concept of coexisting sovereign states in Europe. Because it marks the end of years of conflicts in central Europe, it often directs the study of early modern French political history to events in Europe. However, the conquest of new territories outside Europe requires a global perspective when analysing the movements of people, whether driven by economic logic or by religious conflicts.

Religious tension was high on the agenda of the French monarchy throughout the early modern period. The departure of Huguenots – the name adopted to refer to French Protestants who followed the teaching of Calvin – began during the period of persecution before the 1572 Saint Barthélemy massacre, when thousands of Protestants were killed in Paris and other cities. What is referred to as the 'first refuge' consisted of the departure of French Protestants to London, Geneva and the United Provinces (now the Netherlands). The movement ceased after the 1598 Edict of Nantes, which granted Protestants the freedom of worship. However, in 1685, Louis XIV signed the Edict of Fontainebleau, which banned the public practice of Protestantism in France. 'One king, one law, one faith': it was in the name of this principle that French Protestants were ordered to convert to Catholicism. Faced with persecution, more than a quarter of them preferred to go into exile, leading to the second or 'great refuge' of the seventeenth century.

How many Huguenots left France in the seventeenth century? Like many stories of hiding, the history of the great Protestant refuge is a search for sources. Fugitives did not report their departure. As for those who took them in, they tended to overstate the numbers. One thing is certain, however: the Reformed community in France numbered eight hundred thousand people, and a significant proportion of them fed the many internal resistance movements, particularly in the south.[2] Meticulous work based on arrival registers estimates that a total of two hundred thousand left, which represents a quarter of French Protestants.[3] The losses *en route* were undoubtedly significant, but it remains impossible to measure their scale, as the 1685 Edict of Revocation prohibited departures and forced fugitives into hiding. Otherwise, men were sent to the galleys and women to prison.

---

[2] Philippe Joutard, 'La diaspora des huguenots', *Diasporas. Histoire et sociétés* 1, no. 1 (2002): 115–21.

[3] Samuel Mours, *Le Protestantisme en France du XVIIIe siècle à nos jours* (Paris: Librairie protestante, 1972).

Where did Huguenots go? Following a chain-migration pattern, the departure of French Protestants follows the path set by their sixteenth-century predecessors. They went to Holland, Switzerland, England and Prussia. However, as new territories were conquered and opportunities for settlement developed, the exile of the Huguenots took on a global dimension. Some went as far as southern Africa and the British colonies in the New World.

Insofar as the France of the absolute monarchy was a place of persecution for the Protestants, it also served as a place of protection for the Catholics who were persecuted in their own country. For instance, the Jacobites were English, Scottish and Irish supporters of the Catholic King James II, ousted by the 1688 English Revolution, who joined their monarch after he took refuge in France.

The absolutist monarchy of the early modern period took a rather favourable view of foreigners who settled in France. The kingdom attracted merchants, peddlers, farmers and craftspeople from neighbouring countries. It also called on the services of highly qualified foreign specialists: Italian artists and bankers, Dutch and Castilian merchants and shipowners, typographers and gunsmiths from across the Rhine, for instance. However, they were subject to specific restrictions and taxation. They were forbidden to acquire an office (an administrative position granted by the king) or work in banking and brokerage. They were subject to the law of *aubaine*, which allowed the king to seize the property of foreigners who had died without heirs born in France. A minority were exempt from this duty, whether they lived in port or border towns, or had obtained a naturalization letter (*lettre de naturalité*).

Between the end of the sixteenth century and the French Revolution, the king received an average of around fifty requests for naturalization letters per year, which were often granted. This low number can be explained in part by the very costly process of making a request. In order to obtain it, a number of conditions had to be met: permanent residence in France (for at least one year), economic prosperity and a social base in the Kingdom of France, which the letter helped to increase. In practice, these letters did not radically change the status of foreigners, as they were still subject to taxes on foreigners. However, they were able to avoid the impossibility of holding royal offices and ecclesiastical benefices in the kingdom, as well as the inability to inherit or transmit property.

Finally, in March 1685, exactly the same year as the Edict of Fontainebleau and as part of an attempt to affirm the supremacy of royal power over religious practices, Louis XIV passed a decree (later labelled as the Black Code) on the policing of the islands of French America. Initiated three years before, by First Minister of State Jean-Baptiste Colbert, and bringing together almost fifty years of regulations based on local customs and case law, the decree regulated the status of enslaved people and their relations with their masters while also reaffirming the supremacy of the practice of one religion, Catholicism. Based on this principle, Jewish families established in the colonies had to leave.[4]

The so-called Black Code mainly regulated the status of enslaved people to ensure the economic prosperity of the West Indies, in particular sugarcane production, and did not mention race, nor the terms Black or white but rather the terms masters and slaves.[5] Nonetheless, it established a racial order in the new territories conquered by the French kingdom insofar as it organized relations between individuals based on status and skin colour.[6] Thus, the expression 'free person of colour' referred to freedmen or descendants of freedmen, who did not have the same rights as white French citizens. Finally, the publication in 1718 of a treaty that brought together the ordinances that applied in the various territories of the colonies, entitled the Black Code, leaves little doubt about the link contemporaries drew between skin colour and status, back in metropolitan France.

In terms of numbers, the slave trade represents the largest movement of people in the kingdom during the early modern period. Between 1713 and 1791, one million African captives were sold into slavery and deported to the West Indies, including 773,000 to Saint-Domingue (now Haïti), 217,000 to Martinique and 73,000 to Guadeloupe. So much so that, on the eve of the French Revolution, enslaved people represented more than 80 per cent of the population of the French West Indies. The French were the third largest slave traders, following the Portuguese and the British, who dominated the transatlantic slave trade in the eighteenth century. Le Havre was France's major slave-trading port, followed by Nantes, Bordeaux and La Rochelle. The harbours outfitted ships that transported captives from Africa to the Caribbean islands and the Mississippi Delta, including Louisiana.

In principle, there were no enslaved people in metropolitan France, because the land of the Franks was supposed to set people free. As a result, when slave owners travelled back to France with enslaved people and did not come back to the colonies, the latter became free and formed a Black community. At first, there were not enough of them to cause the government any worry. However, in 1777, a declaration by the king prohibited the introduction into the kingdom of 'Blacks, mulattoes or other coloured people'. Those who arrived despite this ban were arrested and taken to depots, where they were then shipped back to the colonies. Those who had already settled, and, for

---

[4]Patrick Boucheron, *Histoire mondiale de la France* (Paris: Média Diffusion, 2017).

[5]'The term "negro" was used seven times in the edict of March 1685. The term "master" was used sixty-one times but did not refer only to people of European origin, since slave owners could also be non-white' (translated by the author), in Régent, 'Du préjugé de couleur au préjugé de race, le cas des Antilles françaises', 76.

[6]Cécile Vidal, 'Francité et situation coloniale. Nation, empire et race en Louisiane française (1699–1769)', *Annales. Histoire, Sciences Sociales* 64, no. 5 (2009): 1019–50.

some of them, were blood relations of slave owners, had to register before a royal judge. As a result of this compulsory registration, historians estimated that two thousand Black people lived in Paris from 1777 to 1790 and three thousand across all of France (mainly in port cities, such as Bordeaux and Nantes).[7] Most of them were domestics, and their master registered them with the promise that they would return to the colonies soon, but some were craftspeople and held jobs. Although they were far fewer in number than Black people living in the colonies, they proved the existence of a Black presence in France, dating back to the eighteenth century.

The French Revolution of 1789

In 1789, the French Revolution introduced political citizenship, based on the recognition of civil and political rights. With the Declaration of the Rights of Man and of the Citizen, the king's subjects became citizens. Up until then, foreigners could settle in France and even receive a naturalization letter but never become subjects of the Kingdom of France. After the French Revolution of 1789, foreigners could become French citizens provided they took a civic oath and had resided continuously in the country for five years. In other words, starting in 1789, foreigners could naturalize and become French nationals.

The French Revolution ushered in a new era in which it became more important to embrace the new political order than to cling to where a person was born and raised. Guy-Jean-Baptiste Target, a lawyer and representative in the 1790 Constituent Assembly, introduced the decree that allowed foreigners to become French (Decree Target of April 1790). It stipulated that those who had 'worked for freedom' could obtain exceptional naturalization and citizenship. As a result, Thomas Paine, a British-born philosopher and revolutionary, who fled to France in 1792, became a French citizen and was elected to the national Convention in September 1792. By contrast, almost 150,000 French emigrants, who hoped for the return of the monarchy and had fled to neighbouring countries, were stripped of their civil rights and deprived of their property.

Born during the 1789 revolution, the French definition of citizenship is marked by the specific context of the end of absolutism and the advent of a new political order. It is articulated in diametric opposition to everything that was part of the Old Regime, such as the ties that united aristocratic families with the nobility of other European countries, the privileges of birth

---

[7]Richard Brace and Joan Brace, 'The Black Community in Paris: 1777–1790', *Centennial Review* 21, no. 4 (1977): 374–81.

and the notion of intermediary bodies (such as the nobility or the Catholic clergy). The 1789 Declaration of the Rights of Man and of the Citizen called for the destruction of aristocratic privileges. As for the 1791 Le Chapelier law, it enshrined the vertical relationship between each citizen and the state. It banned guilds and group representation. It was also the principle that guided the emancipation of French Jews in Paris (1790) and then in France (1791). Deputies of the National Assembly, such as Robespierre, argued for granting citizenship to 'a multitude of men who live in our midst'. In return, Jews would not form any specific group or political body: '[The Jews] must not form in the State either a political body or an order; they must be individual citizens'.[8] This helped forge the notion of France as a civic nation. In other words, a nation to which everyone could belong, regardless of their origin or religion, as long as they recognized its founding values of justice and equality.

As a result of the new definition of citizenship, regardless of origin or religion, French Protestants who had fled during the great refuge were eligible to return and become French citizens, as well as retrieve their property. In practice, few did, except for one famous returnee, Benjamin Constant, who returned in 1795 and became a major political thinker and a representative in the French Legislative Chamber from 1819 to 1830.

The universal access to citizenship was granted only to free white males, however. First, the Declaration of the Rights of Man and of the Citizen did not apply to women. Olympe de Gouges made this clear in the text she published in 1791, The Declaration of the Rights of Woman and of the Female Citizen in France, and she asked for the Constituent Assembly to accept, to no avail. Not only was her appeal to recognize the failure of the French Revolution to address gender equality disregarded, but Olympe de Gouges was suspected of defending the monarchy because she had dedicated the text to Queen Marie-Antoinette. Later perceived as too moderate a supporter of the French Revolution, she was therefore arrested and sentenced to death by guillotine on 3 November 1793.

Second, when the destruction of aristocratic privileges was discussed in the Constituent Assembly, the question of slavery was barely touched upon.[9] It was the 1791 revolt in Saint-Domingue (now Haïti) that brought the first official abolition of slavery in 1793, in the hope of rallying rebellious slaves to the Republican cause. The decision applied first to Saint-Domingue and was extended to the whole of France in 1794. In practice, historians argue that introducing the concept of equality between citizens made racial distinction

---

[8] Archives of the National Assembly, 23 December 1789, 756. Translation by the author.
[9] Ian Coller, Manuel Covo, Bruno Maillard, Jennifer Palmer, Karine Rance, Éric Saunier and Cécile Vidal, 'Race et Révolution française', *Annales historiques de la Révolution française* 410, no. 4 (2022): 139–62.

all the more necessary to justify the maintenance of slavery in the colonies.[10] As a matter of fact, slavery was reintroduced by Napoleon, less than ten years later, in 1802, when 'people of colour' were no longer enabled to hold the title of French citizen.

Conquest, empire and revolutions, 1799–1870

After the 1799 *coup* that ended the French Revolution and brought Napoleon Bonaparte to power, France redefined the conditions for naturalization, and who qualified as French. The French Revolution and successive constitutions of 1793, 1795 and 1799 firmly asserted *jus soli* with the possibility of foreigners to become French nationals. In contrast, the 1804 Civil Code determined that foreigners had to have lived in the country for at least ten years if they wished to become French citizens (until then, the minimum requirement was five years). Moreover, only a child born out of a French father was considered a French national, which introduced what is referred to as *jus sanguini* – a principle by which nationality is determined by the nationality of one parent. This did not mean that people born in France of parents born abroad could not become French. French nationality remained open, and they just had to ask to become French when they came of age. But, in practice, it seldom did, because it exposed men to fulfil their military obligations, and most remained foreigners residing legally in France.[11]

The 1789 definition of citizenship was marked by the context of the end of absolutism and drew a firm line between French citizens of a free nation, as opposed to aristocrats in exile. In contrast, the Civil Code's definition of who could be French was much more influenced by the context of the Napoleonic Wars and the opposition between French citizens and foreigners, who were suspected of siding with the enemy. As a result, Napoleon Bonaparte granted amnesty to emigrants who had left at the time of the French Revolution, allowing tens of thousands of them to return to France. Conversely, he reinforced control over foreigners. His approach was not without contradiction insofar as he was also driven by the conviction that there can be 'nothing but advantages' in extending the empire of French civil law.[12] However, the introduction of a dose of *jus sanguini* into the definition of nation, solely based on *jus soli* and civil loyalty until then, ushered in the era of modern

---

[10]Cécile Vidal, ed., *Français? La nation en débat entre colonies et métropole, XVIe-XIXe siècle* (Paris: School of Advanced Studies in the Social Sciences Press, 2014).

[11]Patrick Weil, *How to Be French: Nationality in the Making Since 1789*, trad. Catherine Porter (Durham, NC: Duke University Press, 2008).

[12]Weil, *How to Be French*.

nationality law in France: a mixture of automatic attribution based on descent and possibility of acquisition based on residence.

Despite the regime change, foreigners continued to come and settle in France after the revolution. They came in response to the push and pull of the economy. The Industrial Revolution really only began in the 1830s because of the structure of the French agricultural economy. The vast majority of French people indeed lived in the countryside and worked in agriculture. However, the growth of machine production, centralized industrialization, and subsequent urbanization transformed the French economic map. At first, seasonal workers who could only live part-time from agricultural work met the labour force needs of the French Industrial Revolution. Yet, France was the only European country to see its population increase by only 50 per cent during the period from 1800 to 1850. It tripled in Great Britain, and doubled in Belgium, Germany and Italy. So, France ended up attracting landless rural-dwellers from Belgium, Italy, Germany and Switzerland.[13] As a result, France was the leading country of immigration in mid-nineteenth-century Europe. The 1851 census was the first to register foreigners by nationality, and indicated: 128,000 Belgians, 63,000 Italians and 25,000 Swiss nationals. Foreigners made up 1 per cent of the total French population and 6 per cent of the total population living in Paris.

Moreover, France continued to represent a place of refuge for political exiles, such as political liberals from Napoli and Piedmont in 1821, liberal Portuguese in 1829 and finally thousands of Poles after the failure of the November Uprising of 1830. Their coming in greater numbers than their predecessors prompted the parliament of the constitutional monarchy of Louis-Philippe (July Monarchy, 1830–48) to pass the first law on refugees in March 1832. The law combined a concern for help with a desire to control a population regarded as elusive and threatening.[14] The allocation of subsidies to the most destitute went hand in hand with their being placed under house arrest in barracks – under the auspices of the Ministry of War and the Ministry of Interior. The rationale was to house them and keep an eye on them. The necessity to assess their well-founded fear of persecution was articulated from the outset, as shown in Prime Minister François Guizot's appeal to make sure that refugees who benefited from assistance 'had really been forced to leave their country for political reasons'.[15]

---

[13]Moch, *Moving Europeans*.

[14]Delphine Diaz, *Un asile pour tous les peuples?: Exilés et réfugiés étrangers dans la France au cours du premier XIXe siècle* (Paris: Armand Colin, 2014).

[15]Sylvie Aprile and Delphine Diaz, 'Europe and Its Political Refugees in the 19th Century', *Books & Ideas*, 18 April 2016, https://booksandideas.net/Europe-and-its-Political-Refugees-in-the-19th -Century.

Finally, during the Napoleonic Wars of 1803–15, the First French colonial empire, which consisted mainly of territories in the Caribbean and North America, as well as trading posts in South America, Africa, and Asia, declined drastically. In 1803, Napoleon Bonaparte sold Louisiana to the United States and raised the funds needed to wage war in Europe. In 1804, France lost its richest and most important colony, Saint-Domingue, after the massive slave revolt led to the independence of the Republic of Haïti.

However, a new period of conquest began in 1830, with the invasion of Algeria and the overthrow of existing structures of government. The French army captured the strategic port of Algiers on the Mediterranean seacoast, deposing Hussein Dey, the ruler of Algiers, at the time. Algerians resisted the French invasion, particularly under the guidance of Emir Abdelkader in the west. However, in the context of the consolidation of the constitutional monarchy and the search for voters' approval, King Louis-Philippe sought opportunities to offer the country military glory, and a total of one hundred thousand French soldiers were deployed in the conquest of Algeria. With an estimated number of five hundred thousand to one million killed as a result of the fight and disease, the conquest of Algeria is one of the deadliest conquests of the Second French colonial empire.[16] The conquest of Algeria was not fully completed until 1903, when the French managed to control the Saharan lands in the south. However, the civil administration encouraged the settlement of European farmers as soon as parts of the country were pacified, so much so that by 1857, there were one hundred thousand European settlers living in the country, half of them French, half of them from other European countries such as Spain and Italy. They would buy land from native Algerians, estimated to be three million around that time, and farm it.

Meanwhile, in Europe, a revolutionary wind was blowing across the continent. The 1815 Congress of Vienna, which marked the end of the Napoleonic Wars and defined the European map, had curtailed many national and liberal aspirations. French liberals had to face the return of monarchy in France; the Poles, the Greeks and the Belgians had to bear the supervision of the Russian, the Austrian or the Prussian Empire, respectively. In France, the so-called European People's Spring culminated in the 1848 revolution that put an end to the constitutional monarchy and established the Second Republic – a democratic regime that proclaimed direct universal male suffrage on 5 March and abolished slavery in French colonies with the decrees of 4 March and 27 April 1848.

---

[16]Jean-Pierre Peyroulou et al., *Histoire de l'Algérie à la période coloniale, 1830–1962* (Paris Alger: La Découverte, 2012).

The backlash was quick to arrive, however. The Russians and the Prussians crushed rebellious Poles; the Austrians crushed the King of Piedmont, who had launched a crusade to unify Italy; and French citizens elected Louis-Napoléon Bonaparte, Napoleon I's nephew, President of the Republic. In 1852, he proclaimed himself Emperor Napoleon III and put an end to four years of democratic regime.

The French Second Empire lasted from 1852 to 1870, a period during which Napoleon III sought military glory and to emulate his uncle, Napoleon I. He launched several wars. At first, he was successful in Europe, gaining Savoy and Nice in 1860. He then expanded the Second French Empire to three times its original size (one million square kilometres in 1870). He began colonization in Africa (Senegal) and established French rule in Asia (protectorate of Cambodia, 1863).

Napoleon III was determined to make Algeria a settler colony where Arabs and European settlers could live side by side. In 1863, he wrote to the general governor of Algeria, Pélissier and stated, 'I am just as much the Emperor of the Arabs of Algeria as I am of the French'. As inhabitants of the French colonial empire, Arabs of Algeria were French nationals. However, they were not granted French citizenship and the right to vote, unless they decided to give up Muslim laws that governed inheritance and marriage. As a result, very few did, and colonial Algeria consisted of a vast majority of Algerian colonial subjects (estimated three million in 1867) and a minority of European settlers with French citizenship (estimated two hundred thousand). What's more, French naturalization laws applied to non-French European settlers from Spain or Italy, who became French citizens (*Senatus Consulte*, 1865).[17] Algerians, on the other hand, remained colonial subjects and not citizens.

Eventually, Napoleon III's military ambitions led to his downfall when he was forced to surrender in Sedan while fighting the Prussian army. Back in Paris, partly because his fourteen-year-old son was too young to be his successor, but mostly because the legitimacy of the elected assembly was stronger, a group of deputies who supported democracy gathered in front of Paris City Hall on 4 September 1870. Their leader, Léon Gambetta, proclaimed the return of the Republic for the third time since the French Revolution, putting an end to the Second Empire.

This chapter provides the context for some of the key political decisions that will ultimately influence immigration policy. At the time, they translated

---

[17]Hugo Vermeren, *Les Italiens à Bône (1865–1940): Migrations méditerranéennes et colonisations de peuplement en Algérie* (Rome: French School of Rome Press, 2022).

specific economic and political concerns. For the Black Code of 1685, Louis XIV and Prime Minister Colbert wanted to impose the Catholic religion and rationalize sugar cane production in the islands of French America. For the conditions to acquire French citizenship, the Republicans wanted to secure the gains of the 1789 revolution and evict the members of the nobility who were willing to reinstate the monarchy.

Moreover, it was a time of crucial political decisions for the administration of new territories and populations outside Europe. As such, the king drew a clear distinction between what applied in and outside Europe, with particular consequences for inward mobility. The case of the few enslaved people who arrived in France is illustrative of how difficult that division was to maintain. They were freed because the land of the Franks set people free. But they were later arrested and deported because the king prohibited their presence.

Finally, all the political work to define and establish French citizenship in 1789 happened without much consideration for enslaved people in the colonies. This explains why colonized people were never really able to hold the title of French citizen in the empire.

2

Founding the Republic, building an empire, 1870–1940

The First Republic lasted twelve years (1792–1804), the Second Republic four years (1848–52), and the Third Republic seventy years (1870–1940). What could stop the democratic regime of the republic from falling this time around? How come it resisted any attempt to restore the monarchical order or the return of the empire? Historians have been eager to solve this enigma. One could even go so far as to argue that the revival of political history in France derived from the need to address this question.[1] A top-down approach could attribute the success of the Republicans to the divisions between the monarchists: the Legitimists wanted the return of the count of Chambord (House of Bourbon); the Orléanists, the return of the duke of Orléans, son of King Louis-Philippe (House of Orléans-Bourbon); as for the Bonapartists, they wanted the return of Imperial Prince Louis-Napoleon, only son of Napoleon III.

However, the division among the monarchists could not fully explain the gradual acceptance of the democratic regime by the French people. As a result, French historians developed a bottom-up approach to political history to make sense of this phenomenon. They argued that one cannot understand the establishment of democracy without taking into account the critical mass of French citizens who came to accept the new democratic regime and ceased to consider the return of the monarchy as a valid option.[2]

This chapter first explores a remarkable feature of French political history – that is, the extent to which the establishment of democracy was rooted in the values of the Enlightenment, while, at the same time, Republicans maintained the project of colonial conquest and the ensuing subjugation of indigenous populations. This particular paradox is key to understanding why the themes of republican values, such as universalism and secularism, later shaped the politics of immigration in ways that sometimes defied those very principles.

---

[1] Jean-Marie Mayeur, *Nouvelle Histoire de la France Contemporaine., Tome 10: Les Debuts de la Troisieme Republique 1871–98* (Paris: Seuil, 1973).
[2] Serge Berstein, *Les cultures politiques en France* (Paris: Seuil, 1999).

The period from 1870 to 1940 also saw an increase in immigration to France (from 1.5 per cent of the total population in 1872 to 5.6 per cent in 1936). Despite the relative lack of political interest for the issue, the chapter examines several milestones that were reached during the period: the 1889 nationality law according to which a child born in France to a foreign parent becomes French when they reach majority; the 1927 law that created identity cards for foreigners; the 1932 law introducing quotas for the number of foreign workers per sector; and the 1938 decree increasing the surveillance of foreigners and expulsions.

Finally, the chapter looks at the governmental reaction to the contribution of foreigners and the colonial population during the First and Second World Wars. Its central argument is that the Third Republic not only established a new democratic order, but it also laid the foundations for what would shape the politics of immigration in the second half of the twentieth century: a careful mix of liberality in terms of access to rights, notably nationality, and restriction in terms of access to certain professions. But also, a difficulty in taking into account the contribution of foreigners and colonial subjects to national history.

The Third Republic, the Enlightenment and the colonial conquest, 1870–1905

Central to the acceptance of the Republican regime was the making of French citizens through the school system.[3] The Ferry laws of 1881 and 1882 established that school attendance was free and compulsory for all children aged six to thirteen. It centralized the school curriculum and made it secular (*laïc*). The teaching of religious morals was replaced by the teaching of civic morals. Finally, teaching and speaking were in French only. As a result, generations of pupils learned to speak one common language, to distance themselves from religious dogma and to know the history of one common nation.

A good example of the making of French citizens through the school system was the 1877 book *A Tour of France by Two Children*, by Augustine Fouillé, which was widely used in state schools. The book told the story of a brother and a sister whose father died in the French–German War of 1870 and went in search of their family members through France. The book taught about all the different regions of France and was influential in creating a sense of a unified

---

[3] Yves Déloye, *Ecole et citoyenneté. lindividualisme républicain de Jules Ferry à Vichy: controverses* (Paris: Presses de la Fondation nationale des sciences politiques, 1994).

country, the two children being from Lorraine in the North of France. It was also instrumental in maintaining the longing for Alsace-Lorraine – a territory the German Empire annexed following the 1870 war.

The unification of the school system during the Third Republic contributed greatly to the unification of French national identity. Admittedly, the implementation of such a radical change did not happen overnight: resistance occurred, regional languages persisted, and the replacement of religious teachers by laic instructors took time.[4] However, even though the country consisted of many different regional identities and languages, by 1914, one could argue that the French people belonged to the same nation.[5]

The process of national identity formation was not unique to France; the nineteenth century was a time of creation all through Europe.[6] Germany, Great Britain, France, Sweden or Serbia pursued a pan-European trend that consisted of reviving national traditions, popular motifs in music, folkloric costumes and adopting a national language. However, in France, national identity formation was closely linked to the political project of the republic and the acceptance of the new democratic regime. The production of history textbooks dating the birth of the nation to the Gauls – a pre-Roman people living in what is now modern-day France – began around that time. Historian Ernest Lavisse, in particular, popularized the phrase 'Our ancestors the Gauls' (*Nos ancêtres les Gaulois*). In fact, the choice of the Gauls was in opposition to the Franks, and in particular Clovis, the first king of France. It was a republican decision to put the people first, rather than the monarchy.

It was also a republican decision to pursue the colonial conquest. The territory of the French Empire increased by a factor of ten between 1870 and 1940. More precisely, in 1885, the French army was able to secure a large area in western Africa that went from Senegal to Niger (*Afrique occidentale française, AOF*); in 1896, the Confederation of Indochina was created, that consisted in modern-day Vietnam, Cambodia and Laos; by 1897, the colony of Madagascar was founded; and by 1910, the area around the Congo river was established as *Afrique equatorial française* (*AEF*).

The pursuit of colonization might have appeared surprising considering how it was first and foremost a military endeavour characteristic of the Second Empire – a regime, the Republicans had so fervently criticized. As a matter of fact, Republicans, such as Jules Ferry, received strong criticisms from both sides of the Chamber of Deputies. On the right side of the chamber, Monarchists feared that France was losing sight of Alsace-Lorraine. On the

---

[4] Jean-François Chanet, *L'École républicaine et les petites patries* (Paris: AUBIER, 1996).
[5] Weber, *Peasants into Frenchmen*.
[6] Anne-Marie Thiesse, *The Creation of National Identities: Europe, 18th–20th Centuries* (Boston: Brill, 2021).

left, representative Georges Clemenceau famously criticized Jules Ferry and his fellow Republicans for their opportunism and disputable notion that 'superior races' were meant to educate 'inferior races' (speech of 31 July 1885 in front of the Chamber of Deputies). With this charge, Georges Clemenceau, also a strong defender of the Republican regime, but with a more progressive approach to social issues, made an explicit reference to the political rationale that had guided the colonial conquest so far. Together with other representatives on the left wing of the chamber, Georges Clemenceau decried the business of colonization that benefited investors and industrials.

However, the colonial project was closely linked to the establishment of the republic, which explains why the project went through. In a 1885 speech, Jules Ferry clearly articulated the political rationale that guided colonization: the French Republic had to prove that it did not take a monarch or an emperor for a country to hold its ground in the concert of nations. In this perspective, the colonial project could help the French economy prosper, military glory shine, and the Republican regime overcome. Moreover, Jules Ferry argued that it was to bring 'more justice, more light, more order, more public and private virtues' (28 July 1885). This was meant to justify that a democratic regime based on the principle of justice and equality, such as the Third Republic, could continue the conquest of new territories and the subjugation of Indigenous peoples.

As a result, colonization was first and foremost a matter of international influence and economic prosperity. There was little knowledge and discussion about the conditions under which the conquest took place and how order was maintained in the French colonial empire. This explained why the political rationale behind colonization was seldom discussed, except for when the government sought the approval of the parliament on military credits, which was the context of Jules Ferry's 1885 speech. The rest of the time, the colonial conquest continued in a climate of indifference on the part of the politicians, as well as of the citizens.

Colonial rule established by the Third Republic contrasted drastically with the establishment of democracy in metropolitan France. A case in point is the evolution of nationality law at that time. The law of 26 June 1889 reintroduced *jus soli*: a child born in France to a parent born in France is French by right from birth. In metropolitan France, the aim was to prevent French children born to foreign parents from abandoning French nationality to avoid military service. Military service lasted five years at that time. The French army was not able to recruit enough soldiers during the Franco-German War of 1870. As a result, the enlargement of conscription – the act of forcing people by law to join the armed services – was a strong motive for the return to nationality based on place of birth, as opposed to nationality based on descent.

However, in the colonies, indigenous populations remained subjects of the empire, not citizens. Only in the settler colony of Algeria did the law of 26 June

1889 apply, but only to non-French European settlers and only because the French colonists feared being outnumbered by foreign Europeans. Other than that, the indigenous population received a specific treatment, detailed in a 'native code' (*Code de l'indigénat*) – a set of laws and regulations that first applied to Algeria, and was later extended to all colonies. The native code replaced the no-longer-existing Black Code by organizing the sanctions against the rebellious indigenous population and defining a taxation system. It was only abolished in 1946 and lasted throughout the entire Third Republic. It did not implement the law according to the same principle of justice and freedom as in metropolitan France.[7]

Another good example of discontinuity between territories is the establishment of equal rights for all citizens, and particularly religious freedom. In 1905, the Republican regime passed the law separating the churches from the state. To this day, the 1905 law guarantees religious freedom – understood as the freedom of belief and disbelief and ensures the freedom of public institutions from the powerful Catholic Church. It discourages religious involvement in government affairs and, conversely, prohibits the state from funding any religion.

The context of the nineteenth century is crucial in understanding the establishment of state secularism (*laïcité*) in France. The Catholic Church, as an institution, posed a reasonable threat to the democratic regime, as higher religious officials were in favour of a return to monarchy. Indeed, the Catholic Church benefited from a strong territorial network throughout the country, and Republicans feared they could influence people's votes.

However, the power dynamic was different outside France. As such, the 1905 law did not apply in Algeria. In the settler colony, the French authorities sought to control the practice of Islam through the formation of an official clergy.[8] The full separation between religious authorities and public institutions was not necessary. Thus, one of the fundamental principles of the Enlightenment – the fight against religious dogma – took a back seat when it came to controlling conquered territories.

As a result, the Third Republic pursued the project of colonial conquest, for reasons of national grandeur, even though it contradicted its founding principles. What's more, it did so without applying in the conquered territories the principles it defended on its own soil. From this point of view, the advent of democracy with the establishment of the regime of the Third Republic did not put an end to a process that had already begun under the Old Regime: what applied in France did not apply elsewhere in the empire.

---

[7]Olivier Le Cour Grandmaison, *De l'indigénat: Anatomie d'un 'monstre' juridique: le droit colonial en Algérie et dans l'Empire français* (Paris: Zones, 2010).

[8]Raberh Achi, 'La séparation des Eglises et de l'Etat à l'épreuve de la situation coloniale. Les usages de la dérogation dans l'administration du culte musulman en Algérie (1905–59)', *Politix. Revue des sciences sociales du politique* 17, no. 66 (2004): 81–106, https://doi.org/10.3406/polix.2004.1017.

Immigration and the Dreyfus affair: the making of the enemy within, 1893–1914

At the end of the nineteenth century, France was in need of labour because of lagging population growth. In 1896, there was a fertility rate of 2.2 children per woman; by contrast with 3.9 in Great Britain and 5.09 in Germany, the same year. Moreover, the French Revolution facilitated access to property and French peasants did not have to leave their land in the same proportion as Germans and British peasants. The transformation from rural to urban population that took place in Great Britain in the eighteenth century, and in Germany from the 1870s, did not happen similarly in France. Yet, industrialization required ever more intensive use of the means of production, and therefore, ever more labour. As a result, the proportion of foreigners living in France continued to increase. By 1901, there were 330,000 Italians and 323,000 Belgians among the one million foreigners living in France, representing 2.7 per cent of the total metropolitan population.

Despite the flow of immigrant workers going back and forth from neighbouring Belgium or Italy, it would be an overstatement to consider immigration in France as purely economic and temporary. On the contrary, labour migration leads to settlement more often than not. First, foreigners living in France were 40 per cent women, some of whom arrived on their own and worked as maids, for instance. However, some others came as families. Moreover, since the 1889 nationality law, foreigners could acquire French nationality after five years, and their children were automatically French when they came of age. Finally, freedom of movement made circulation, installation and naturalization easier than in any other European country at the time. For instance, Great Britain passed the Aliens Act of 1905, which introduced immigration control and restricted immigration by those who did not have the means to support themselves. In France, one could come, settle and look for a job. A situation that suited employers who could therefore resort to cheap foreign labour force, sometimes even going so far as recruiting them directly (e.g. the recruitment of foreign workers in Poland).[9]

Free movement and a constant need in the labour force did not mean that the settlement of foreigners in France did not cause any trouble. On the contrary, the first expressions of xenophobia took shape around that period. Employers pitted foreign and French workers against each other, using the former to drive down the wages of the latter. As a result, riots took place

---

[9]Ponty, *Polonais méconnus*.

among workers, one of the deadliest and most well-known of all being the ones that took place in Aigues-Mortes in 1893.[10]

The town of Aigues-Mortes in the south of France was famous for the salt marshes operated by the *Compagnie des Salins du Midi*. In the summer of 1893, the company began recruiting workers for the threshing and lifting of salt on a smaller scale than usual. An economic crisis was raging throughout Europe. However, many workers in the region relied on the job, as did Italians from northern Italy who had grown accustomed to finding employment there during the summer. As soon as work began, brawls broke out between the French and Italians, which quickly degenerated despite the intervention of the police. At the end of two bloody days, the official death toll was nine, with fifty injured workers, while the Italian press reported seventeen additional missing bodies and fifty more injured workers.

However, what made the Aigues-Mortes massacre infamous was not so much the scale of the event as the profoundly unfair judicial treatment it received. Four months later, a criminal court clearly established the guilt of sixteen suspects. Yet, their actions were reclassified as attempted murder, instead of murder. Moreover, the circulation of the prejudice that Italians were troublemakers, wielding knives at the slightest opportunity, helped support the theory that victims were, in fact, agitators and that the suspects were merely defending themselves.[11] As a result, when the jury of the criminal court handed down their verdict, they bowed to nationalist pressure and handed down a general acquittal of the sixteen suspects.

The violence that erupted among workers, such as the one in Aigues-Mortes, was a reflection of a broader xenophobic discourse that developed in the late nineteenth century.[12] It came from journalists, politicians, and elected representatives, and can be understood as an exercise in boundary drawing, in a context of intense national identity formation. In a process of defining who French nationals were and what French national identity was, politicians and intellectuals engaged in the definition of a significant other. While on the labour market, the sworn enemy was the Italian who came to take the job of French workers; at the highest levels of the military hierarchy, the enemy within was Captain Dreyfus.

The Dreyfus affair began as a banal story of espionage, even though it ended up calling into question power distribution within the Third Republic. In the wastepaper basket of a German lieutenant, Lieutenant-Colonel von Schwartzkoppen, stationed in Paris, the French intelligence services (through the intermediary of an accomplice housekeeper) found a piece

---

[10]Gérard Noiriel, *Le Massacre des Italiens* (Paris: Fayard, 2009).
[11]Enzo Barnabà, *Mort aux Italiens!: 1893, le massacre d' Aigues-Mortes* (Toulouse: Editalie, 2012).
[12]Laurent Dornel, *La France hostile* (Paris: Hachette Literature, 2004).

of paper written in French that indicated several attached documents (a note on Madagascar, a note on artillery preparation) – the *bordereau*. The piece of paper referred to 'notes', which were thought to be administrative, even though it later appeared that this was the term used by the author to designate various documents in which he had given his opinion on various issues. Nevertheless, Major Henry, in charge of the investigation, immediately interpreted the finding as a case of high treason which had come from the General Staff, the higher rank of the army. Investigators carried out writing tests, but the person who had written the note could not be found among the General Staff. Investigation moved on to the interns, among them a young artillery captain, Alfred Dreyfus.

Captain Alfred Dreyfus graduated with highest honours from artillery school in 1892, two years prior to the investigation. Born in Mulhouse in 1859, Alfred Dreyfus came from a family that had to leave Alsace-Lorraine after German annexation if they wanted to keep French nationality, which they did. However, they first settled in Switzerland, in Basel, where Alfred Dreyfus attended high school, after which he relocated to Paris and attended military school, starting in 1877. Moreover, Alfred Dreyfus was of Jewish ancestry, even though his family was not religious. Despite his brilliant academic record, his origin in Alsace and schooling outside France attracted the suspicion of the military official in charge of the investigation. On 15 October 1894, Dreyfus was summoned to take a writing test. Some of the words in the *bordereau* appeared to be written in the same way, and he was arrested. On 5 January 1895, Alfred Dreyfus was found guilty in a swift court-martial trial, stripped of his army rank and sentenced to life imprisonment on Devil's Island, in the French colony of Guiana.

In 1895, the first trial of Alfred Dreyfus ended with the almost unanimous conviction of his guilt and the legality of his court-martial. The government of the time did not question the accusation. The army, through the administration of the War Ministry, appeared to be all-powerful. Army officials went out of their way to strike the opinion with Dreyfus' conviction. Dreyfus had his rank insignia cut from his uniform and his sword broken, before silent ranks of soldiers. Moreover, the circulation of the prejudice that Jews had connections abroad and were unpatriotic helped support the idea that Dreyfus could be a traitor. Most newspapers at the time rarely used antisemitic arguments *per se*.[13] However, they were affected by the tidal wave of antisemitism that emerged around that time.

---

[13]To the notable exception of *La Libre parole* (Free Speech), the newspaper funded by Edouard Drumont in 1892 that positioned itself as 'anti-Jews'. Édouard Drumont authored *Jewish France* in 1886 and proceeded to identify Jews in the administration and the media. He was instrumental in developing a racial antisemitism that attributed moral characteristics to physical traits.

Several currents were at the origin of this nineteenth-century version of antisemitism: an old Catholic anti-Judaism originating in the biblical fact that the Jews killed Jesus; a conservative antisemitism that associated Jews with Freemasonry and blamed them for the secularization of society; an anti-capitalist antisemitism, associating Jews with financial capitalism and considered they were getting rich at the expense of all French people; and finally, a nationalist antisemitism that considered Jews as having no homeland and in constant danger of betraying the country. Jews were few in number – seventy-one thousand in 1897, including forty-five thousand in the Paris region. However, together with foreigners, they became the enemy within, who had to be defeated. An affirmation of patriotism, against a backdrop of antisemitism, therefore turned Alfred Dreyfus into the ideal culprit.

The Dreyfus affair that shook the very foundations of the Third Republic only took over in 1898. On the one hand, Alfred Dreyfus's family, convinced of his innocence, had established a counter-investigation that dismantled the burden of proof. On the other hand, in 1895, Colonel Henry's successor discovered that false documents had been produced to incriminate Alfred Dreyfus at his trial and that the author of the document was another officer in the army, Major Estherazy. However, at the end of a second court-martial, the army decided not to back down and to declare Major Esterhazy not guilty. It was then, and only then, that the affair became *the Affair*: because the army chose not to question its judgement; because it put its own interests before the imperative of justice on which the republican regime was founded; and because it thus affirmed its ability to operate according to its own rules. It prompted the writer Emile Zola to address a letter to Felix Faure, the President of the Third Republic, famously published on the front page of *L'Aurore* (The Dawn), in which he called on him to exert his power as president and set the record straight. It was only after a third trial in 1899 that Alfred Dreyfus was offered a pardon by the president of the Republic, and released from jail, and in 1906, he was officially exonerated by a military commission.

Antisemitism fuelled a crisis that called into question power-sharing within the fledgling democracy. After Dreyfus's first conviction, the government of the Third Republic gave the impression of being under the thumb of the Ministry of War, and in particular, its administration. The omnipotence of the army, which included many Royalists, gave rise to fears of a *coup* in the crisis affecting the regime. From this point of view, the president's pardon in 1899 sent out a strong signal: The executive was distancing itself from the power of the army. The rehabilitation of Alfred Dreyfus in 1906 followed an inquiry that proved his innocence, based on a claim for truth and justice.

Moreover, by making Alfred Dreyfus an enemy within, antisemitism led the authorities to indulge in the easy option of accusing an ideal culprit, without making the effort to find the real culprit. In a famous speech, Socialist politician Jean Jaurès demonstrated that, by refusing to stand down and going so far as to fabricate a false accusation against Dreyfus, it was the army that had played into the hands of foreigners, not the other way around. To right-wing nationalists sitting in the legislative assembly who accused him of supporting 'the party of foreigners' because he defended Dreyfus, Jean Jaurès notoriously replied that *they* were 'the real party of foreigners' (6 April 1903).

On the eve of the First World War, the republican regime was finally confirmed. The Dreyfus affair had strengthened republican culture, for it marked the victory of justice and transparency over arbitrariness and secrecy. However, new fault lines had also emerged that defined a new political game based on structuring ideas, such as nationalism and the rejection of the Other.

A war of nations and colonial encounter, 1914–18

The First World War (1914–18) was a war of nation-states, and for the first time, twenty-one thousand foreign residents of enemy countries were interned in camps when the war was declared. The French government passed the April 1917 decree that created the first identity card in an effort to keep a record of all foreigners living in France. The administration recorded their civil status, place of birth and commune of residence. The card was also used to assign foreigners to economic sectors such as industry, agriculture or crafts. This was the first time the authorities attempted to identify all foreign residents. It revealed a major change in the mentality of the authorities and the police. From this period onward, the police took on the task of identifying and controlling foreigners on French territory.

Many foreigners (e.g. Italians and Poles) took part in the war effort and were recruited into the Foreign Legion – an assault troop created in 1831 to recruit foreign soldiers who did not hold French nationality. Moreover, one of the key features of the First World War was the use of colonial subjects in addition to the recruitment of foreign workers to support the war economy (450,000 in agriculture and industry, 1915–18).[14] France resorted to 668,000 colonial subjects from Algeria, Morocco, Tunisia, West and Central Africa, Madagascar

---

[14]Laurent Dornel, *Indispensables et indésirables: Les travailleurs coloniaux de la Grande Guerre* (Paris: La Découverte, 2025).

and Indochina, of which 480,000 fought in the army (which represented 6 per cent of the total soldiers called to arms) and 188,000 worked in factories. They recruited an additional thirty-seven thousand Chinese people to work in factories. The Chinese were not subjects of the empire. However, the French government had been accustomed to recruiting Asian workers, mainly from China, to work on farms in the colonies after the abolition of slavery. The practice was, therefore, extended when it came to recruiting labour during the war.

The first contact between the colonized and metropolitan France was based on methods developed in the colonies. The management of those recruited to work in the factories was entrusted to officers who had worked in the colonies and were considered to know them better. Employers were given meticulous instructions on how to assign them to different tasks depending on their origin. A process of racialization operated, which consisted of assigning specific traits to each group.[15] Some were deemed to be more skilful and therefore mostly sent to work (Indochina, China and Morocco), while others were perceived as hard workers and mostly sent to combat (Algeria, Tunisia, Madagascar, West and Central Africa). The latter were attached to troupes of *tirailleurs* (skirmishers), a type of light infantry soldiers meant to take part in short, unexpected fights. They suffered major casualties with a death toll of seventy thousand (14 per cent), and many were injured.

TABLE 1 Recruitment of Fighters and Workers in the Empire and China, During the First World War[16]

	Fighters	Workers
Algeria	172,000	78,560
Morocco	37,000	35,500
Tunisia	60,000	18,250
West and Center Africa	134,000	–
Madagascar	34,000	4,500
Indochina	43,000	49,000
China	–	37,000
TOTAL	480,000	225,000

---

[15]Laurent Dornel, 'L'appel à la main-d'œuvre étrangère et coloniale pendant la Grande Guerre: un tournant dans l'histoire de l'immigration?', *Migrations Société* 156, no. 6 (2014): 51–68.
[16]Marie-Claude Blanc-Chaléard, *Histoire de l'immigration* (Paris: La Découverte, 2001).

The first direct experience of colonial encounter came to an abrupt end in 1919, when the authorities sent colonials back home. This did not prevent some of them from staying or coming back later – starting a new migration route promised a long future. However, it proved the differential approach to European versus non-European war recruits. On one hand, Europeans from Italy, Spain and Portugal had a temporary title of sojourn and were also destined to come back home after their contribution to the war but enjoyed free circulation. On the other hand, subjects of the colonial empire did not enjoy free circulation, and their return home was supervised by French authorities.

A country of immigration and protection, 1918–40

The interwar period saw an unprecedented rise in migratory flows. The census recorded 1,532,000 foreigners in 1920 and 2,715,000 in 1931, which was an increase from 3.9 per cent to 6.6 per cent of the total population. As migratory flows increased, so did the complexity of trajectories and experiences. While much of the movement of people was the result of the push and pull of the economy, political unrest also contributed to the picture, and a new status emerged, that of refugee. The term 'immigration' covered a number of contrasting realities during this period.

First, there were the push and pull of the economy. Following the end of the First World War, France's weakening demographics (because the war had wiped out a large proportion of men of working age) and increasing need for labour force due to devastation in the northern and eastern parts of the country operated as a pulling force for immigrants. By contrast, economic recession in Poland and Italy pushed people out. Some of them left their country for the United States, but others went to France.

Moreover, the United States passed immigration laws in 1921 and 1924 that restricted arrivals from Eastern and Southern European countries. The US political decision to restrict immigration led to the redirection and increase of migration flows to France. In twenty years, the country's foreign population almost tripled, from just over a million to nearly three million, surpassing the United States' rate of foreign population growth. In 1931, the French census counted 2.7 million foreigners, of which the most numerous were Italians (808,000), Poles (507,000) and Spaniards (351,000). The proportion of foreigners reached 6.6 per cent of the total population – the highest since the census operation began counting foreigners in 1851. A demographic shift unknown in other European nations around that time.

As for colonial migrants, even though they were officially nationals, the French census differentiated them from the rest of French nationals and identified them as 'French subjects from North Africa'. There were 102,000 in 1931. Most of them were former soldiers who had been discharged from their duties as soldiers during the war.

Second, there were political reasons for the arrival of foreigners in 1920s France. Coming from Hungary and Poland, Jews were fleeing persecution, as were Armenians from Turkey. Russians were fleeing the Soviet revolution and the subsequent change in power holders. As a result, the 1931 census identified 36,100 foreigners from Turkey, 44,500 foreigners from Eastern and Central Europe, and 71,900 foreigners from Russia.

In addition to this, the new government of the Soviet Union revoked the citizenship of Russians living abroad, who found themselves stateless. In an attempt to address the issue, the League of Nations created the first refugee passport for them, the Nansen Passport, after Fridjof Nansen, a Norwegian polar explorer and diplomat who headed the High Commission for prisoners of war and refugees. In 1924, the Nansen Passport was extended to Armenians fleeing Turkey, and in 1928 to Assyrian and Bulgarian refugees.

The various reasons for leaving their country of origin did not prevent newcomers from facing the same realities of housing, healthcare, finding a job and raising a family. When the French economy required additional labour, settlement was challenging but possible, as newcomers could find employment. When the economic situation worsened, the difference in status (i.e. economic versus political immigrants) became more salient.

Economic migrants may have seemed better off than political refugees in some respects. The needs of reconstruction imposed a logic of labour recruitment that involved signing bilateral agreements with countries of

TABLE 2 Number of Foreign Residents and Colonial Subjects by Country of Birth, 1931

Belgium	253,000	Southern Europe	100,000
Central and Eastern Europe	44,300	Spain	351,900
Germany	71,700	Switzerland	98,500
Italy	808,000	Czech	47,400
North Africa	102,000	Turkey	36,100
Poland	507,000	United Kingdom	47,400
Russia	71,900	Other	175,500

Source: INSEE, French Census

emigration.[17] For example, in Marseilles, in the 1920s, Italians arrived under bilateral treaties and as such benefited from access to medical care and assistance for the elderly, mothers and children. Armenians, on the other hand, despite recognition of their refugee status by the League of Nations, were considered stateless and therefore ineligible for national treaties. They were not entitled to medical aid. In her research in the archives of two cities that received a subsequent share of foreigners, Mary Dewurst Lewis found a letter from the Marseille deputy mayor who wrote to the mayor of Lyon that Armenians 'were not accepted at the hospice under any pretext'.[18] She highlights a series of factors on which the application of migrants' rights depends: origin, geographical situation, type of work, proof of long-term residence and the vicissitudes of administration. All these factors determine migrants' access to social benefits, demonstrating how social rights organize the lives of migrants as much as, if not more, the law in the legal sense of the term.[19]

As for colonial subjects, their right to claim to be part of the French nation, after many of them fought for France during the First World War, was scrupulously circumvented to deny workers the right to travel to France, have access to social assistance and enjoy full citizenship. From 1924, a circular made it compulsory for Algerians to hold a legal document authorizing them to travel to France, in the same way as a passport. In 1936, Prime Minister Léon Blum and Maurice Violette, governor general of Algeria, instigated a plan to grant full French citizenship to a fraction of the population of French Muslims in Algeria. The mayors of the Algerian towns violently opposed the Blum-Violette project and voted massively against the reform.

What's more, the economic and political arguments in favour of restricting the movement of Algerians to metropolitan France kept considerable traction within the French political class. First, French Muslims who had come to work in France for much higher wages than in Algeria were threatening to become property owners in their own right; second, politicians were aware of political demands that threatened the integrity of the French empire. In 1927, Messali Hadj had already founded the North African Star Movement (*Mouvement de l'Etoile Nord Africaine*) and was active in Algerian workers' circles. The creation of social services to help colonial migrants, such as North African Indigenous Affairs Services (*Services des Affaires Indigènes Nord Africains, SAINA*), was

---

[17]Mary Dewhurst Lewis, *The Boundaries of the Republic: Migrant Rights and the Limits of Universalism in France, 1918–1940* (Stanford, CA: Stanford University Press, 2007).

[18]Lewis, *The Boundaries of the Republic*, 23.

[19]Thomas Humphrey Marshall, *Citizenship and Social Class: And Other Essays* (Cambridge: Cambridge University Press, 1950).

part of a desire to exert political control over colonial migrants while they were on metropolitan soil.

Finally, the economic crisis that began in the United States in October 1929 and hit France in 1931 considerably worsened opportunities for immigrants. The number of unemployed was still low, but there was nonetheless a widespread feeling of underemployment. Xenophobia was on the rise, with the return of the idea that foreigners were taking the jobs of French workers. However, what was new in the 1930s compared with the 1890s was that this logic of exclusion reached the ranks of the Chamber of Deputies, and the government passed a series of legal provisions aimed at protecting the French workforce. The law of 10 August 1932 regulating salaried labour introduced quotas for the number of foreigners in each business sector or region. Moreover, the decree of 8 August 1935 subjected immigrant business-owners to the same obligations. It required the possession of a special identity card, a mechanism that made it possible to regulate the number of foreign workers.

What is remarkable is how the passing of the law was met with general approval in the Chamber of Deputies: the 1932 law was adopted without a single vote against it. During parliamentary debates, right-wing deputy Louis Fourès reportedly stated that 'if foreign workers left France, the unemployment problem would be solved' (23 March 1933). As for employers still wishing to resort to foreign labour, the legislator referred them to branch-by-branch agreements.

The laws regulating the foreign workforce (1932) and foreign business (1935) had a considerable impact on immigration flows and the number of foreigners who lived in France. From 1936 to 1946, the share of immigrants in the total population went from 6.6 per cent to 5.6 per cent. Companies contributed to the return of immigrants. One of the most spectacular events was the Anzin mining company (North of France), which organized the return of thousands of families to Poland via train.[20]

However, not all foreigners could or would return home, and a lot of them turned to other employment opportunities, in agriculture, for instance, or naturalized. The naturalization legislation of 1927 had reduced the residency qualification to three years. As a result, from 1927 to 1940, six hundred thousand foreigners became French (including those who naturalized through marriage). It was particularly the case for Italians and stateless refugees. One out of four naturalized French citizens was an Italian national.

In 1936, foreign workers enjoyed a brief respite when a coalition of left-wing parties (the centre-left Radical Party, the left-wing Socialist Party and the extreme left-wing Communist Party) came to power under the banner of

---

[20]Ponty, *Polonais méconnus*.

the *Front Populaire*. Improvements to workers' lives (the first introduction of a two-week leave per year and a reduction in the working week to forty hours) benefited immigrants with stable jobs. In addition, deportations of foreign nationals who lacked legal papers were slowed down.

However, the end of the *Front Populaire* government in 1938 put job protection for French workers and surveillance of foreigners back on the agenda. The decree of 2 May 1938 allowed for increased surveillance of foreigners and expulsions. In 1938 alone, the Aliens Department arrested 2,100 foreigners, turned back 8,813 and expelled 1,465.[21] Moreover, after deciding not to come to the aid of the Spanish Republicans driven out by the *coup d'état* of July 1936, the French government was faced with the arrival of hundreds of thousands of Spaniards fleeing the regime's repression in 1939. Camps were set up to receive them. The government respected the principle of the right of asylum, and five hundred thousand Spaniards entered France. However, no refugee status was created for them (as in the case of Russians and Armenians), and they were crammed into camps where they lived in very poor conditions. In the end, the return of 50 per cent of them was organized in 1940, while two hundred thousand remained on French soil and were naturalized. In the run-up to the war, the naturalization office was all the more inclined to grant the precious ticket to French citizenship as the country needed able-bodied men to face the enemy.[22]

The interwar period was therefore marked by several new situations from the point of view of immigration: the considerable increase in labour migration; the arrival of political refugees, some of whom were stateless; and the fact that some colonial subjects who fought in the First World War remained on French soil. Politicians sometimes responded in a concerted manner (such as the creation of a status of refugee), but sometimes also in fits and starts, giving ground to protectionist and xenophobic reflexes.

Selection and resistance, 1940–5

The Second World War and the advent of the Vichy regime confirmed the protectionist and xenophobic tendencies that had emerged between the wars. On 10 July 1940, a majority of 569 elected representatives of the Third Republic out of 700 voted for an article that granted Maréchal Pétain authority to promulgate a new constitution and subsequently assume in his own name full legislative and executive powers. The Third Republic had gone

---

[21]Clifford D. Rosenberg, *Policing Paris: The Origins of Modern Immigration Control Between the Wars* (Ithaca, NY: Cornell University Press, 2006).
[22]Weil, *How to Be French*.

through decades of attempts to restore the monarchy and a world conflict. Eventually, the members of parliament voted to give full power to Marshal Pétain, relinquishing the very power that had been hard-won over the past seventy years. Eighty voted against, and eighteen abstained. The advent of the Vichy regime marked the victory of the camp of the most acerbic critics of the Third Republic: those who denounced its parliamentary character and were on the right of the political spectrum; those who included the most ardent nationalists, xenophobes and antisemites, too.

Nationalism, xenophobia and antisemitism were particularly intertwined in the summer of 1940, as France was a place of refuge for many German Jews seeking to escape the Nazi regime. At the start of the war, as in 1914, France interned foreign nationals from enemy countries present on its soil, including Jews from Germany. After the armistice, these camps became internment camps for all foreign Jews and continued when the Vichy regime took part in the Final Solution. French Jews were not spared, even if they were less easy to locate than foreign Jews, as there were no registers for them. Following on from the protectionist measures of the 1930s, the Vichy regime excluded Jews from the civil service, the press and the cinema (Statute of 3 October 1940). The Aryanization of businesses was then decreed in the summer of 1941, and the police raids of 20 and 23 August affected both foreign and French Jews.

The Vichy regime also set about withdrawing nationality from foreigners who had acquired it far too easily in their view since 1927. Analysis of the denaturalized files shows that most of them concerned foreign Jews.[23] Out of all the naturalized foreigners who were identified as Jews, 78 per cent of them were stripped of French nationality. Although there was no way of identifying people of the Jewish faith (no French administrative document listed a person's religious denomination), the services relied on the consonance of the surname, first name and sometimes original identification documents from the country of birth, which included this information. For instance, identity papers issued by the government of the Ottoman Empire indicated religious denomination.

Moreover, foreigners who were not of the Jewish faith could lose their nationality if the commission considered that they had demonstrated political activity against the interests of the French state. Some naturalized French citizens threatened with denaturalization set about challenging the administrative decision. Remarkably, French writer Louis Ferdinand Céline wrote a letter in support of his friend George Montandon, citing not only his lack of 'Marxist, Bolshevik or anarchist feeling' but also 'his antisemitic works',

---

[23]Weil, *How to Be French*.

concluding, 'Professor Montandon is certainly the most resolute antisemite I know' (16 January 1941). Antisemitism, as a political opinion, therefore played the role of a guarantee of loyalty to the French state.

Despite the very xenophobic backdrop, the contribution of foreigners and colonials was essential to the resistance and liberation of the country – a fact that only began being acknowledged and celebrated in the twenty-first century.[24] Many foreigners had come to France because they were political opponents in their countries of origin. An instance of this was the communist networks FTP MOI (for *Franc-tireur partisans – Main d'oeuvre immigrée*). In 1943, the police stopped a group of twenty-three FTP MOI in Paris, tried them and sentenced them to death for treason. In February 1944, they published a propaganda poster, the Red Poster (*L'Affiche Rouge*) listing ten of the twenty-three fighters, their country of birth (Poland, Hungary, Armenia, Spain, Romania) and their Jewish denomination.

The Red Poster propaganda aimed to demonstrate that the resistance was unpatriotic and headed by foreigners. The movement was therefore a foreign conspiracy against French sovereignty. After the end of the war, the French Communist Party became known as the party of the executed (*parti des fusillés*), due to the large number of Communists who died during the resistance. However, it was not made clear at the time that the vast majority of those shot were foreigners, and it took decades before the proportions of foreign-born were acknowledged in the fight.[25] Eventually, on 21 February 2024, the remains of their leader, Missak Manouchian, an Armenian refugee who arrived in France in 1925, and his wife, Mélinée Manouchian, also a resistance fighter, were transferred to the Panthéon during a national tribute.

The coordination between resistance networks, the Allied forces and the Free French Forces eventually led the country to liberation. Initially, the so-called Free French Forces (*Forces françaises libres*, FFL) were soldiers and civilians who refused the armistice by answering General de Gaulle's call on 18 June 1940. A few territories of the colonial empire joined them (French Equatorial Africa, in particular). The end of the Third Republic and the advent of the Vichy regime in metropolitan France were reflected in different ways in the empire. There were many adjustments depending on the territory, including in Algeria, albeit a settlement colony, and the change of regime could only be achieved by preserving the hard-won local balances.[26] The territories that joined the Free French Forces gave them a territorial base. It enabled them to

---

[24]Béatrice Gurrey, 'Missak et Mélinée Manouchian entrent au Panthéon à l'issue d'une cérémonie émouvante et engagée', 22 February 2024.
[25]Denis Peschanski, *Des étrangers dans la Résistance* (Paris: L'Atelier, 2013).
[26]Edenz Maurice and Raberh Achi, 'Le régime de Vichy face aux sociétés coloniales: adaptations et recompositions locales', *Genèses* 120, no. 3 (2020): 3–7.

continue fighting against the Italians and Germans in Libya, for example, and thus maintain the Franco-British alliance against the Axis forces.

Moreover, subjects of the empire paid a heavy price. Of the 1.8 million soldiers taken prisoner in 1940, seventy thousand colonials were interned in labour camps in France, as the German authorities did not want to see 'men of colour' on German soil. They were swiftly sent back home after the end of the war.[27] Moreover, 120,000 soldiers from North and sub-Saharan Africa joined the Free French Forces as early as July 1940. After the Allied landings in North Africa in 1942, these troops distinguished themselves in Tunisia, Italy, Corsica and during the French campaign. Finally, African soldiers contributed to the liberation of Paris with the 2nd armoured division in the summer of 1944.

However, the Army Staff ordered fifteen thousand African riflemen to 'leave their place' to soldiers of the Free French Forces shortly before the end of the combat. The riflemen had to leave their weapons and equipment behind and were repatriated to the south of France and then to their homeland.[28] Several arguments have been put forward to justify the 'whitening' of troops, which was counterintuitive from a military point of view. Indeed, the African riflemen were better trained and experienced than the FFL fighters. Undisclosed papers reveal that the British and American commanders conditioned the participation of French troops in the liberation of Paris on the provision of white-only divisions. In order to ensure that a division of the French army would be present at the liberation of Paris, the General Staff relented and went ahead with the formation of a white-only infantry division.[29]

At the end of the Second World War, the French presence among the winners owed a great deal to the empire: because it provided the territorial base needed to keep the fighting going between 1940 and 1944, and because of the heavy toll paid by the indigenous population, both as prisoners and as combatants. However, for reasons that had as much to do with the balance of power at the international level – such as the order of whitening the French troops was a condition imposed by the American General Staff – as with the need to re-establish democracy after the authoritarian regime of Vichy, the account of the victory that was given did not fully reflect it. The story of France's victory focused on the metropolitan part of the conflict, both in terms of territory and who played a key part in the events.

---

[27] Armelle Mabon, *Prisonniers de guerre Indigènes: Visages oubliés de la France occupée* (Paris: La Découverte, 2010).

[28] Claire Miot, 'Le retrait des tirailleurs sénégalais de la Première Armée française en 1944. Hérésie stratégique, bricolage politique ou conservatisme colonial?', *Vingtième Siècle. Revue d'histoire* 125, no. 1 (2015): 77–89, https://doi.org/10.3917/ving.125.0077.

[29] Mike Thomson, 'Paris Liberation Made "Whites Only"', 6 April 2009, http://news.bbc.co.uk/2/hi/europe/7984436.stm.

This chapter demonstrated the necessity of including the empire in the narrative of the Third Republic in order to comprehend the exclusionary dynamics that agitated French political life in the years preceding 1940. Moreover, the chapter highlighted how the rationale behind the colonial conquest and the brutality of colonial rule foreshadowed the difficult inclusion of colonial fighters in the victory of 1945. Finally, it shed light on the political response to the arrival of immigrants from numerous regions of the world. It showed that exclusion was already evident in public opinion and legal action against foreigners. These factors are important to consider, as they provide a better understanding of the dynamics that ultimately shaped immigration politics in the post-war period.

3

After the war, 1945–54

After the war, France was no longer the sole country of immigration in Western Europe. The end of the Second World War saw unprecedented movements of people: soldiers returning from the various fronts; prisoners of war and camp survivors returning home; and population movements in reaction to regime change. Around fifteen million people were transferred from one country to another, many of whom were forced to relocate as a result of boundary changes (e.g. Germany, Poland and former Czechoslovakia). A distinctive feature of the post-war period was the new relevance of national and international political dynamics in shaping population flows. Two narratives organized the story of migration in post-war Europe.[1] The first was the economic narrative, with the need for an additional labour force consequent to the destruction of the war. The second was the narrative of the state, as maker of war, recruiter of labour and controller of borders. The two intersected and created three types of migration regimes: labour, colonial and refugee migration regimes.

After the war, the British, Belgian, Swiss and Dutch governments joined the French government in actively recruiting labourers. As for Germany, the Federal Republic was initially able to rely on the twelve to fourteen million descendants of German citizens, scattered all around the former German Empire, who were forced to leave and resettled in Germany.[2] However, these flows began to slow by the mid-1950s and eventually stopped by the time of the building of the Berlin Wall in 1961. The government of West Germany began organizing recruitment. Over the period from 1949 to 1973, net immigration for Western Europe reached around ten million (compared with the net outflows of four million for the period 1914–49).[3] In France, with the return to republican legality, a new legal text, the ordinances of 1945, defined the conditions of access to nationality, entry and residence for foreigners.

---

[1] Moch, *Moving Europeans*.

[2] R. M. Douglas, *Orderly and Humane: The Expulsion of the Germans after the Second World War* (New Haven, CT: Yale University Press, 2012).

[3] Peter Stalker, 'Migration Trends and Migration Policy in Europe', *International Migration* 40, no. 5 (2002): 151–79, https://doi.org/10.1111/1468–2435.00215.

From then on, the government began to recruit the foreign labour needed for reconstruction.

After the war, citizens of the French and British empires also came for economic reasons. However, their circulation was made possible by governmental decisions that did not aim directly at recruiting the labour force but rather at maintaining control over their respective empires. In 1946, the French government created the Citizenship of the French Union, which included free circulation within the overseas territories. Algerians, in particular, came in great numbers. They went from twenty thousand in 1946 to two hundred thousand in 1954 in the French census. Along the same lines, the British government created the Citizenship of the United Kingdom and Colonies, which prompted the migration of citizens from the New Commonwealth (India, Pakistan, Bangladesh and the West Indies). Citizens from the West Indies arrived first: Fifty-five thousand came in from 1951 to 1956.[4] As for the Netherlands, three hundred thousand Dutch and Indo people came from the Dutch East Indies during Indonesia's struggle for independence in the second half of the 1940s.

Finally, the turmoil of the post-war period put the issue of refugees back on the agenda of European governments. Already in 1945, the French government had initiated discussions to identify and grant asylum to individuals in need of protection.[5] Eventually, France joined the efforts to organize the help and refuge to people fleeing communist regimes and signed the Geneva Convention of 28 July 1951.

This chapter presents the three pieces of legislation that governed each migration regime in France successively: the two ordinances of 1945, which defined the status of foreign workers and the conditions to become French; the ordinance of 1946, which created a colonial citizenship; and the fact that the French government signed the Geneva Convention of 1951, which established a status for refugees. In doing so, the chapter looks at policymakers within the state apparatus and highlights the disagreements and the balance of power between them. It shows how political decisions on immigration bear the mark of the post-war context. Then, the chapter looks at the experts and the scientific knowledge on which policymakers base their policies. Its central argument is that the need for migration regulation prompted policymakers to decide and define the migrants they wished for. In doing so, they outlined a new narrative of who Frenchmen and Frenchwomen should be.

---

[4] Claude Moindrot, 'Les vagues d'immigration en Grande-Bretagne', *Population (French Edition)* 20, no. 4 (1965): 633–50, https://doi.org/10.2307/1528584.
[5] Weil, *La France et ses étrangers*.

The ordinances of 1945 and the emergence of a new labour regime

Already in the interwar period, the will to regulate the presence of foreigners had emerged among policymakers. They wanted to strike a balance between two opposite, yet pressing, concerns: on the one hand, the economic need for a labour force; and on the other, the political need for foreign surveillance. To this aim, centre-left Philippe Serre was appointed under-secretary of state for immigration and foreigners in 1938. His team included Georges Mauco, who wrote a PhD dissertation entitled 'Foreigners in France: A geographical study of their role in economic activity' in 1932.[6] Based on Mauco's analysis, Serre proposed several projects that aimed at sorting the wheat from the chaff, identifying the needs in agricultural and industrial work for each region; sorting out the pressure on crowded professional branches such as shopkeepers and independent professions; and identifying the useful labour stock accordingly.[7] However, the center of power under the Third Republic was in Parliament, and the instability of the government and the lack of influence of the legislature meant that none of their projects came to fruition.

After the war, the Provisional Government of the French Republic put the migration regulation project back on the agenda. Chairman of the government, Charles de Gaulle, pronounced a programmatic speech in March 1945 that clearly articulated the French demographic recovery to a proactive birth policy, along with an attractive immigration policy:

To bring to life the twelve million beautiful babies that France needs in ten years, to reduce our absurd rates of infant and juvenile mortality and morbidity, to introduce over the next few years, methodically and intelligently, good elements of immigration into the French community, a great plan has been drawn up.[8]

With clear direction given by the highest level of government and no legislative approval required,[9] the officials in charge of elaborating a policy managed to gain approval, and Charles de Gaulle signed the ordinance relating to the conditions of entry and residence of foreign nationals in France on

---

[6]Albert Demangeon, 'Les étrangers en France', *Annales de géographie* 41, no. 232 (1932): 408–11.
[7]Philippe Rygiel et al., *Le bon grain et l'ivraie: La sélection des migrants en Occident, 1880–1939* (La Courneuve: Aux Lieux d'être, 2006).
[8]Charles de Gaulle, 'Le discours du Général De Gaulle devant l'Assemblée consultative', *Le Monde*, 5 March 1945.
[9]From its proclamation in 1944 to the establishment of the Fourth Republic in 1946, the Provisional Government was able to pass ordinances without seeking approval from the legislative chamber.

2 November 1945. However, the establishment of the text was the result of intense debates and involved contrasting opinions on the issue of migration, which we discuss below.

Following up on his interwar project, Georges Mauco was appointed head of a Higher Committee on birth and population and pushed for a selection policy. Until then, he had been mainly concerned with economic activity. But with the new objective of demographic growth, he clarified his position and advocated selection based on geographical origin in his proposal for a new legislation: 'We need to limit the influx of Mediterranean and Oriental immigrants, whose influx has profoundly altered the human structure of France over the last half-century'.[10]

Mauco's reference was the Immigration Act, which the United States issued in 1924. The law required quotas to be allocated to countries in the same proportion that the American people traced their origins to those geographical areas. The quotas were therefore based on the composition of the American population of the late nineteenth century – mainly European immigrants from the northern and western parts of Europe. The quota board issued a list that aimed at keeping the number of arrivals of southern and eastern Europeans low, while the number of arrivals from the rest of Europe was higher. For instance, in 1929, the quota for British immigrants was as high as 25,957, and the quota for Italian immigrants was as low as 5,802.[11]

Similarly, Mauco argued for selecting immigrants based on their origins and established a hierarchy among them. His work found some echo among demographers, notably Alfred Sauvy, head of the newly created National Institute for Demographic Studies (*Institut national d'études démographiques, INED*), who favoured the input of Europeans among the French population.

However, senior civil servants in the administration and ministers were not in favour of selecting immigrants. Already in 1944, after the country had been liberated, Interior Minister Adrien Tixier had lectured the police, who continued to hunt down foreigners as required by the Vichy regime. According to him, this had led to the 'unacceptable' arrest of many foreigners who had fought in the Resistance.[12] The policing of foreigners was not so legitimate after they had proved their commitment to the nation, in some cases with their lives. Moreover, the State Council (*Conseil d'État*) redrafted the proposal before presenting it to Charles de Gaulle. As legal adviser to the executive branch, the governmental body did not include checks on the origin or geographical location of foreign nationals who applied for entry or residence in France.

---

[10] Weil, *La France et ses étrangers*, 71.

[11] Mae M. Ngai, *Impossible Subjects: Illegal Aliens and the Making of Modern America – Updated Edition*, Revised édition (Princeton, NJ: Princeton University Press, 2014).

[12] Weil, *La France et ses étrangers*, 66.

As a result, the State Council issued an ordinance relating to the conditions of entry and residence of foreign nationals in France, which listed the types of stay possible in France (one-year, one to three-year and ten-year renewable stays) and set up a National Immigration Office to organize the recruitment of foreign workers. Eventually, the ordinance of 2 November 1945 did not copy the Immigration Act of 1924. It established France's first labour migration regime, one that organized the stay of foreigners in France, regardless of where they came from.

Moreover, Charles de Gaulle also signed the ordinance on the French nationality code on 19 October 1945, which re-established *jus soli* with a requirement of a five-year residency. The new legislation no longer provided for the possibility of withdrawing nationality, as had been the case under the Vichy regime. With the reintroduction of *jus soli*, the spirit of the nationality law of 1889 was back, but with a new twist: peopling the nation. The objective was not so much to make sure young, able foreign-born individuals became French nationals and possible military recruits, as in 1889, but rather to ensure that newcomers established and started a family. As a result, incoming foreign spouses became French after only three years. French women marrying foreigners did not lose their French citizenship anymore, as had been the case since 1803.[13] Finally, naturalization was only examined if the applicant fulfilled four conditions: effective residency, good health, good morality and 'assimilation'.

The 1945 French nationality code introduced the condition of assimilation and, in doing so, drew new boundaries of French national identity.[14] The 1927 legislation had already introduced the notion of assimilation, but it was not conditional on the examination of the application. Moreover, path dependency and a general lack of understanding of the ways in which assimilation should be assessed jeopardized the whole process. As deplored in a memo from the minister of justice to the staff responsible for registering naturalization applications, the latter did not provide sufficient information about the applicant's ability to 'adapt to our culture and customs' (11 October 1930). As of 1945, assimilation became a criterion for eligibility. The authorities had to ensure that the departments responsible for registering applications knew how to assess this new eligibility criterion: it would be determined on the basis of the candidate's command of the French language.

---

[13]Linda Guerry, *Le genre de l'immigration et de la naturalisation. L'exemple de Marseille (1918–1940)* (Lyon, ENS Editions, 2013).

[14]Abdellali Hajjat, *Les frontières de l'"identité nationale": L'injonction à l'assimilation en France métropolitaine et coloniale* (Paris: La Découverte, 2012).

There were two reasons for the decision to assess assimilation on the basis of language proficiency.[15] The first stemmed from the colonial context. For the most part, the indigenous population hold French nationality, but not the citizenship and political rights that go with it. However, the colonial authorities could never completely bring themselves to prevent the indigenous elites from acquiring full French nationality. From this point of view, knowledge of the French language represented a formidable filter, given the low level of schooling of the indigenous population in the French system. This practice, dating back to the early twentieth century in the empire, anchored the idea that mastery of the French language completed the process of assimilation in the mind of the legislator.

The second stemmed from the metropolitan context. For the Republican elites, mastery of the French language was the best way to keep foreigners away from the stronghold of the Catholic Church. They feared that Spanish and Italian Catholic Churches controlled their fellow foreign nationals. As a result, a new regime of naturalization emerged after the war.

The advocates of selection by national origin certainly did not win the day when it came to defining a new immigration regime in 1945. At no point does the ordinance of 2 November 1945 actually refer to this principle. However, a dose of nationalism was introduced into the conditions for naturalization as laid down in the ordinance of 19 October 1945. The reasons for this may have been politically justified – fear of the influence of the Catholic Church, for example. The fact remains that the 1945 French nationality code introduced assimilation as one of the eligibility criteria, and the assessment of this criterion was based on a command of the French language. This permanently distanced naturalization from an essentially civic procedure, based on adherence to common values, as it had been in 1789. Those in favour of introducing the assimilation criterion, based on language, may well have argued that French was the best vehicle for transmitting republican values. Nevertheless, after 1945, not only did one have to speak French to become French, but what's more, one would have to be able to prove it to the administrative employee responsible for registering their naturalization application.[16]

Finally, although the 1945 immigration regime may not have been selective in theory, in practice, it offered leverage to administrative officials who sought to favour some national origins over others. They opened immigration

---

[15]Abdellali Hajjat, '2. La barrière de la langue. Naissance de la condition d'assimilation linguistique pour la naturalization', in *Les nouvelles frontières de la société française*, Poche / Sciences humaines et sociales (Paris: La Découverte, 2012), 53–77, https://doi.org/10.3917/dec.fassi.2012.03.0053.
[16]Spire, *Etrangers à la carte*; Didier Fassin and Sarah Mazouz, 'Qu'est-ce que devenir français? La naturalization comme rite d'institution républicain', *Revue française de sociologie* 48, no. 4 (2007): 723–50.

bureaus (*Office national d'immigration*, ONI) in European countries where they wanted to recruit foreign workers (such as Italy). After his last attempt at implementing a selective immigration law based on ethnicity, Georges Mauco kept his position at the High Commission on Population and Family but ceased to influence the discussions.

However, Alfred Sauvy, who was an economist and a statistician by training – he graduated from the prestigious Ecole Polytechnique in 1920 – enjoyed an influential position as director of the National Institute for Demographic Studies from 1945 to 1962. He contributed to the debate on immigration policy by bringing a populationist perspective – the idea that certain individuals were more desirable than others for France's population growth. Less concerned about the difference between northern and southern Europeans than Mauco was, Sauvy reacted mainly to the arrival of non-Europeans, and in particular Algerians. The latter were not actively recruited by ONI but arrived following the creation of the status of citizens of the French Union.

The constitution of 1946: From empire to French union

Towards the end of the Second World War, there were rising demands for independence among local elites in the colonies. In 1941, the American and British governments issued a joint statement, known as the Atlantic Charter, which proclaimed the right to self-determination and self-government – a statement that aimed at combating the German occupation of parts of Europe at the time, but that ended up giving credentials to nationalist movements across empires. Moreover, in Algeria, the establishment of the capital of Free France in Algiers gave hope for Algerian nationalists. In 1943, nationalist leader Ferhat Abbas published the Manifesto of the Algerian People that claimed the right of Algerians to have a constitution. After the end of the war and the subsequent signing of the 1946 Charter of the United Nations, which established the right of all people 'to develop self-government', nationalist movements forced the British to hand over control of India (1947) and the Dutch to free Indonesia (1949). However, French officials resisted the attempts and interpreted the UN Charter as a call to develop the ability of colonized people to administer themselves, rather than to move toward independence.[17] In Algeria, French colonial authorities brutally repressed the nationalist demonstrations that took place in Setif, following German capitulation (8 May 1945). In Indochina, France

---

[17]Todd Shepard, *The Invention of Decolonization: The Algerian War and the Remaking of France* (Ithaca, NY: Cornell University Press, 2008).

launched a military campaign after Ho Chi Minh proclaimed independence on 2 September 1945.

The re-establishment of the Republican order with the passing of the 1946 constitution proposed a new system that knit together the republic and empire into the French Union. The October 1946 constitution of the Fourth Republic created French Union citizenship, which extended to all French citizens and colonial subjects, eliminating the latter term from official administrative categories. As such, the official administrative category for colonial migrants from Algeria living in metropolitan France became 'Muslim French Citizens from Algeria' (*Français musulmans d'Algérie, FMA*). Eliminating the categories of colonial subjects and indigenous populations prompted the end of native codes that had structured the administration of all colonies since the abolition of slavery in 1848. As a result, the 1946 constitution implied the equality between all civil law codes. Muslims who resided in metropolitan France came under French civil law and enjoyed all the rights attached to the quality of French citizenship, including political rights. As such, they could register on voting lists, even though few have done so.[18] Finally, France renamed its colonies 'Overseas France'. Guadalupe, Martinique, Reunion and Guiana became Overseas Departments (*départements d'outre-mer, DOMs*). Other colonial holdings in Africa, Asia and Oceania became Overseas Territories (*territoires d'outre-mer, TOMs*). The whole system constituted the French Union, and the term empire was no longer in use.

The post-war order was articulated in terms of 'citizenship', 'equal rights' and 'union', instead of 'empire', 'indigenous' and 'colonial'. As argued by Frederik Cooper, 'the old claims to colonial authority, based on racial superiority and civilization were thoroughly discredited by the experience of Nazism and fascism'.[19] As such, French reforms parallel the concomitant changes in the British Empire. Westminster passed the 1948 Nationality Act, which created the status of Citizenship of the United Kingdom and Colonies (CUKC). It came into effect on 1 January 1949 and put Britain's colonial subjects on equal footing with those living in Great Britain (namely, free circulation within the British Empire and political rights). However, both British and French reforms emerged as a desire of metropolitan elites to retain control over their empires, rather than to develop their right to self-government.

A side effect of the 1946 citizenship of the French Union was the arrival of newcomers from French overseas, and particularly from Algeria, in

---

[18]Spire, *Etrangers à la carte*, 49.

[19]Frederick Cooper, *Decolonization and African Society: The Labor Question in French and British Africa*, African Studies (Cambridge: Cambridge University Press, 1996), 173.

metropolitan France.[20] It was a side effect, because granting free circulation to citizens of the French Union so that they could come and settle in metropolitan France was not the formal aim of the law. However, this did not mean that employers did not see it as fitting to rely on their labour force. As a matter of fact, the recruitment system set up by the 1945 decree proved to be complex: immigration bureaus abroad would recruit, set up contracts, run health checks and finally arrange for the transportation of foreign workers. By contrast, after the passing of the 1947 Lamine Gueye law that formally legalized the presence of Muslim French citizens of Algeria in France, employers could rely on a workforce available more quickly. Add to this the fact that demographic and economic trends in Algeria combined a high birth rate with a labour market unlikely to absorb the surplus labour. The conditions were ripe for the departure of many Algerians to metropolitan France. As a result, from 1946 to 1949, the National Office for Immigration (ONI) managed to organize the arrival of 214,000 foreign workers (of which 67 per cent were Italians); while the General Government of Algeria declared that 265,000 Algerian workers had left for metropolitan France.

To be sure, the relatively low number of foreign workers recruited by the National Office for Immigration was not only due to Algerian competition. France was not the only country to call for foreign immigration. In the immediate post-war period, some former emigration countries, which turned into immigration countries after the war, such as Belgium and Switzerland, were also calling on foreign immigrants, sometimes using less complex procedures than those put in place by the French immigration bureaus abroad. Moreover, France was experiencing a major housing crisis at the time, and French families were unable to find accommodation – let alone foreign families. Finally, after the war, France was also a country with a high number of refugees; a matter that was addressed through the creation of a new refugee regime.

Signing the 1951 Geneva Convention for Refugees

During the interwar period, the arrival of Russians fleeing the advent of a Soviet regime, followed by Armenians fleeing Turkey, had already led to the creation of a specific status. Dedicated offices based in France were able to issue Nansen Passports to Russian refugees, starting in 1922, and then Armenian refugees in 1924. One of the main aims of the Nansen Passport

---

[20]Georges Tapinos, *L'immigration étrangère en France: 1946–1973* (Paris: University Press of France, 1971).

was to enable stateless people to hold identity papers. However, this case-by-case allocation policy was not extended to Spanish Republicans fleeing the Spanish Civil War in 1936. They were admitted to France under the principle of the right of asylum but were not granted any specific status. Those who remained swelled the number of naturalizations after 1945.

After the war, however, it was necessary to deal with foreigners who had sought refuge in France. In 1948, the International Organisation for Refugees estimated they were six hundred thousand; an overestimation, according to the French census bureau, the National Institute of Statistics and Economic Studies (*Institut national de la statistiques et des études économiques, INSEE*), which issued the number of 360,000 in 1949. In any event, they could not fall within the scope of the 1945 ordinance. The ordinance was designed to actively recruit workers and their families to populate France, not to regularize people already on French soil. The population dimension was not absent from this logic either: these refugees of all ages were not the young and able-bodied immigrants the authorities were looking for. Last but not least, they were not the same authorities. The decisions that accompanied the creation of a system of refugee migration stemmed from international commitments rather than from economic planning. The two did not follow the same logic. In terms of economic planning, separating the wheat from the chaff consisted of identifying economic sectors in need of labour and recruiting workers accordingly; in terms of international law, the challenge was, above all, to assess refugees' well-founded fear of persecution in their origin country.

The issue of defining a refugee migration regime was made all the more complex by the wide variety of people who could fall within its scope. They could be pre-war refugees who had fled the advent of Nazism in Germany, fascism in Italy or Francoism in Spain, but also Displaced People (DP) such as Poles or Hungarians, who had been deported by fascism and Nazism out of their country of origin, during the war. Finally, political opponents were fleeing the advent of communist regimes in Southern and Eastern European countries following the victory of the Allied Forces.

Eventually, France's foreign affair ministry signed the 1951 Geneva Convention related to the Status of Refugees, agreeing to recognize as refugees all individuals who: 'Owing to a well-founded fear of being persecuted for reasons of race, religion, nationality, membership of a particular social group or political opinion, is outside the country of [their] nationality and is unable or, owing to such fear, is unwilling to avail [themself] of the protection of that country' (Article 1 of the 1951 Refugee Convention).

The convention applied only to Europe and was strictly limited in time to all events before 1 January 1951. This was to evolve in 1967 with the New York protocol that extended the perimeter of the convention to the whole world. However, at the turn of the 1950s, the stakes were high to make sure that refugees were not sent back to the country they were fleeing. In this respect, the signing of the Geneva Convention by the French government meant that most foreigners fleeing persecution could be assured they would not be sent back. The main contribution of the international agreement was to establish the principle of non-refoulement. Despite the international dimension of the convention, the office in charge of reviewing applications was a national bureau placed under the authority of the French Ministry of Foreign Affairs. The French Office for the Protection of Refugees (*Office français de protection des réfugiés et apatrides, OFPRA*) was created on 25 July 1952. Finally, legal protection was not enough: refugees had to be able to make a living. In this respect, the entry into force of the Convention enabled people with refugee status to obtain a permanent work permit after three years of residence in France.

The logic of economic planning was perhaps not the same as that of international aid when it came to granting a formal status. Yet, from the perspective of the individuals, the boundaries between economic logic and political factors were much more tenuous. The definition of the three migration regimes characterizes the policing of immigration in the post-war period. The politics of immigration, however, entered a new era. With the need for a labour force and concern for population growth, policymakers and experts articulated a new narrative of how newcomers should mix, or not, with French national identity.

Experts and the issue of population mixing

An inquiry into the production of scientific knowledge on immigration in France reveals the rearticulation of the politics of immigration after the war and gives insight into the origins of the way in which the issue was subsequently addressed.

In the drafting of the 1945 ordinance regulating the entry and stay of foreigners in France, economist Alfred Sauvy may have failed to impose his view on the selection of immigrants; this did not mean, however, that he gave up on his will to impact French immigration policy. As director of the newly created National Institute for Demographic Studies (INED), he was editor in chief of the journal *Populations* that aimed at informing academics, but also senior civil servants and policymakers on demographic issues. Already in 1947, INED published a study entitled *A Possibility of Italian Migration*, advocating a more proactive Italian immigration policy. In 1950, Alfred Sauvy published a series of two articles assessing the needs and possibilities of immigration in France. Finally, in 1953 and 1954, INED published a series of surveys entitled *French and Immigrants*, which analysed both the opinion of French people on immigrants and the social conditions of Poles, Italians and Algerians living in France. These publications aimed to base Sauvy's advice to policymakers on scientific knowledge.

The story of the production of these surveys is revealing of the scientific mindset that shaped post-war immigration policies.

Within the National Institute for Demographic Studies, historian Louis Chevalier was in charge of researching immigration as head of the history and geography section. A specialist of Paris, he developed a psychological approach to population history. From 1944 to 1951, he prepared a PhD dissertation on Paris that was later published under the title *The Working and Dangerous Classes in Paris in the First Half of the Nineteenth Century* (1958). As a result, his main concern was to impact policymakers on the issue of immigrant populations in relation to urban development. As an instance of this, he taught classes on immigration at the newly created National School for Administration that was to train the future higher civil servants of the country. Moreover, Chevalier's psychological approach to population issues translated into a deep belief in psychological differences between ethnic groups.[21]

As soon as he was appointed head of the history and geography section in INED, and while researching his PhD dissertation, Louis Chevalier began publishing pieces to alert policymakers on their laissez-faire policy in terms of immigration and the complete lack of immigrants' selection. Although it is difficult to assess the role of racial hierarchy in his writing, how he assigned innate differences to groups definitely amounts to a process of racialization, understood as the categorization of a group of people by others.[22] In 1947, he published a piece on population growth in Algeria, alerting the authorities to the imminent arrival of large numbers of Algerians and describing their religious denomination, 'Islam', as 'a way of being, of feeling, of understanding, a temperament in short, a psychology that creates, behind all the secondary appearances of Europeanization, a profound refusal of any assimilation'.[23] Not only did Chevalier assign specific traits to Algerians ('a way of being') in his work, but he also asserted their inability to mix with the French population ('refusal of any assimilation'). This meant that Algerians could not be considered a valid prospect for contributing to French population growth.

Chevalier's provocative tone and accusatory writings ended up damaging Sauvy's original plan to influence politicians. In 1950, the director for the recruitment of workforce wrote directly to Sauvy, blaming him for his lack of

---

[21]Paul-André Rosenthal, *L'Intelligence démographique: Sciences et politiques des populations en France* (Paris: Odile Jacob, 2003).

[22]Michael Banton, *The Idea of Race* (London: Tavistock, 1977).

[23]Robert Colin, 'Louis Chevalier. Le problème démographique nord-africain', *Politique étrangère* 13, no. 2 (1948): 197–8.

pragmatism: 'Beside ideals, it is necessary to take into account more pragmatic imperatives such as the priority of recruitment among French citizens, the economic situation, the reaction of the public opinion, finally and *above all*, the need in workforce. . . .'[24] Sauvy therefore reassigned the topic of immigration to another unit within the institute, the psycho-sociology section, headed by Jean Stoetzel and Alain Girard, both sociologists and polling specialists.

However, it is important to note that it was not so much the content of Chevalier's comments on the Algerians that drew the wrath of the policymakers but rather the way in which he compromised the country's economic recovery by hindering the recruitment of foreign labour forces. The publication of Girard and Stoetzel's research results confirmed the preconceptions formulated by Chevalier regarding Algerians. In the general presentation to the survey on Algerians living in metropolitan France, published in 1954, they referred to 'the problems posed by this immigration' as about its distinct 'ethnic origins and family, civil, religious and cultural traditions [bound] to cause difficulties'.[25]

The racialization of Algerians is rendered difficult to assess as the term race completely disappeared from scientific and political vocabulary after the war. In the aftermath of the war and the realization of the extremities to which a mobilization of racist thinking could lead, scientists set about to eradicate racism and the very use of the term race.[26] Crucial to this strategy were discussions that took place in meetings organised by the United Nations Educational, Scientific and Cultural Organisation (UNESCO). French scientists who attended these meetings included Sauvy, Chevalier and Stoetzel. They began replacing the previous biological understanding of difference associated with race with a culturally based understanding of difference. Finally, UNESCO set up a large conference on the topic of 'the cultural assimilation of immigrants' in 1949. As a consequence of this, 'cultural assimilation' became a new criterion for evaluating and selecting immigrants. Following up on his intention to impose his view on the selection of immigrants, Sauvy adopted this new vocabulary. In his foreword to the INED study on immigrants, he distinguished between the Italians and the Poles, the latter being less likely to assimilate than the former. As for Algerians, according to him, 'there can hardly be any question of assimilation'.[27]

The eradication of the term race did not put an end to the categorization of people by others. In the case of immigration specialists, it even prompted

---

[24]Viet, *La France immigrée*, 157.

[25]Alain Girard and Jean Stoetzel, *Français et immigrés. Nouveaux documents sur l'adaptation. Algériens – Italiens – Polonais. Le Service social d'aide aux émigrants. Travaux et Documents. Institut national d'études démographiques. Cahier no 20* (Paris: University Press of France, 1954), 15.

[26]Lentin, *Racism and Anti-Racism In Europe*.

[27]Girard and Stoetzel, *Français et immigrés. Nouveaux documents sur l'adaptation*, 12.

a new research agenda, with new methods of analysis and new disciplinary approaches. The aim is to measure immigrant integration, or lack thereof.[28] Gone were the historical and geographical analyses of ethnic groups and their ways; now was the time for a psycho-sociological approach to individual opinions and social interactions.

French and immigrants after the war

INED surveys on the French and immigrants are a rare account of immigrants living in France after the war. It is worth recalling their most significant findings, bearing in mind that they also revealed the prejudices of the time.

INED surveys of 1953 and 1954 focused on the two most important groups in proportion at the time, the Italians and the Poles (28 per cent and 25 per cent of the foreign population in the 1946 census) and studied them in different settings: Italians in the Paris region versus Italians in the southwest of France; and Poles in the mining industry versus Poles in agricultural sector, in the north.[29] However, it is important to bear in mind that surveys on Poles and Italians were drafted with the objective of evaluating immigrants' capacity to assimilate and eventually mix with the French population. As such, they examined their presence in the labour force, as well as their habits in terms of language acquisition, customs and clothing, religious practice, rates of intermarriage, naturalization and relation with their country of origin.

In their study, Girard and Stoetzel highlighted how immigrants had established themselves throughout the years. Among Italians, the longest-established group, there was a longer-term perspective in terms of upward economic mobility. The survey on Italians living in the Paris region showed that many of the factory workers who arrived as agricultural workers (23 per cent) became skilled workers (72 per cent); as for those who worked as shopkeepers and craftsmen, 43 per cent of them were previous factory workers who managed to establish themselves throughout the years.[30] Regarding rates of intermarriage, 20–28 per cent of Italians living in the Paris region married a French woman (as opposed to 5 per cent Polish mining workers in the north).

Moreover, Italians were compared to the Poles when it comes to their adaptation to French society. The study points out how both Polish and

---

[28]Angéline Escafré-Dublet and Lionel Kesztenbaum, 'Measuring Immigrant Inclusion: The Genesis and History of the Girard-Stoetzel Surveys, 1945–1953', *Geneses* 84, no. 3 (2011): 93–112.

[29]A total of 300 Italians were interviewed in Paris and in the South of France by trained professional interviewers, both in French and Italian; 223 Poles were interviewed in the North of France by schoolteachers who spoke Polish.

[30]Girard and Stoetzel, *Français et immigrés*, 69.

Italians dress as French but keep cooking Italian and Polish dishes and keep reading news in Polish or Italian. As for religious practice, they distinguish between Italian factory workers living in the Paris region, who are further from Catholicism (57 per cent of them declare being nonpracticing Catholics), as opposed to Italian shopkeepers and agricultural workers, along with Polish immigrants who are devoted Catholics.[31] Both Italians and Poles kept strong ties with their country of origin, with numerous exchanges of letters and parcels. Italians were able to come back to their area of origin every year. Finally, both Italians and Poles had rather low rates of naturalization.

Finally, census results showed that 27.4 per cent of Italians and 25.3 per cent of Poles naturalized in 1946. Considering that naturalization was open to most of them, the surveys explored both Italians' and Poles' attitudes towards naturalization.[32] One out of three expressed hostility towards naturalization, either because they didn't see the point (their situation was already stable) or because they considered the acquisition procedure tedious. They opposed the situation in the United States, where naturalization was compulsory after a five-year period, which made it less of a 'painful moral dilemma'. It is therefore an interesting counterpoint to the assimilationist standards underpinning the 1945 ordinance on national acquisition – a criterion to which, apparently, immigrants did not necessarily wish to conform.

The authors concluded their study with the fact that Italians and Poles had 'adapted' rather than 'assimilated' to French society, by which they meant that they had managed to achieve a stable economic situation, and included French practice in their everyday social life (speaking, reading and to a lesser extent, eating, French), yet remained different, considering they kept ties with their country of origin, did not necessarily wanted to become French citizens and kept higher rates of religious practice. The feature appeared in local monographs issued later. Polish immigrants tended to keep a strong attachment to their national identity, and Italian immigrants settled and stabilized in the French workforce, while maintaining links with their country of origin.[33]

However, Girard and Stoetzel's conclusion of the study remained positive about immigrant settlement and prospects for population growth, particularly about the socioeconomic characteristics of the children of these immigrants. The surveys included questions about the children of Italians and Poles that showed high rates of language acquisition (94–100 per cent spoke French only or both French and Italian or Polish), high rates of intermarriage (24–84 per cent)

---

[31]Girard and Stoetzel, *Français et immigrés*, 84.

[32]Girard and Stoetzel, *Français et immigrés*, 92.

[33]Ponty, *Polonais méconnus*; Blanc-Chaléard, 'Les Italiens dans l'Est parisien des années 1880 aux années 1960'.

and encouraging rates of upward mobility (3–15 per cent pursued a college education).

As a result, Girard and Stoetzel demonstrated that immigrants did adapt to French society, but what was more important was that their children mixed with French people and therefore contributed to French population growth. Their study matched Sauvy's objective: supporting an active immigration policy.

In addition to the surveys on immigrants, the volume included an opinion poll that measured French people's attitude towards immigrants. The survey put into practice new polling techniques developed by Jean Stoetzel. It was based on a representative sample of 2,463 French nationals over twenty years of age and was by far the most sophisticated scientific piece of the whole volume. The results were rather bleak in terms of the French people's openness to foreigners. While 50 per cent thought foreigners were useful to the country, 58 per cent thought they caused difficulties. Their attitude varied greatly from one origin group to another. According to the poll, French people held Belgians or Swiss in sympathy; neither liked nor disliked Italians, Poles or Spaniards; but did not hold in sympathy Austrians, North Africans and above all, Germans. Despite the negative response to immigrants in French opinion, the authors clearly chose to remain optimistic. They identified higher rates of immigrant acceptance among French people living in areas with higher rates of immigrant presence. A process they identify as encouraging: the more they know foreigners, the more the French accept them. They drew on the contact hypothesis developed by psychologists at the time, that is, the notion that intergroup contact reduces prejudice between majority and minority group members.[34]

The arrival of 'Muslim French citizens from Algeria'

The production of a survey on Algerian immigrants stood in sharp contrast with that dedicated to the Italians and the Poles. It reveals the extent to which scientists, and subsequently the authorities, considered this group of immigrants to be different.

The INED survey on Algerian immigrants consisted of a series of 140 interviews conducted and analysed by Leo Bogart, an American Fulbright student, who had just completed his PhD in sociology at the University of Chicago. Bogart met Sauvy at UNESCO and informed him of his interest in researching Algerians in France. In four months, the American scholar organized the interviews, analysed the questionnaires and wrote a report. He drew up

---

[34]Gordon Allport, *The Nature of Prejudice* (New York: Addison-Wesley, 1954).

a questionnaire containing around a hundred questions on work, social life, reasons for leaving Algeria, life in France, relations with the French and leisure activities. Bogart even received support from the French administration, which put him in touch with three North African interviewers who conducted the interviews in Arabic. They were to present the survey as coming from the United Nations to 'get to know [North Africans] better' and 'help' them.

The consultation of Bogart's working papers demonstrates his interest in documenting the lives of Algerians living in France.[35] However, the presentation of his research revolves around Algerians' ability to assimilate. It is entitled *Algerians in France. Successful and Non-Successful Adaptation.* The analysis does not follow the same structure as for Poles and Italians. Regarding professional occupation, only the category of unskilled worker (60 per cent) features, with no other options, such as shopkeeper or skilled workers. No question allows for assessing their upward mobility, customs and attitude to religion. Arguably, the sample was half as numerous as for the surveys on Italians and Poles. However, several questions featured exclusively in the survey on Algerians, such as phenotypical questions (such as eye colour, skin complexion, hair colour, lip size and nose shape) or questions testing their psychological profile (such as reasonable versus unreasonable prospects; self-centred versus open to others). As for questions regarding social interactions, instead of opposing immigrants and French people, as in the case of the surveys on Poles and Italians, they opposed Europeans and North Africans.

The survey protocol, therefore, appeared to be organized according to a racial construction of the other: Algerians were described as different owing to their belonging to a group physically distinct from Europeans. It shows that the term race was not in use anymore in the French scientific context. But the scientific practice of describing physical traits in a study on the ability to assimilate remained.

Moreover, Leo Bogart organized his analysis into social types to determine the profiles most likely to adapt successfully to life in metropolitan France. He distinguished between those who meant to settle in France and therefore displayed some faculty to adapt to French society, as opposed to the vast majority of them (90 out of 140) who did not mean to settle. As a result, only a third of the Algerian sample could be regarded as likely to adapt successfully. More precisely, Algerians who were deemed more likely to successfully adapt were Algerians who expressed a desire to settle in France (95 per cent of them declared they wanted to stay in France); were more likely to marry or live with a French woman (48 per cent); and were going to Algerian and French

---

[35]Leo Bogart, 'Leo Bogart Papers, 1912–2010 and Undated', 62.0 Linear Feet, Archives & Manuscripts (Duke University Libraries, s.d.), RL.10146, https://archives.lib.duke.edu/catalog/bogartleo.

cafés alike. On the other hand, Algerians less likely to adapt were the ones who would rather live in Algeria (54 per cent) or in another Muslim country (23 per cent) than in France (19 per cent); were married, or would only marry, a Muslim woman in Algeria (64 per cent); and only went to Algerian cafés (40 per cent).

It should be noted that responses to open-ended questions revealed negative experiences of life in France, such as episodes of discrimination in the workplace or in certain public places. As for their status as Muslim French, the fact that they were still considered foreigners was bitterly resented. As one said: 'They put F. M. on our identity cards, which stands for French Muslim, and therefore temporary French'; or another one, 'I cannot consider myself French when I feel that I am only needed to wage war'. However, the negative experiences of Algerians, their feeling of not being considered fully French, despite their status as French citizens in metropolitan France and the heavy price they paid during the war, are only visible in Leo Bogart's working documents. They were not included in the volume published by Girard and Stoetzel, with a foreword by Sauvy. As a result, the survey on Algerian immigrants is a better account of how officials perceived them at the time than an indication of their living conditions in the period.

Sociologist Andrée Michel did issue an account of the living conditions of Algerian immigrants living in France, although it did not receive as much echo among administrative officials.[36] Based on a series of 170 interviews conducted with Algerian workers in the Paris region, she also pointed out the difficult experience of living and working in France. Her approach was distinct, however, in the sense that she pointed out the colonial dimension of their situation in France and stressed the discrimination they experienced. Algerians came in great numbers to work in mining, metallurgy and construction because there was a strong demand. This did not mean, however, that they always found work. First, because, as opposed to ONI foreign workers, they came freely and under no specific agreement. Second, because they were kept assigned to unskilled and temporary tasks due to enduring prejudices towards them. As a result, they were surplus employees and experienced numerous periods of unemployment.[37] Moreover, although they were French citizens and were eligible for social benefits, they did not always receive them. There was a one-year residency requirement that they rarely met, either because they lacked the necessary documentation or because they had been back in Algeria for a short period of time.

---

[36]Andrée Michel, *Les travailleurs algériens en France* (Paris: National Center for Scientific Research Press, 1956).
[37]Emmanuel Blanchard, *Histoire de l'immigration algérienne en France* (Paris: La Découverte, 2018).

Finally, Algerians lived in the most run-down areas of the working-class neighbourhoods of Paris, Lyon and Marseille or in industrial centres (particularly in the north and the coal-rich east). Single men sometimes shared rooms in cheap hotels and rented a bed. As for families, when they could not find a room to rent, they settled in the shanty towns (*bidonvilles*) that began to appear on the outskirts of the big cities.[38] Often presented as being made up mainly of men, Algerian immigration after the war also included women and families who joined them in greater numbers at the turn of the 1950s. According to the 1954 census, out of the 208,540 Algerians living in France, 14,920 were women.[39] For a while, French authorities regarded Algerian family settlement as 'the hope for Algerian integration' – drawing on older arguments about the vital role women played as a stabilizing force and modernizing agent.[40] As a result, they developed social aid programmes for Algerian families.

However, as the colonial dimension of the Algerian presence in France became more politicized and the perspective of decolonization took over, the attention shifted from integration to surveillance and control.

Ten years after the war, a total of 1,765 million foreigners lived in France, including 1.4 million Europeans.[41] This was not the rapid increase of European migration the government had hoped for, since there were already 1,744 million foreigners living in France in 1946.

But essentially, economic recovery was slow, and the politics of immigration departed from their very proactive tone. The director of INED, Alfred Sauvy, ceased to impose his view on the topic of immigration selection. As for policymakers, much of their attention was soon to be redirected towards the political activity of Algerians in France.

However, what we saw in this chapter is that the main features of what was to become French immigration policy were already present within the state apparatus: a concern for population mixing, and the idea that immigration policies could play a role in the process; a racial divide between Europeans and non-Europeans that no policy of granting citizenship could make up for.

---

[38]Marie-Claude Blanc-Chaléard, *En finir avec les bidonvilles: Immigration et politique du logement dans la France des Trente Glorieuses* (Paris: Sorbonne, 2016), 43.

[39]Muriel Cohen, *Des familles invisibles: les Algériens de France entre intégrations et discriminations (1945–1985)* (Paris: Sorbonne, 2020).

[40]Lyons, *The Civilizing Mission in the Metropole*, 71.

[41]Institut national de la statistique et des études économiques France, *Recensement général de la population de mai 1954: population légale (résultats statistiques) population, superficie, densité de population des principales circonscriptions administratives, migrations apparentes, logements et maisons* (Paris: INSEE, 1956), 45.

TABLE 3 Foreigners by Nationality of Origin and Algerians (Labelled as 'Muslims from Algeria')

Austrian	3,790	Dutch	9,985
Belgium	76,500	Polish	92,160
Bulgarian	1,432	Portuguese	7,220
Danish, Norwegian and Swedish	3,328	Romanian	6,528
Estonian, Latvian and Lithuanian	2,800	Spanish	28,720
German	53,760	Swiss	45,595
Greece	10,187	Czech	11,300
Hungary	8,135	British	19,349
Italian	294,480	Yugoslavian	17,159
Luxembourg	6,872	Other nationality	3,761
Muslims from Algeria	208,540		

Source: 1954 Census

4

From empire to country of immigration, 1954–68

On 1 November 1954, a series of bombs exploded throughout Algeria, killing nine people, an action later claimed by the armed branch of the National Liberation Front of Algeria (FLN). The attacks targeted institutions, military buildings and representatives of the French government. The authors of the attacks issued a statement demanding 'the restoration of the Algerian State, sovereign, democratic and social, within the framework provided by Islamic principles'.[1] Algerians had long voiced their demand for an independent state, and the members of the FLN were dissidents from the banned Movement for the Triumph of Democratic Liberties (MTLD). With this attack, however, the nationalist movement embarked on an armed struggle against colonial authority. The shift to armed violence reflected the greater obstacles encountered by the inhabitants of settler colonies in achieving independence. The process by which power was transferred had already taken place in other colonial possessions: Laos and Cambodia became independent in 1953, North Vietnam in 1954. But French authorities maintained that Algeria was French and that the situation elsewhere in the empire did not compare. However, a wind of change was blowing across the world, and Algerians' claim was framed in comparable nationalist terms as most colonized countries at the time. FLN delegates came and represented Algeria at the 1955 Bandung Conference that condemned colonialism and advocated for a third way between the Eastern and Western blocs. Eventually, Algeria became independent in 1962.

The impact of the Algerian War on French political life was tremendous. Despite their willingness to resist decolonization, the French government could not avoid accepting the Algerian claim for independence. However, it took a change in regime in 1958 and a redefinition of the French nation, without its empire.

In the meantime, the economy was finally taking off, and France entered an era of mass immigration. The politics of immigration therefore found themselves at the heart of two very distinct issues in the years between 1954

---

[1]Shepard, *The Invention of Decolonization*, 43.

and 1968: on the one hand, the Algerian War and the surveillance of Algerians in France; and on the other hand, the arrival of numerous immigrants from Southern Europe (Spanish immigrants overtook Italians, and Portuguese immigration began) and North Africa (Morocco and Tunisia).[2] Yet, the two issues became intertwined as administrative officials and organizations of social aid took over and invented a policy of immigrant reception. We shall see in this chapter that, in doing so, they shaped a narrative of immigration in France as a necessary, yet temporary phase for non-European migrants and their families, while at the same time encouraging the settlement of European migrants.

This chapter focuses on governmental and non-governmental actors who initiated the first public action scheme to help immigrants. From 1954 to 1968, the issue of immigrant reception was rarely discussed, despite a steady increase in the number of arrivals.[3] Journalists did not pay much attention to the living conditions of immigrants, and there was little television coverage during the period.[4] Politicians were concerned with the Algerian War, but not so much with the living conditions of Algerians living in France. Only a few administrative officials in the government, and some non-governmental actors in the field of social aid, took an interest in the living conditions of immigrants.

What's more, the chapter shows that many of the governmental and non-governmental actors involved in public action to help immigrants had a previous experience of living in the colonies. As a result, their role in initiating the first public action scheme to help them led to a continuity of institutional practices between the colonial and metropolitan worlds.[5] This chapter aims to discuss the extent to which France's original approach to immigrant policies was shaped by a colonial point of view. It takes into account the specific context of the Algerian War and, in doing so, points to the lasting impact of decolonization on the politics of immigration in France.

The chapter first explains how and why the government initiated public action towards Algerian immigrants in France, and how this was invested with strategies of control as the war intensified. It then shows that the independence of Algeria did not put an end to this type of governmental initiative and, on the contrary, gave birth to a new kind of policy to manage the reception of newcomers to France. The chapter highlights the complexity of people's move in response to decolonization, such as the repatriates or

---

[2]By 1968, there were 605,624 Spaniards; 565,024 Italians; 295,508 Portuguese; 473,252 Algerians; 79,176 Moroccans; and 60,688 Tunisians (Paris: National Institute of Statistics and Economic Studies, 1962 Census).

[3]Tapinos, *L'immigration étrangère en France*, 47.

[4]Édouard Mills-Affif, *Filmer les immigrés: Les représentations audiovisuelles de l'immigration à la télévision française* (Brussels: De Boeck, 2004), 14.

[5]'La colonie rapatriée'.

the colonial veterans who could claim French citizenship. They added to the increasing number of immigrants coming from Southern Europe, in particular Portugal.

Taking care of colonials in metropolitan France, 1954–8

The presence of Algerian immigrants in metropolitan France can be seen as the trigger for the French government to design a policy of immigrant reception as early as the 1950s. This is due, on the one hand, to their status as French citizens, which made them eligible for social benefits in metropolitan France, and on the other hand, to the question of their adaptation to French society, which experts considered to be particularly challenging. This did not mean, however, that the government created dedicated public services for them, but rather that administrative officials relied on a series of non-governmental organizations that formed a network of welfare services specialized in providing aid to colonial migrants.

France's immigrant reception policy stood in sharp contrast with its active immigrant recruitment policy, called for by de Gaulle himself in 1945. There was no specific department dedicated to it (such as the Office for National Immigration for immigrant recruitment, for instance), nor any allocated budget. But this aligned with how the most vulnerable populations were dealt with at the time: a form of 'mixed economy of welfare', where local government and private organizations filled the gap left by top-down national policies.[6] The only difference was that, in the case of colonial migrants, local private organizations received funding from the Ministry of the Interior rather than the Ministry of Social Affairs, which was commonly responsible for welfare. The whole government of the three French departments of Algeria came under the authority of the Algerian Office at the Interior Ministry, and so did the Algerians residing in metropolitan France. As a result, by 1956, the Interior Ministry partially funded 135 private initiatives throughout the country.[7]

It is striking to observe the extent to which the people involved in this mixed economy of welfare based their expertise on a previous experience in the colonies. Indeed, soon after the end of the war, people with professional experience in the colonies began to set up private organizations for colonial migrants arriving in Paris, Lyon, Marseille and northern France. For instance,

---

[6]Axelle Brodiez-Dolino, 'The Conjunction of Social and Health Considerations in Policies against Poverty and Vulnerability in Twentieth-Century France', *Le Mouvement Social* 242, no. 1 (2013): 9–29.
[7]Lyons, *The Civilizing Mission in the Metropole*, 45.

in 1948, Father Jacques Ghys, a former missionary priest in Tunisia, began to run Moral Assistance to North Africans (AMANA) in the Paris region. In 1950, Louis Belper, who had been a colonial officer in Algeria, founded Aid to Overseas Workers in Marseille (ATOM). In 1952, a former military officer in Morocco, and senior civil servant in the Interior Ministry, Pierre Lamy, founded the Lyautey Committee in memory of Marechal Lyautey, the first governor of Morocco, and his wife, who had herself been involved in a charity organization for Moroccan soldiers back in Rabat.[8] As such, the experience of living in the empire shaped their understanding of migrants' needs and ability to adapt to French society. They provided social aid to Algerian workers and their families in the form of food, clothes and health care. But they also included activities centred around language acquisition and adaptation to life in metropolitan France.

When the French government initiated a programme of housing construction, specifically dedicated to Algerian immigrants, they called on the expertise of these private organizations and entrusted them with the task of helping Algerian immigrants adapt to life in metropolitan France. In fact, the only reason government officials designed a specific housing policy for Algerians and allocated a specific budget for it was that they believed that Algerians had specific needs and needed specific help to adapt to French society.[9] As such, the National Construction Society for Algerian Workers (SONACOTRAL) was created in 1956, with the idea that it would build transitional housing for Algerians and their families. Algerians would live there for a short period of time, during which they would adapt to the French way of life, after which they would move into permanent housing with the rest of the general population. SONACOTRAL would build hostels (*foyers*) for single male workers living in France (namely, buildings with rooms for rent and a shared kitchen) and living units for families.

AMANA was such an organization entrusted with the task of helping Algerian immigrants adapt to life in metropolitan France. A focus on this organization helps understand how ideas that were rooted in the empire continued to influence the management of immigration issues in metropolitan France.[10]

AMANA officially addressed the needs not only of Algerians but also of all 'North Africans', as per the name of the organization. The choice of words may

---

[8]Angéline Escafré-Dublet, 'Le Comité Lyautey et l'accueil en gare des migrants (1952–1975)', *Migrance*, no. 46 (2015): 43–54.

[9]Lyons, *The Civilizing Mission in the Metropole*, 124.

[10]Angéline Escafré-Dublet, 'Aid, Activism and the State in Post-War France: AMANA, a Charity Organisation for Colonial Migrants, 1945–1962', *Journal of Modern European History* 12, no. 2 (2014): 247–61, https://doi.org/10.17104/1611-8944_2014_2_247.

stem from the fact that Father Ghys had previously been posted in Tunisia and was therefore concerned about the fate of all North Africans living in France. However, Algerians were ten times more numerous than Moroccans and Tunisians at the time, and both former colonial protectorates became independent in 1956. As a result, Moroccans and Tunisians never qualified as French citizens, eligible for social services in metropolitan France. In fact, the practice of referring to Algerians as North Africans was widespread in the working documents of the administration and the non-governmental organizations – a practice that might have come from a certain indifference to distinguish between them, combined with a reluctance to recognize Algerian nationalist claims, particularly in the context of the war of independence.[11]

The acronym AMANA stands for Moral Assistance to North Africans but also means 'trust' in Arabic. Father Jacques Ghys, who led AMANA from 1948 to 1991, was a member of the White Fathers, a missionary order that had been founded in Algiers in 1882. The White Fathers wore the traditional robe (*gandoura*) and learned the language of the indigenous population. Their action was informative, and they produced detailed accounts of life in Algeria that ethnographers would later be able to rely on.[12] However, the bulk of their action was educational; they ran a parochial school and from 1867 to 1890 had been at the head of a vast campaign of conversion of Algerian orphans to Catholicism. They had since given up on the conversion project, but White Fathers remained knowledgeable on the issue of Algerian adaptation (if not full assimilation), at least in the view of the officials. Hence, the support they received to develop literacy classes, vocational-skills training, orientation and aid in navigating the bureaucracy, as well as collecting information on Algerian immigrants living in France and publishing the *North African Papers* – a quarterly journal that documented the life of North Africans living in France, written by Jacques Ghys and social workers who kept in touch with AMANA.

Starting in 1953, AMANA published a series of French-language methods entitled *Ali Learns French, Ali Improves in French, and Ali Writes to His Parents and Friends*. They were aimed at being a support for the literacy classes they developed. The pedagogical resources reinforced pervasive stereotypes.[13] Instruction materials only depicted occupations such as construction, mining and factory work. Grammar examples conveyed ideas that Algerians had to improve themselves if they were to adapt successfully. An example of

---

[11]On official and non-official categories in use to refer to Muslim French citizens from Algeria, see Angéline Escafré-Dublet, Lionel Kesztenbaum, and Patrick Simon, 'La greffe coloniale en métropole. Les Français musulmans dans le recensement de 1954', *Sociétés contemporaines* 110, no. 2 (2018): 35–59, https://doi.org/10.3917/soco.110.0035.

[12]Pierre Bourdieu, Mouloud Mammeri, and Yacine Tassadit, 'Du bon usage de l'ethnologie | Cairn. info', *Actes de la recherche en sciences sociales*, 2003.

[13]Lyons, *The Civilizing Mission in the Metropole*, 89.

grammar for learning the conditional tense read as followed: 'I would find work if I were a skilled worker, You would find a job if you knew French, He'd find friends if he was nicer, We'd find friends if we went to the hostel, They would find a situation if they knew how to read and write'.[14] As for safety in the workplace, it was made clear that it was the responsibility of the worker to follow the rules. Yet, nothing mentioned the possibility of filing a complaint or joining a union.

Welfare providers in general, and AMANA director Jacques Ghys in particular, were especially eager to make the fate of North Africans less ignored and more visible. As Historian of Algerian immigration, Philippe Dewitte wrote about the North African Papers, later on, in 2005, 'The simple fact that they took interest in the fate of invisible, often ignored, workers was in itself a sign of true solidarity'.[15] However, colonization placed AMANA in 'the paradox of emancipation and domination' that Michael Barnett has described regarding the humanitarian venture.[16] What stands out from the specific example of AMANA is that what appeared to be a relatively straightforward charity or welfare provision at first sight can reveal complex colonial subtexts that can be traced back to missionaries and humanitarian work in North Africa. As a result, bonds that had been created in the empire maintained an unequal repartition of power in metropolitan France: the Muslim colonial subjects on the one hand, and the European social workers on the other – a power dynamic that became ever more crucial as welfare provision became the social arm of France's final attempt at keeping Algeria French.

Winning the 'hearts' of the Algerians, 1958–62

As soon as the 1954 attacks were announced, the French government reacted with a strategy of maintaining order and economic development. Accounts of life in Algeria – as, for instance, Albert Camus's 1939 report on poverty in Kabylia – contributed to this economic interpretation of the problem.[17] However, the intensification of the FLN's terrorist actions in

---

[14]Laurent Gervereau, Pierre Milza and Émile Témime, *Toute la France: histoire de l'immigration en France au xxe siècle* (Paris: Somogy, 1998), 126.

[15]Philippe Dewitte, '1950–2000. Des Cahiers nord-africains à Hommes & Migrations', *Hommes & migrations* 1257, no. 1 (2005): 62–8.

[16]Michael Barnett, *Empire of Humanity: A History of Humanitarianism* (Ithaca, NY: Cornell University Press, 2011).

[17]Albert Camus and Arthur Goldhammer, *Algerian Chronicles* (Cambridge, MA: Harvard University Press, 2002), https://doi.org/10.2307/j.ctvjf9xg8.

Algeria and the French army's response meant that the situation could no longer be considered as one of maintaining order but rather as one of war. The year 1957 was particularly violent, with an increase in terrorist violence and the French army's use of force in response. From January to October 1957, the French military succeeded in dismantling terrorist networks and important leaders by combing the city of Algiers and resorting to torture. This was the famous *Battle of Algiers*, brought to the screen by Italian director Gillo Pontecorvo, who won the Golden Lion at the 1966 Venice International Film Festival and Critics' Choice award at the Cannes Film Festival but whose movie was banned in France until 1971. In fact, the use of torture as a method of fighting the terrorist guerrilla depicted in the movie provoked national and international condemnation. The United Nations questioned the French government on the situation and the use of torture, to which the French government did not respond, arguing that the maintenance of order in Algeria was a matter of domestic security, not international scrutiny. As for French public opinion, although criticism of the use of torture was becoming increasingly pressing in intellectual circles,[18] it was above all the commitment of the conscripts that struck people's minds. Otherwise, the situation was of limited concern to the population of metropolitan France, unlike the Europeans in Algeria who formed the main opposition to Algerian independence, organizing demonstrations and voicing their discontent.

In a situation of rising criticism on the international scene and opposition coming from Europeans in Algeria, the French government struggled to remain in power. The Fourth Republic was a parliamentary regime, still quite similar to that of the Third Republic, where the legislative power largely prevailed over the executive. In times of crisis, when disagreements were particularly acute in the National Assembly, prime ministers and their governments struggled to hold on to power. From 1954 to 1958, prime ministers of the Fourth Republic came and went: first Pierre Mendès France (1954), then Edgard Faure (1955), Guy Mollet (1956), Maurice Bourgès-Manoury (June–September 1957), Felix Gaillard (November 1957–April 1958, and finally Pierre Pfimlin (14–28 May 1958). Eventually, President René Coty called in Charles de Gaulle, who only agreed to return to power if the constitution was amended and greater power was given to the executive branch. After his inauguration on 2 June 1958, de Gaulle instructed the government to draw up a new constitution, which was approved by referendum on 28 September 1958. The 1958 Constitution

---

[18]Jean-Paul Sartre, *Situations, V Colonialisme et néocolonialisme* (Paris: Gallimard, 1964). The book is a collection of essays French philosopher Jean-Paul Sartre wrote from 1954 to 1958 about colonization, decolonization, terrorism, torture and censorship.

established the regime of the Fifth Republic, in which the powers of the executive branch (president and prime minister) were greatly strengthened.[19]

The very fact that special powers were granted to Charles de Gaulle and that it was necessary to go through a change of regime clearly proves the situation of deep political crisis. Once in power, however, President de Gaulle kept the original strategy of focusing on economic and social development. On 3 September 1958, the French government launched the Constantine Plan. The programme consisted of extending industrial and welfare policies in Algeria. It was meant to lead to a preference for a French solution in Algeria. What's more, the Constantine Plan had a 'metropolitan arm' that intended to 'integrate progressively French Muslims of Algeria in the economic and social life in France'.[20]

Initially steered by the Algerian Office at the Interior Ministry, the management of social welfare for Algerians became the responsibility of a special agency under the responsibility of the prime minister. The Social Action Fund for Muslim French citizens of Algeria (*Fonds d'action sociale pour les Français musulmans d'Algérie et leurs familles*) was created in 1958. It was entrusted to Michel Massenet, a senior civil servant who had just published an essay advocating for social development as a strategy to keep Algeria French.[21] Indeed, the less official objective of the Social Action Fund was to expand its reach to as many Algerians as possible and counter the popularity of the National Liberation Front for Algeria (FLN, *Front de libération nationale*). The FLN proved a fierce rival to the French administration not only in Algeria itself but also in appeals to the immigrant population of metropolitan France. Although the FLN competed with the National Algerian Movement (*MNA, Mouvement national algérien*), it was effective in extracting money from Algerian workers under the promise of social and educational opportunities.[22]

During the Algerian War, the lives of Algerians residing in metropolitan France were particularly difficult.[23] They continued to arrive in France, mainly because they were fleeing the violence of war on Algerian soil. Their flow began to slow down in 1956, when France made it compulsory for those wishing to transit between the two territories to request authorization. Intended to give a better idea of the number and identity of Algerians arriving in France, the formality had the effect of curbing the number of entries. However, the

---

[19]Initially elected by indirect universal suffrage, the President of the French Republic has been elected by direct universal suffrage since 1962.

[20]A. H. Lyons, 'Social Welfare, French Muslims and Decolonization in France: The case of the Fonds d'action sociale', *Patterns of Prejudice* 43, no. 1: 65–89.

[21]Michel Massenet, *Contrepoison ou La morale en Algérie* (Paris: Grasset, 1957), 79.

[22]L. Amiri, 'La bataille de France. La guerre d'Algérie en métropole' (Paris: Robert Lafont, 2004).

[23]Benjamin Stora and Linda Amiri, *Algériens en France: 1954–1962: la guerre, l'exil, la vie* (Paris: Autrement, 2012).

census carried out at the beginning of 1962 put the number of Algerians living in France at 350,224 (83 per cent men) – a steady rise since 1954 (250,000).[24] Two-thirds of them concentrated in the Paris region, the remaining third were located in the region of Lyon, Lille and the Northern and Eastern parts of the country, where they work in the mining industry.

Algerians were still only able to find housing in the most run-down areas of the cities: those with cheap hotels or in the shanty towns, on the outskirts of the cities. In Nanterre, west of Paris, two thousand single workers rented a bed in a dormitory, and eight hundred families had built or bought their own unit in 1961.[25] Living in the shantytowns meant living in an unpaved, muddy area where rubbish was not collected, and where access to water and electricity was restricted. Shantytowns were isolated from the rest of the city. In her account of life in the Nanterre bidonville called 'La Folie', activist and social worker Monique Hervo described a 'black hole' in comparison with the brand-new social housing emerging from the ground a few hundred metres away.[26] The place was somehow lively with shops, cafés and hairdressers. It was also a space where Algerians experienced solidarity. They shared tips, food and news from back home. Moreover, children were able to go to the nearby French public schools. However, women who did not work outside the shantytown experienced great isolation from the rest of society. Finally, access to healthcare was limited, as few doctors entered the area, no ambulances drove in, and residents had to go into town for dispensaries.

Faced with the difficult living conditions of Algerians, the welfare network of services established before continued to operate, under the supervision of Social Action Fund director Michel Massenet. However, organizations had few resources at their disposal and, as a result, were limited in their actions. Moreover, the ultimate goal of the French government's support for social development was control. French language courses and vocational training were intended to reach out to Algerians and influence their choices. Visits by social workers were intended to gather information about them.

As a case in point, the organization AMANA, which not only provided language courses and vocational training but also published studies on Algerians, received the support of the administration and the full confidence of Michel Massenet, who considered it to be a model to follow.[27] As such, AMANA opened new centres in the northern and eastern parts of the country

---

[24]By 1962, there were 441,4478 Spaniards; 623,156 Italians; 49,930 Portuguese; 350,224 Algerians; 33,260 Moroccans; and 26,529 Tunisians (Paris: National Institute of Statistics and Economic Studies, 1962 Census).

[25]Muriel Cohen, 'Les bidonvilles de Nanterre', in Stora et Amiri, Algériens en France, 27.

[26]Monique Hervo, Chroniques du bidonville: Nanterre en guerre d'Algérie (Paris: Seuil, 2001).

[27]Escafré-Dublet, 'Aid, Activism and the State in Post-War France'.

in 1959. The director never fully took sides with public authorities. It has even been argued that, despite their attempts to appear apolitical, caritative organizations, including missionaries who had been in touch with the reality of the colonial empire, could be regarded as favourable to decolonization.[28] However, AMANA, along with other private initiatives, could not escape the political situation and the fact that, for the French government, social aid was a way of maintaining a form of control over the colonial population. They contributed to the general social control over the colonial population.

Finally, the violence of the war was significant on Algerian soil, but the fight was not absent from metropolitan France. The FLN collected large sums of money from Algerians living in France, when the latter were not directly involved in fighting and organizing.[29] As a result, police exerted intense surveillance, and many arrests took place.[30] So much so that the first curfew, established in September 1958, which had fallen into disuse, was finally reinstated on 5 October 1961. Algerian Muslim workers were 'advised' to 'refrain from going out at night in the streets of Paris and its suburbs, particularly between 8.30 pm and 5.30 am'. As a result, Algerian immigrants residing in metropolitan France experienced difficult living conditions not only from a social point of view but also psychologically, as they were at the centre of opposing political strategies.

On the evening of 17 October 1961, Algerians in the Paris region demonstrated against the curfew imposed by Paris police chief Maurice Papon. The call came from the French Federation of the FLN, but the watchword was peaceful protest. However, in several places, the police charged, injuring many and killing dozens of Algerians. A few months later, on 8 February, this time in response to a joint call from the French Communist Party, the Socialist Party and the trade unions, an equivalent demonstration took place, including French demonstrators. This time again, police charged, killing nine French people fleeing through the entrance of the Charonne metro station. The tragedy in the Charonne metro, which killed nine French people, long overshadowed the repression of the demonstration on 17 October 1961, which killed dozens of Algerians. The double standard in repression at the time, and how the events were remembered, both reflect the colonial dimension of the conflict that led to the eventual independence of Algeria.

Eventually, on 1 July 1962, six million people residing in Algeria were asked whether or not they were in favour of the independence of Algeria in

---

[28]Florence Denis, 'Entre mission et développement: une expérience de laïcat missionnaire, l'association Ad Lucem 1945–1957', *Le Mouvement social*, no. 177 (1996): 29–47, https://doi .org/10.2307/3778951.

[29]Stora and Amiri, *Algériens en France*, 9.

[30]Blanchard, *La police parisienne et les Algériens*.

a referendum vote, to which 93 per cent answered 'yes'. What had been a long and bloody battle finally ended in the ballot box with the affirmation of the Algerian people's right to self-determination. Indeed, a year after taking office, General de Gaulle had changed his views on the situation in Algeria and asserted the right of the Algerian people to 'decide their own destiny', on 16 December 1959. However, he had also met with considerable resistance from the Europeans in Algeria, who could not see themselves leaving their country and had won the support of certain members of the French army. Despite an attempted coup in Algeria by Generals Salan, Challe, Jouhaud and Zeller in April 1961, the French government launched independence negotiations with the FLN, resulting in the Evian agreement of 18 March 1962 and ultimately the proclamation of Algerian independence on 5 July 1962.

Independence and the unexpected rise in arrivals from Algeria, 1962–4

Despite the efforts put into negotiating the continued stay of Europeans in Algeria during the 1962 Evian discussion, most of them left.[31] France experienced the largest wave of settlement in such a short period: from 1960 to 1965, a million Europeans from Algeria settled in France.[32] The vast majority (80 per cent) of the French citizens repatriated from Algeria were born there and had not previously lived in France; either because their parents or grandparents had moved to Algeria many years ago, or because they were of Spanish, or Italian descent, or else, because they were Algerian Jews who had acquire full French citizenship following the 1870 decree Cremieux.

Moreover, Algerian independence did not put an end to the presence of Algerians in France. On the contrary, Algerian immigration to France continued, and by 1968, Algerians amounted to 473,252 according to the French census. This may come as a surprise, for Algerians had clearly expressed their wish to break away from France and gain independence. However, exploring the reasons behind the phenomenon highlights the paradoxes of immigration in general, and postcolonial immigration in particular. In theory, the new Algerian state needed brains and manpower for the new country, but, in practice, for those who had left Algeria several years ago, it was not necessarily easy to find a situation when they came back. As a result, among the Algerians who

---

[31]Yann Scioldo-Zürcher, *Devenir métropolitain: Politique d'intégration et parcours de rapatriés d'Algérie en métropole* (Paris: School for Advanced Studies in the Social Sciences Press, 2010).
[32]In 1954, there were 984,000 French citizens and 60,000 European foreigners living in Algeria, which constituted a tenth of the total population of Algeria.

travelled back from France to Algeria in the years that followed, many returned and re-established themselves in France afterwards.[33] In addition, massive European departures, the closure of industries and the withdrawal of capital contributed to weakening the Algerian economy.

The difficulty of overhauling an economic system originally based on colonial exploitation is fundamental to understanding the economic strains that Algeria subsequently experienced. As a result, many Algerians continued to embark on the well-established route of migration to France in pursuit of better economic prospects. Finally, for those Algerians who had settled in France with their families, it was becoming increasingly difficult to envisage returning to Algeria, as their children were now at school and had their lives on this side of the Mediterranean. This did not mean that a continued stay in France did not lead to conflicting feelings among Algerian nationals towards their newly independent homeland. In fact, many of them suffered living in a society that had repeatedly denied their own identity. However, as argued by Algerian sociologist Abdelmalek Sayad, they proceeded to downplay their suffering and kept living in France.[34]

In Algeria, European Algerians and Algerians lived together, knew each other, and sometimes even worked together. Yet, they did not hold equivalent status and only mingled up to a certain extent. As a case in point, a 1957 administrative inquiry estimated that the number of mixed households only amounted to seventeen hundred.[35] As much as their fate differed greatly from that of the Algerians in Algeria, so did their move to France in the 1960s. In 1961, the French government voted a law defining the status of repatriates from the French overseas departments 'who had to leave or felt they had to leave a territory [under French sovereignty] where they were established' (Law of 26 December 1961). This law enabled hundreds of thousands of French citizens established in the colonies – and particularly in Algeria – to benefit from assistance to settle in France. The French government deployed a major reception and settlement aid scheme, ranging from reassignment to civil service jobs, accommodation in transit centres, and the allocation of specific allowances based on income.

However, the history of repatriation from the colonies is that of a drama of misunderstanding between metropolitan France and the empire. French people had a distorted image of colonial settlers, who were easily seen as rich landowners with vast estates. They were unaware of the important social and economic stratification of colonial society. As a result, they were ill-

---

[33]Tapinos, *L'immigration étrangère en France*, 61–2.

[34]Abdelmalek Sayad and Pierre Bourdieu, *The Suffering of the Immigrant*, trad. David Macey (Cambridge: Polity, 2004).

[35]Scioldo-Zürcher, *Devenir métropolitain*, 32.

prepared for the arrival of repatriates, whom years of discourse on the colonial empire had doomed to appear exotic in their eyes. In the case of Algerian repatriates, they felt that the panic and violence in Algeria was far from being understood in metropolitan France. Moreover, public opinion was, in many respects, hostile towards them. This may account for the construction of a *pied-noir* identity, in opposition to the metropolitan perception of repatriates, which revolved around cuisine, music and popular figures, in the following decades.[36] Nevertheless, the government allocated considerable means to aid their installation on French soil. The government did not necessarily show it off, for it was meant to channel the discontent of repatriates who felt betrayed by France's abandonment of Algeria.

Finally, hundreds of thousands *harkis* fled Algeria in fear of retaliation.[37] *Harki*, which means a group of soldiers in Arabic, is the term used to refer to Muslim French citizens of Algeria who served as soldiers in the French army. Some of them had been regular soldiers, such as the riflemen (*tirailleurs*) who had served during the Second World War, but some were recruited as militia and based throughout Algeria. The reasons for their enrolment in the French army could be varied; sometimes it could reflect a preference for French Algeria, but most of the time it was a way to secure family and property in a context of guerrilla warfare across the country. Nonetheless, by taking sides with the French army, and even though the Evian agreements stated that no measure of retaliation would officially be taken against them, they were at risk, and many of those who did not flee died at the hands of the winner.[38]

Although they were in danger and had served France, the French government did not facilitate the Muslim veterans' escape. During the Evian discussions, the French authorities had specifically negotiated that nothing would happen to them so as not to have to organize their reception. As a result, many of them were isolated in reception camps where they settled with their families, while others came to join the areas where Algerian immigrants had settled. Despite services rendered to the country, the fate of the *harkis* in France was therefore more like that of Algerian immigrants than that of repatriates.[39]

The complexity of people's move in repercussion of decolonization in general, and the Algerian War in particular, was unmatched: the repatriates who hold French citizenship and were eligible to governmental aid, yet had never lived in France, nor were especially well perceived by the French population;

---

[36]Eric Savarese, *L'invention des Pieds-Noirs* (Paris: Séguier, 2002).

[37]An estimated 270,000 of which only half came legally. See Blanc-Chaleard, *Histoire de l'immigration*, 64.

[38]Alistair Horne, *A Savage War of Peace: Algeria 1954–1962* (New York: Viking, 1977), 537.

[39]Sung-Eun Choi, *Decolonization and the French of Algeria: Bringing the Settler Colony Home* (Basingstoke: Palgrave Macmillan, 2015).

the Muslim veterans who could claim French citizenship but were not eligible to the same kind of governmental aid and experienced considerable push back from officials; and, finally, Algerian nationals who continued to come and settle in France in search for better economic prospects, despite experiencing guilt for abandoning their newly independent homeland.

Moreover, the construction of a welfare state happening at the same time renders the differences between each group particularly salient. The efforts the French government put – or did not put – in organizing their settlement reflect political choices to include or exclude certain groups. The case of the *harkis* is particularly revealing in this sense. That Algerian immigrants were not particularly assisted in their settlement in France could be regarded as deriving from their new status as foreign nationals. However, the fact that Muslim veterans who had fled Algeria for fear of retaliation, in a state of mind, probably comparable to that of Europeans, eventually experienced pushback from the French government does not follow any rational logic, except for the irrational logic of racial division. Thus, as much as Algerians had been kept apart from becoming full French citizens during colonization, their fate would be different from the rest of the former inhabitants of the empire after decolonization.

Managing immigrant reception, 1965–8

The unrest that followed decolonization and the subsequent influx of repatriates did not prevent net migration from remaining high throughout the 1960s. Between 1956 and 1965, the National Immigration Office recorded three times as many workers entering the country as in the previous decade (966,000 compared with 325,000). Arrivals from Spain were at the top of the list for the period 1962–5. But there was also an increase in the number of arrivals from Portugal, whereas the number of arrivals from Italy decreased. These arrivals were largely linked to France's economic needs. In fact, the arrival of the repatriates did not meet France's needs in the labour force. They were families, with people of all ages and skills spread across all professional fields. Rather, their arrival increased the demand for housing and the need for labour in the construction industry. This need was matched by foreign labour, and hence prompted an increase in economic immigration from Southern Europe. Foreigners went from 4.67 per cent to 5.27 per cent of the total population from 1962 to 1968. Among them, Spaniards were the most numerous: 605,624, in 1968.

Faced with an increase in the number of immigrants on French soil, the French government reinvested the previous expertise in the management of colonial migrants in a policy of immigrant reception. Admittedly, the French government also aimed at retaining a form of control over the Algerian population, which remained suspicious in their view, and which was no longer under its authority. However, it was the very same expertise developed to deal with them as colonial migrants that was maintained and extended to all foreign migrants. This did not mean that governmental and non-governmental organizations treated foreign immigrants arriving from Europe in the same way as they had treated colonial migrants. Quite the opposite, in fact, how governmental and non-governmental organizations went about organizing the reception of European immigrants reveals what they thought of them, and the extent to which they favoured them over non-Europeans, particularly Algerians.

At the highest levels of the state, the negotiation of movement and labour agreements is indicative of the governmental preference for Europeans, and up to a certain extent, Caribbeans or Africans, provided they were *not* Algerians. In 1963, the National Office for Immigration extended its active recruitment policy to Morocco, Tunisia and Portugal. In 1965, labour agreements were signed with Turkey and Yugoslavia. As for nationals of the former French colonies of sub-Saharan Africa, immigrant workers could enter freely, provided they went through a health check, in exchange for which they would benefit from access to French social security services.[40]

Moreover, in 1963, former prime minister and de Gaulle long-time collaborator Michel Debré, who had just been elected deputy in the Island of Reunion, organized the recruitment and travel of men and women from the French Caribbean islands, Guiana and Réunion. Between 1963 and 1982, 160,000 French citizens from the overseas departments travelled to metropolitan France under the BUMIDOM scheme, the Office for the Development of Migration within Overseas Departments (*Bureau pour le développement des migrations dans les départements d'outre-mer*). They came and worked in the construction industry, but also in public services, such as the health service, the post office and local administration. Specific programmes organized the deportation of children – some orphans, but others not – from Réunion to repopulate declining rural areas, specifically in central France (such as La Creuse).[41]

As for Algerians, the French government signed the Nekkache-Grandval agreement in 1964 that aimed at restricting new arrivals in France. Algerians who had previously worked in France could come freely, provided they had proof of their previous employment in France. Others had to obtain a work permit from the National Office of Algerian Labour (*Office national algérien de la main d'oeuvre*, ONAMO). Should they wish to visit France as tourists,

---

[40]Agreements signed on 5 March 1965, for Senegal; 11 March 1965, for Mali; 22 July 1965, for Mauritania. See Tapinos, *L'immigration étrangère en France*, 64.

[41]Ivan Jablonka, *Enfants en exil: Transfert de pupilles réunionnais en métropole* (Paris: Seuil, 2007).

they had to show a round-trip ticket and prove they could provide for their own needs (have a minimum of 500 francs).

In terms of implementing social action, in contact with immigrants, the difference in approach is observable in the means implemented to receive European immigrants, as opposed to Algerians. As such, the Social Action Fund was preserved, and its reach was expanded to the entire immigrant population. More than half of the Social Action Fund's budget was dedicated to the construction of dwellings for immigrants, and the other half to social development. The administration wanted to keep its control over Algerians who were now foreigners but also continued the work and extended it to all foreign immigrants. In a board meeting of the Social Action Fund in 1965, director Michel Massenet advised that organizations were to 'develop, particularly for the benefit of the Portuguese and Spanish, the operations hitherto carried out for the benefit of North African workers'.[42] In line with this new political orientation, AMANA extended its literacy classes to immigrants of all origins, and in 1965, the *Cahiers Nord Africains* were renamed *Hommes et Migrations*.

The Lyautey Committee is a good example of how resources and skills developed for colonial migrants were reinvested in programmes to organize immigrant reception at railway stations.[43] When it was set up in 1952, the Lyautey Committee aimed to guide migrants from North Africa as they got off the train, and immediately enlisted the help of the National Railway Service (SNCF) to provide premises at Paris-Lyon, Paris-Austerlitz, Metz, Nancy and Lyon railway stations. It helped that Guillaume de Tarde, a former official in Morocco and board member of the Lyautey Committee, was a senior civil servant and board member of SNCF.[44] It was also following his intervention that former SNCF staff were asked to provide orientation and welcome services in stations.

Starting in 1967, the Lyautey Committee, which had been a privately funded organization until then, began to receive funding from the Social Action Fund and extended its activities to all foreigners arriving at the station, particularly Portuguese migrants. More precisely, the work of the reception staff stationed at the stations consisted of informing migrants as they got off the train about the transport they needed to take to reach their final destination, as well as directing them towards other aid structures (such as emergency

---

[42]Board meeting of 17 November 1965, Archives of the Social Action Fund (National Archives number: 1985–0021, article 19).

[43]Escafré-Dublet, 'Le Comité Lyautey et l'accueil en gare des migrants (1952–1975)'.

[44]Olivier Büttner and Bénédicte Héraud, 'L'accueil en gare. Pratiques de l'entre-soi du Comité Lyautey', in *Le sens pratique de l'hospitalité. Accueillir les étrangers en France, 1965–1983,* (Paris: CNRS, 2021).

accommodation offered by Catholic Relief) and preventing them from falling into clandestine channels, or ending up in shanty towns. It was a question of conveying practical information to them, and also a question of language. The network of agents consisted primarily of men and women speaking French and Arabic, at first. They were joined by Spanish and Portuguese speakers afterwards.

However, French government support for the Lyautey Committee reception programme in railway stations should be understood in the specific context of Portuguese migration, which Portugal was trying to prevent. In fact, Portuguese authorities officially refused the 1963 labour agreement with France, and many Portuguese left their country illegally.[45] France, for its part, wanted to encourage migration from Portugal because of the purported assimilative qualities of its nationals. The resources deployed to welcome them were designed to encourage them to come and join the French job market. To this end, the Portuguese-speaking agent stationed at Gare d'Austerlitz, where most of them arrived on the Hendaye-Paris train, was to be able to provide them with a list of employers' addresses. The Lyautey Committee, with the support of the Social Action Fund, therefore implemented means that were unparalleled in the action they had put in place for North Africans.

This chapter showed that, far from being a rupture with the colonial period, the management of immigrant reception in the 1960s bears witness to its continuity. In both cases, the French and Algerians lived together except under distinct regimes, one being that of colonization, the other of immigration. However, in both cases, differentiation took place. This is illustrated by the fact that the colonial regime of racial distinction that kept Algerian Muslims apart from the possibility of becoming full French citizens turned into an immigration regime of racial preference, where European immigrants – and more specifically Portuguese – were favoured because of their capacity to assimilate into French society. This chapter, therefore, highlighted how the politics of immigration can tell the story of a paradigm shift, from the civilizing mission of the French Empire to the need for immigrant assimilation in the Fifth Republic.

---

[45]Victor Pereira, *La dictature de Salazar face à l'émigration: L'état portugais et ses migrants en France* (Paris: Sciences Po University Press, 2012).

5

Politics of protest, 1968–81

From North America to Europe, a new type of protest cycle began in the 1960s. The aim of these popular movements was not to overthrow governments, like the revolutions of the nineteenth century. Rather, they opened up new possibilities to make way for a new society.[1] In the United States, the Free Speech student movement against universities' restrictions on political activities gave way to a larger movement against the war in Vietnam. In Belgium, student protests against the church hierarchy in higher education contributed to the emergence of Left Catholicism, which affected the politics of the Left durably. In Italy, protests erupted in solidarity with Vietnam and turned into a general mobilization against police repression of political activism. In the United Kingdom, student activism reconstructed the world of university students and raised public awareness on issues such as the threat of nuclear weapons, racism, sexism and injustice. In France, students' revolt added to the working-class protests and opened new avenues for the articulation of social demands.

Among the unprecedented social demands of the decade that followed the political protest of May '68, a movement for the rights of migrant workers emerged that would eventually alter the fabric of the politics of immigration in France. At first sight, the mobilization of immigrants to defend their rights was a reaction to the passage in 1972 of new regulations limiting their stay. However, they can also be seen as part of a more general trend towards the mobilization of identities in politics – that is, the articulation of political demands and the representation of interests of social groups with which people identify, such as race, class, gender, sexual orientation or ethnicity. The recognition of an identity claim is often regarded as impossible in the French context, as it would operate a breach of the Republican principle of equal treatment among citizens.[2] However, a closer attention to immigrants' claims

---

[1] Gerd-Rainer Horn, *The Spirit of '68: Rebellion in Western Europe and North America, 1956–1976* (Oxford: Oxford University Press, 2008).
[2] Article 1 of the 1958 Constitution that the republic guarantees the equal treatment of all citizens, regardless of their origin, race or religion.

and action repertoire helps identify patterns of group-based mobilization on the ground of a common immigrant experience.[3]

The 1970s were a decade of political turmoil, as well as the beginning of the politicization of immigration in France. From street protests to the media and political debate, discussion about immigration began, but it was also greatly misunderstood. It was during this period that politicians began to present immigration restrictions as a way to end the economic crisis and reduce unemployment. The politics of immigration entered a confrontational phase that opposed governmental restrictions of immigration flows, against the fight for immigrant rights, and resulted in the political polarization of the topic.

Eventually, the proportion of immigrants rose from 6.5 per cent in 1968 to 7.4 per cent in 1982. Among them, Portuguese and Algerian nationals were the most numerous.[4] Yet, the Portuguese authorities entered the process of application to the European Union in 1977, which distinguished the fate of Portuguese nationals as opposed to Algerian nationals in France. As a result, the politics of immigration selection entered a new era, in which European immigrants were welcome to stay, while North African immigrants – and more specifically Algerians – were encouraged to return.

The chapter explores how the redefinition of the French Empire into a nation of immigration affected the politics of protest in France. First, it describes the participation of immigrants in the event of May '68 and clarifies why it was so difficult for an immigrant-specific claim to emerge. It then turns to the politics of immigration restriction and explains why they were a clear sign of a new politicization of immigration. Finally, it takes the vantage point of immigrant cultural life and artistic expressions to highlight how the issue of immigration was politicized in France.

The participation of immigrants in the events of May '68

What is referred to as May '68 in France consisted of a series of demonstrations, workers' strikes and building occupations that eventually led to President Charles de Gaulle dissolving the National Assembly on 30 May and calling parliamentary elections on 23 June 1968. The specificity of

---

[3]Riva Kastoryano, *Negotiating Identities: States and Immigrants in France and Germany* (Princeton, NJ: Princeton University Press, 2002).

[4]From 1968 to 1982, the number of Algerian nationals almost doubled (from 473,252 to 805,116), and the number of Portuguese nationals more than doubled (from 295,508 to 767,304).

French political protest of the late 1960s relied on workers' protest happening alongside the student revolt.[5] That the two movements intersected was carefully staged by student organizations and workers' unions, when up to one million people marched throughout Paris, on 13 May 1968. However, the solidarity between the students and the workers during the events remains the topic of much debate, despite Marxist positions on both sides. In fact, it is rather that student organizations expressed solidarity with workers in an effort to legitimize their fight, when striking workers may have felt estranged by students' demands: workers went on strike and occupied factories demanding better pay and working conditions, while students demonstrated and occupied university buildings, claiming participation in university government. Workers' mobilization eventually led to the passing of a new labour legislation allowing significant wage gains for workers (the Grenelle agreements of 27 May 1968). As for students, they managed to obtain access to representation in university bodies.

The violence that occurred in street fights between opposing students and the police, as well as the general strike that halted the economy of the country, made a lasting impression on public opinion. When parliamentary elections took place in June 1968, de Gaulle's party called for a return to order and ended up winning the vote. Nevertheless, demonstrating, going on strike and occupying buildings proved fruitful in advancing political demands, and that was probably one of the outcomes of May '68, which explains the series of protests that ensued.

The participation of immigrants in the 1968 protest has now been established as proportionate to their presence in France.[6] For a long time, historians had hypothesized that they had kept out of trouble, or even returned home, out of fear or disapproval of the movement in general. Indeed, anti-communism was rampant among immigrant workers, and some of them associated the events with a political culture they did not approve of. However, after closer scrutiny and examining archives of the unions and intelligence services, it seems rather that the minority that did leave may have left for economic reasons (there was a lack of employment due to the strikes) and for fear of deportation, as police forces threatened to arrest and deport foreign demonstrators. As for those who stayed, their participation in the strikes was indeed in proportion to the size of their group living in France.

---

[5]A transnational perspective on the history of social movements in the 1960s highlights how there were mainly students movements in Northern Europe (Belgium, Germany and the United Kingdom, in particular); while they were happening in conjunction with workers mobilizations in France, Italy and Spain (see Horn, *The Spirit of '68*).

[6]Daniel A. Gordon, *Immigrants & Intellectuals: May '68 & the Rise of Anti-Racism in France* (Pontypool: Merlin, 2012), 66–70.

Moreover, foreigners very soon became the target of specific police scrutiny.[7] This made them all the more victims of police repression when they demonstrated. As far as students are concerned, the emblematic figure of Daniel Cohn-Bendit is often mentioned. A student activist of German nationality, he was indeed threatened with deportation by the French authorities because of his role in the events of May 1968. However, Cohn-Bendit was born in France, of German parents, grew up there and spoke French without an accent. In contrast, police reports show that foreign students were arrested in greater numbers than French students, for police officers were trained to pursue them. Moreover, officials intended to demonstrate that the event stemmed from 'an element foreign to France and outside the university'.[8] As for Algerians, they had been the target of police repression a mere six years before the events of May '68, and those who did participate took great risks.

However, it is important to distinguish between the participation of immigrant workers in the movement and the articulation of immigrant-specific claims. Within the labour movement, Marxist ideology dictated that workers of the world should unite. Along this theoretical line, the immigrant workers represented the paragons of capitalist and imperialist exploitation, and therefore the most deserving of attention and worthy of fighting for. In practice, it was the general interest of the working class that was at stake, and few concerns were expressed about the specificity of immigrant working conditions, and even more so, their specific living conditions. Except for a few leftist activists and intellectuals, the specific features of immigrant living conditions (difficulty in finding housing, access to public services, low wages, and repeated periods of unemployment) were seldom known to the larger working-class movement. Not to mention the fact that the ruling elite had traditionally pitted immigrant workers against French workers in an attempt to divide the working class and ensure low wages. Finally, the media coverage of immigrant life, particularly the shanty towns, was scarce. When it did happen, it did not give much voice to the experience and concerns of immigrants and showcased silent images of desperation.[9]

It was only because immigrants began protesting against their difficult living and working conditions that the immigrant-specific claim found its way into French politics.

---

[7]Rosenberg, *Policing Paris*.
[8]Gordon, *Immigrants & Intellectuals*, 74.
[9]Mills-Affif, *Filmer les immigrés*.

The difficult articulation of immigrant-specific claims, 1968–72

In the wake of May '68, residents of immigrant hostels (*foyers*) built by Sonacotra or other private companies began protesting against rising rents and poor quality of living. The residents of the hostels were mostly Algerians (especially since Sonacotra was initially created to build transitional housing for them), but also sub-Saharan Africans who arrived in France, following the signing of a labour agreement with Senegal and Mali (1965).[10] Facing increased risk of unemployment following the economic turmoil of May '68, they found themselves in dire economic conditions and experienced difficulties paying hostel rent. Yet, the hostels' administration kept increasing rents. Moreover, most immigrant hostels were managed and controlled by officers who exerted impartial control on them and their obligations to respect curfew. As a result, several hostel residents went on a 'rent strike' – that is, they stopped paying rent as a way to oppose the rent increase and the forms of control exercised by the authorities over residents. Rent strikers risked eviction from their homes and even from the country. In doing so, they received the support of leftist movements, who turned the issue of immigrant housing into a scandal.

However, in 1969, only a few dozen rent strikes took place around the country, and those initiatives did not succeed in linking up at the national level and forming a general movement. It was not until 1974, when some immigrant hostel residents were able to emerge as spokespersons for the cause, that the gap between the cause and the people representing it was eventually closed.[11]

A lack of spokespersons who were themselves immigrants can also be observed in a series of 'foreign workers' strikes' which took place in the industry throughout the years of 1971 and 1972. Partly because employers kept speeding up production and partly because May '68 had proved that strikes were efficient in advancing one's cause, foreign workers began massive strikes in January 1971. They opposed exploitative working situations and articulated immigrant-specific grievances, such as working longer hours

---

[10]In 1971, 8 per cent of foreigners from Algeria, Morocco and Tunisia lived in hostels, against 76 per cent of foreigners from sub-Saharan Africa. Foreign worker hostels were therefore the primary type of housing for sub-Saharan African immigrants in France. However, North African immigrants were still the most numerous in this type of housing, as they were present in greater number in France at the time: 613,616 in 1968, when the National Office of Immigration recorded 10,525 entries from sub-Saharan Africa in 1971.

[11]Choukri Hmed, 'Challenging an Institution in the Case of an Unlikely Mobilization: About the "Rent Strikes" in the Sonacotra Hostels in the 1970s', *Societes contemporaines* 65, no. 1 (2007): 55–81.

for less pay and facing more precarious employment status than their French counterparts. Ultimately, the strike in the still-making Peñarroya factory led to the passing of a law recognizing lead poisoning as an illness caused by the workplace. Moreover, it was a formative experience for many immigrant workers who became eligible for employee representation after the passing of the law of 27 June 1972. However, they also complained that trade unions tended to speak on their behalf in political discussions and radio interviews.[12]

Indeed, one may differentiate not two, but four types of key players in analysing immigrant protest in these years. One may distinguish a first group of French leftist intellectuals, particularly Maoists, who saw immigrant workers as the ultimate victims of capitalist exploitation and contributed to making the situation of immigrant workers residing in hostels visible. French workers and unionists who regarded them as fellow fighters in the battle against employers constitute a second group. Moreover, a third group consisted of foreign students coming from North African countries or the Middle East who had come to study in France because they were opponents to the political regime in their country of origin. Originally primarily interested in politics back home and international issues (particularly the Palestinian cause), they gradually reoriented their interest towards the defence of immigrants in France. However, there was a major class divide between this third group and the fourth group of immigrant workers, who constituted the bulk of immigrants living in France. Both immigrant students and immigrant workers eventually connected when they were equally affected by the increase in immigration restrictions, as we shall see below.

Immigration restrictions and the birth of an immigrant movement, 1972–4

In response to a slowdown in economic growth, the government chose to curb labour migration in the early 1970s.[13] In 1972, the Labour Ministry, together with the Interior Ministry, passed the Marcellin-Fontanet circulars that made the issue of a residence permit conditional on obtaining a work contract and accommodation. Although seemingly aimed at prospective migrants, this type of legislation has actually had the effect of weakening the

---

[12]Gordon, *Immigrants & Intellectuals*, 142.
[13]Sylvain Laurens, *Une politisation feutrée: Les hauts fonctionnaires et l'immigration en France* (Paris: Belin, 2009).

position of immigrants already in France. Those who could not prove that they had a contract of employment or accommodation were unable to have their residence permit renewed after the expiration date.

This was the beginning of the making of the undocumented migrant and the enduring misconception attached to it. Indeed, the common image associated with undocumented migration is the illegal crossing of the border. However, it is rather the case that many undocumented migrants have entered the country legally but were not able to renew their residency permit ultimately.

Insofar as restrictive policies on migratory flows affected immigrant workers and students alike, they had the unexpected effect of creating a common awareness of the immigrant cause, in particular the cause of undocumented migrants.[14] As a case in point, activists such as Saïd Bouziri, who until now had been more involved in human rights issues in his country of origin (Tunisia), shifted their focus to defending the rights of immigrants, and in particular, undocumented migrants. As he was unable to renew his residence permit and was threatened with deportation, Said Bouziri and three other immigrants facing expulsion embarked on a hunger strike on 6 November 1972. The choice of a specific type of action – the hunger strike – underlines the difficulty immigrants had in making their voice heard. Left-wing intellectuals helped to publicize the struggle: Michel Foucault, Jean-Paul Sartre or Gilles Deleuze. They saw in the situation of undocumented migrants the expression of a power that had been exercised without sharing since the beginning of the Fifth Republic. Since 1958 and the return of Charles de Gaulle as president of the Republic, only right-wing governments had been in place, with no alternation to a left-wing government.

However, among immigrant workers, there was a growing awareness that they shared a common experience of exploitation and otherness in French society. The voice of this emerging awareness is particularly visible in a series of artistic experiments that accompanied the struggles. As a case in point, renowned Algerian poet Kateb Yacine wrote the play 'Mohamed, Take Your Suitcase' (*Mohamed, prends ta valise*) and toured immigrant neighbourhoods all around the country in 1972. Yacine wrote and directed the play in French and Algerian Arabic, so that mainly Algerian immigrants could understand it. He aimed to denounce the illusions of immigration. The play attacked both French employers who recruited Algerian workers at low wages, and the brand-new Algerian state, which encouraged its nationals to leave, drawn by the prospect of migrants' remittances. Using a series of clever puns and articulated around the traditional comedy trope of the farce, it staged a clueless Mohamed who goes from one deception (such as fighting in the French army) to another

---

[14]Johanna Siméant, *La cause des sans-papiers* (Paris: Sciences Po University Press, 1998).

(working for a greedy French employer). The names of the French employers are *Pompez-tout* and *Pompez-tout-doux,* which literally mean 'pump it all' and 'pump it all gently', and sound like the name of the president of the Republic at the time, Georges Pompidou.[15]

The play, *Mohamed prends ta valise,* was part of a tradition of Algerian popular theatre that had already been used during the fight for independence by Kateb Yacine's own cousin, Mustapha Kateb, then director of the FLN theatre company. Nevertheless, how it was showcased in small community halls of predominantly Algerian neighbourhoods across the country, and what it demonstrated, ushered in a new protest cycle. The difficult living conditions of immigrants, the collusion between rulers and capitalism, and the ultimate need to fight back were at the core of the play. In the years that followed, theatre was again used to publicize the cause of immigrants. Some immigrant workers wrote a series of sketches that they showcased during the occupation of the LIP factory in 1973. The occupation of the French watch factory in eastern France was a unique experiment in self-management that gave rise to a number of on-site experiments, including militant theatre performances. Among them, Mokhtar Bachiri, a Moroccan-born worker, presented his sketches with five other immigrant workers, and met two leftist activists, Geneviève Clancy and Philippe Tancelin. Together, they formed *Al Assifa,* a theatre group that aimed at raising awareness on immigrant-specific living conditions. One of their plays was entitled, 'It Works, It Works and Keep Its Mouth Shut' (*Ça travaille, ça travaille et ça ferme sa gueule*). It depicted the conditions of exploitation of immigrant labour, along with the obstacles encountered living in France, such as interaction with the bank, social services and the national unemployment agency. *Al Assifa* performed at militant gatherings, in the streets and in immigrant neighbourhoods, not only to publicize the immigrant cause but also to mobilize immigrants themselves.

Al Assifa participated in the activism of the Arab Workers Movement (*Mouvement des travailleurs Arab, MTA*), a group of activists that emerged from the National Conference of Arab workers of June 1972.[16] The Arab Workers Movement represented the meeting of two types of actors: immigrant workers and activists in exile; all from Algeria, Morocco, Tunisia, Lebanon and Syria. Some of them had met through a gathering in support of the Palestinian cause earlier in 1970 (such as Said Bouziri). However, the

---

[15]Born in 1911, Georges Pompidou was a long-time companion of Charles de Gaulle. Prime minister from 1962 to 1969, he was then elected president of the Fifth Republic in 1969. He died of cancer in 1974.

[16]Abdellali Hajjat, 'Le MTA et la "grève générale contre le racisme" de 1973', *Plein Droit,* no. 67 (2005): 35–40.

movement aimed at defending immigrants living in France. The use of the term Arab referred to all Arabic-speaking peoples from the Atlantic Ocean to the Arabian Sea and can be understood in the Cold War context, when pan-Arabism referred to a cultural, economic and political movement that sought to ensure the solidarity between Arab countries in opposition to the Western World. Advocates of pan-Arabism generally espoused socialist principles, and for this reason, the term Arab workers could resonate with the French Labour movement. The Arab Workers Movement soon spread among immigrant workers around the country. For instance, the movement called for a general strike against racism, following the off-duty police officer's assassination of Lhadj Lounès, in Marseille. The strike began on 3 September 1973, when close to thirty thousand workers went on strike in Marseille, La Ciotat and Aix-en-Provence.

The year 1973 proved particularly intense in terms of racial tensions.[17] Even though Portuguese immigrants were now as numerous as Algerians (there were 758,395 Portuguese and 709,785 Algerians in the 1975 census), the latter were the target of most of them. When an Algerian immigrant suffering from mental health issues stabbed a tram driver in Marseille, violence erupted, and numerous appeals to violence ensued. Although the minister of justice had passed the Pleven law of 1972, condemning racism and incitement to racial hatred, political groups had formed that made racism their rallying cry. In particular, reinvesting the networks that had been created in the defence of French colonial rule in Algeria, Jean-Marie Le Pen had created the National Front in 1972. It became one of the most vocal advocates for anti-Arab racism.

However, anti-Arab racism was not the only monopoly of extreme right political groups. In the 1970s, the acknowledgement of racism among the French population became the topic of much discussion in the media and political debate. After Georges Pompidou stated in a government meeting that France should not engage in the slippery slope of racism, the weekly magazine *Paris-Match* asked: 'Are French people racist?' on its cover of a September issue. So much so that in September 1973 Algerian President Houari Boumediene called for a stop to emigration from Algeria to France.

The decision of the Algerian government to discourage emigration to France reveals the salience of the topic of immigration in relation to racism in France. The decision was scarcely followed by action, which most likely resulted from the lack of proper sanction and the long-established route of exchange between the two countries. However, the mere fact that the

---

[17]Yvan Gastaut, '1973, l'année intense', *Hommes & migrations. Revue française de référence sur les dynamiques migratoires*, no. 1330 (2020): 9–13, https://doi.org/10.4000/hommesmigrations.11346.

government thought of acting on migration flows is revealing of this strong connection between the topics of immigration and racism.

The will to put an end to migratory flows came from the host country in the years that followed, anyway. And that was not to put an end to racism but rather for what was presented as, economic concern.

Putting immigration to a halt, 1974

In 1974, France issued a halt on immigration, as many other European countries that had relied on labour migration in the past decades (such as the United Kingdom in 1971 and Germany in 1973). The decision followed soon after the oil shock of 1973, when the price of oil increased drastically. The fact that other countries responded similarly does not mean that this decision was inevitable, however. It has rather been argued that immigration restriction was presented as a crisis-resolution tool, when in fact there was no such quick fix to a complex economic situation.[18] In fact, senior officials in the Interior Ministry had long wanted to restrict immigration and saw the opportunity to finally see their project come to fruition.[19] Moreover, trade unions were in favour of the decision that they had been advocating for since 1973. The halt to immigration formally put an end to the active recruitment of foreign workers through the National Office of Immigration (ONI). Trade unions such as the communist-leaning CGT considered foreign workers' recruitment as unfair competition for French workers and a cause of unemployment. The only exception was the French Democratic Confederation of Labour (CFDT), formerly tied to the Catholic Church and involved in charity-oriented work towards immigrant families. Together with organizations for the defence of immigrants' rights, they were quick to contest the decision to restrict the movement of foreign children and spouses who wanted to join a family member in France. The government came to issue a specific authorization for immigrants who could prove sufficient resources to support the family member willing to join them and therefore recognized the right to family reunification (Decree of 29 April 1976).

In 1974, the decision to bring immigration to a halt was a sign of a new politicization of immigration. To be clear, immigration was not a topic of debate during the 1974 presidential campaign. After the sudden death of President

---

[18]Yvan Gastaut, 'Français et immigrés à l'épreuve de la crise (1973–1995)', *Vingtième Siècle. Revue d'histoire* 84, no. 4 (2004): 107–18, https://doi.org/10.3917/ving.084.0107.
[19]Weil, *La France et ses étrangers*, 117–21.

Georges Pompidou in 1974,[20] former minister of economy Valéry Giscard d'Estaing campaigned with a call for the modernization of society that implied a centre-right positioning, economic liberalism and societal reforms. As for Jean-Marie Le Pen of the National Front, he essentially focused his campaign on anti-communism and anti-abortion rights. A very marginal force at the time, the National Front only accounted for 0.75 per cent of the vote in the first round of the presidential election.

When in office, forty-eight-year-old President Valéry Giscard d'Estaing appointed Jacques Chirac as prime minister and proceeded to implement change in French society: the government changed the age of majority from twenty-one to eighteen years of age; dismantled the state monopoly on television broadcast and abolished censorship. The composition of the government itself was thought to illustrate change, with four women, including health minister Simone Veil, who proposed and passed the law that decriminalized abortion (law of 17 January 1975). Finally, the 1974 government marked state intervention in new areas of public policy, with the creation of a state secretary for immigrant workers. Immigration, therefore, became a category of state intervention policy after the election of Valéry Giscard d'Estaing, as president of the Republic, in 1974, before which it was not a topic of political debate, nor an electoral issue for that matter.

Interestingly, the beginnings of this new turn in French immigration policy proved rather chaotic: the first state secretary of immigrant workers only lasted six weeks. Senior civil servant and former Resistance fighter André Postel-Vinay was initially appointed for his economic and social expertise. A former member of the financial market authority, he had also been part of the French development agency and an institution responsible for monetary issues in the overseas departments. He participated in the decision to put a halt to labour migration on 3 July 1974. However, he was deeply concerned with the lack of means allocated for the social dimension of immigration policies and resigned on 22 July 1974. After which, he was succeeded by Paul Dijoud until 1977.

The somewhat bumpy beginnings of the state secretary of immigrant workers are indicative of the tensions already underpinning the politics of immigration in France. On the one hand, elected representatives were keen to demonstrate their ability to limit migratory flows in response to the economic crisis, the government putting immigration on hold a mere four weeks after being appointed. On the other hand, the practical consequences for immigrants were neglected, or more precisely, deliberately hindered to distinguish the wheat from the chaff. Those regarded as of good stock were

---

[20]The illness of the president, even though he was already diagnosed in 1972, was hidden to public opinion and the news of his death came as a surprise in April 1974.

welcome to assimilate and become French. As for those whose resources were less stable, whose status was more dubious and who were regarded as less assimilable, they were encouraged to leave. A closer attention to the state secretary for immigrant workers' cultural programmes is revealing of its carefully planned strategy to encourage the return of (some) immigrants back home.

Government control over immigrant cultural life, 1975–8

As part of its new take on immigration issues, the state secretary designed an immigrant policy that included a 'cultural policy adapted to immigrants' (*une politique culturelle adaptée aux immigrés*). This meant that when meeting with his team, Paul Dijoud assigned one of his technical advisors the task of coming up with a specific programme that would deal with the cultural life of immigrants living in France. In theory, all state intervention in relation to culture and the arts comes under the prerogative of the French Ministry of Culture, created in 1959. In practice, officials in the culture ministry seldom attended the meetings organized by the state secretary for immigrant workers, for the development of an audience-specific programme did not fall under the universalistic reach of the ministry's mandate.[21] As a result, Dijoud's adviser liaised with the already active private initiatives dealing with immigrants and their welfare and came up, on its own, with a project to create an office aimed at furthering immigrant cultural advancement (*Office national pour la promotion culturelle des immigrés, ONPCI*).

Opened in 1975, the office was placed under the supervision of a diplomat and former cultural advisor to the French embassy in Algeria, Stephen Hessel. A double national (he was born in Berlin and acquired French nationality in 1937), he was also the son of artists, Franz and Helen Hessel.[22] Despite noble intentions to develop immigrants' access to the arts, the office achieved little in this regard. The team enlisted the help of Sylvia Monfort, a famed actress

---

[21]The decree of 24 July 1959, states that the mission of the ministry is to 'make accessible the capital works of humanity, and first of all of France, to the greatest possible number of French people, to ensure the widest audience for our cultural heritage and to promote the creation of works art and the spirit that enrich it'.

[22]The life of Franz and Helen Hessel (born Grund), and their friendship with French writer Henri-Pierre Roché was famously portrayed in Henri-Pierre Roché's book *Jules et Jim* published in 1953 and later brought to screen by François Truffaut (1962).

and theatre director, who organized a festival in the spring of 1976. She invited theatre groups created by immigrants, but no activist groups, such as the aforementioned *Al Assifa*, for instance. Moreover, it was concentrated in the Paris region and had little impact on immigrant audiences. After the office bussed a few dozen Moroccan immigrants to a performance by the Moroccan King Theatre troupe in downtown Paris, the director admitted they had only reached one tenth of their target audience.

In fact, the office aimed to compensate for France's restrictive turn in terms of immigration policy. The government intended to demonstrate that it was also concerned about the difficult living conditions of immigrants. After all, Valéry Giscard d'Estaing had only been elected president of the Republic by a narrow margin against Socialist candidate François Mitterrand (50.81 per cent), following a campaign during which the question of the distribution of wealth was central. Giscard d'Estaing had famously challenged his opponent by telling him that he did not have 'a monopoly on the heart'.[23] In 1977, Paul Dijoud's office contributed to the first urban development programme that aimed at improving the state of the unfit housing stock and the lives of the inhabitants, of which a subsequent share were immigrants (*Habitat vie sociale*).[24]

With the Office for Immigrant Cultural Advancement, the state secretary honoured a promise made during the president's campaign. Moreover, the office was also a gesture aimed at countries of emigration. To understand this, we need to consider the economic interests that the sending countries shared with France. Migration benefited sending countries from an economic point of view: it eased pressure on the labour market, migrant remittances meant an influx of foreign currency, and workers returned with professional skills acquired in the host country. However, the situation only benefited sending countries in the case of short-term migration. By settling more permanently in the host country, immigrant families would send less money back home; with the birth and schooling of their children in France, the chances of them returning would diminish.

As such, one of the office's functions was to prepare for the return of immigrant families back home. It was complemented by a system for children of immigrants that consisted of teaching immigrant languages in state-funded schools. The programme (*Enseignement des langues et cultures d'origine, ELCO*) was implemented by the Ministry of Education as part of agreements signed by the Ministry of Foreign Affairs with sending countries (such as

---

[23]'Vous n'avez pas le monopole du cœur', inter-round presidential debate of 10 May 1974.

[24]Angéline Escafré-Dublet and Christine Lelévrier, 'Governing Diversity without Naming It: An Analysis of Neighbourhood Policies in Paris', *European Urban and Regional Studies* 26, no. 3 (2019): 283–96, https://doi.org/10.1177/0969776417750439.

Portugal in 1972, Tunisia in 1974, Morocco in 1975 and Turkey in 1978).[25] Both programmes aimed at making sure sending countries would benefit from the eventual return of their nationals. Adults would come back with skills acquired in France. As for children born in France, they would come back knowing the language and culture of their parents. Language classes took place after school in neighbourhoods with a predominantly immigrant population and were taught by consulate employees.

However, through these language and culture programmes, immigrants were identified as foreigners and assigned specific cultural traits. European immigrants were presented as having closer cultural traits to French nationals than North African immigrants. When designing and implementing this 'cultural policy adapted to immigrants', administrative officials rearticulated a racialized understanding of immigrant capacity to assimilate into French society.

Finally, the office launched a TV show entitled *Mosaïc,* which became its biggest achievement and lasted ten years. *Mosaïc* aired every Sunday morning from 10.30 am to 12.30 pm on the third public television channel (FR3). The secretary of state had initially thought of a Muslim television programme, and Paul Dijoud had announced its creation during a trip to celebrate the Mouloud festival in 1975. However, the idea of a cultural programme aimed at all immigrants seemed more appropriate for a show that would rest entirely on the budget of the state secretary for immigrant workers. Indeed, French public television rejected the idea of financing a show that targeted a specific audience.

Throughout the ten-year broadcast (1976–86), the administration in charge of immigrants organized production, paid the broadcasting costs and controlled the content of the show. The show consisted of music performances and embassy reports on the cultural life of the sending countries. Long before it was possible to access television programmes via satellite dishes, *Mosaïc* made it possible for immigrants to see people speaking their own language and watch images from back home. In this respect, *Mosaïc* certainly filled a great need. In 1977, an audience study measured that 54 per cent of immigrants watched the show.

The continued existence of the show *Mosaïc* was not only due to its success among immigrant TV viewers but also because it was useful in terms of political communication as the politics of immigration took on an even more restrictive turn. In 1977, Lionel Stoleru was appointed state secretary for immigrant workers with a mission to further reduce foreign presence in France. Unemployment appeared to be one of the top concerns of the French,

---

[25]Thomas Douniès, 'The Time of Origins: The Rise and Fall of a Diversity Policy Toward Migrant Pupils in France (1960s–1990s)', *European Journal of Cultural and Political Sociology* 12, no. 3 (2025): 226–47.

and the idea that immigrants leaving France could be a solution to the crisis, despite no evidence to show for it, continued to spread. To speed up the departure of immigrants, Lionel Stoleru introduced a policy of return migration that consisted of allocating the sum of 10,000 francs to all immigrants who agreed to return permanently to their country of origin. In this context, *Mosaïc* was an opportunity to present news reports on immigrants who had returned home, and, at times, allowed for the government to communicate on the legislation. For instance, the archives of the show include the script from a declaration by State Secretary Lionel Stoleru that reads as such: 'Rumours are circulating about work permits and residence permits, as if the French government had hidden plans to carry out mass and brutal expulsions, and I have come here today to explain this to you very clearly so that you know the truth. . . . For the moment, nothing has been decided'.[26] Through this televised appearance, the secretary of state sought to mitigate criticism of his political decisions.

Mosaïc was conceived as 'entertainment without politics', in a context of increased protest against immigration restrictions.[27] Denounced as 'the Stoleru million', the government policy of return migration was highly contested, as we shall see now.

Resistance and immigrant artistic expressions, 1975–8

Following up on the actions of the early 1970s, the immigrant fight went on. Gathered around the House of Immigrant Workers (*Maison des travailleurs immigrés, MTI*) created in Puteaux, in 1973, several immigrant movements organized demonstrations and meetings to protest their difficult living conditions. In 1973, the House of Immigrant Workers consisted of Moroccan (*Association des Marocains en France, AMF*), Senegalese (*Union Générale des travailleurs sénégalais en France, UGTSF*) and Portuguese groups. In 1975,

---

[26]'Un certain nombre de bruits circulent sur les cartes de travail et les cartes de séjour comme si le gouvernement français avait des intentions cachées de procéder à des renvois massifs et brutaux et je viens aujourd'hui m'en expliquer devant vous de manière très claire pour que vous connaissiez la vérité. . . . Il n'y a pour l'instant, rien de décidé' (translation by the author), in Francis Bouquillon Papers, Déclaration de M. Lionel Stoleru, actualité no 3, Paris, 24 April 1979. (Francis Bouquillon was director of the office, when it turned into Information, Communication and Immigration (ICEI) from 1977 to 1981.)

[27]Catherine Humblot, 'Divertissement sans politique', *Le Monde*, 12–13 March 1978.

they were joined by an Algerian group (*Comité des travailleurs algériens, CTA*); in 1977, by two sub-Saharan groups (Mouvement des travailleurs ivoiriens de France, MTIF; and *Fédération des travailleurs immigrés d'Afrique Noire, FETRANI*); and in 1978, by a Tunisian group (*Union des travailleurs immigrés tunisiens, UTIT*). All these groups were activists who mobilized on a national basis, even though they all gathered around the defence of immigrants living in France.

The groups that took part in the House of Immigrant Workers were dissidents in more ways than one. They were opposed to the French government and its restrictive measures towards immigrants, but they were also resisting the control of each of their respective countries of origin. Countries of origin exercised a form of control over their nationals through their representatives in France (at embassies and consulates).[28] Some countries had set up organizations they called *Amicales.* They were network societies that kept an eye on their nationals, under the guise of organizing cultural events, national celebrations or matters such as arranging the repatriation of deceased bodies. For instance, the *Amicales des Algériens en Europe* was created in 1966 by reinvesting the network of activists who fought for the independence of Algeria, in France (*Fédération française du FLN*). In 1973, the Moroccan authorities also created a network of Moroccan societies for workers and shopkeepers in order to counter the influence of the opponents to the Moroccan regime who were in exile in France.[29] Finally, in 1975, the Senegalese authorities encouraged the creation of a trade union that would be an alternative to the UGTSF, as they considered the latter too close to French leftist activists.[30]

Following on the same pattern of autonomous representation initiated in the early 1970s, and because they were eager to differentiate themselves from the official organizations set up by each of their respective countries of origin, immigrant movements organized meetings that included theatre and musical performances. In 1975, the first festival of immigrant workers took place in Suresnes (outside Paris) and featured numerous theatre performances depicting the difficult living conditions of immigrants in France (including a theatre play by Al Assifa). It was followed by festivals that took place in several other cities around France in 1977 and 1978. Notably, the 1978 festival of immigrant workers' opening concert that took place in downtown Paris

---

[28]Angéline Escafré-Dublet, 'Préserver les loyautés nationales. Le rôle des États d'origine dans l'immigration en France, 1962–1975', *Annales de démographie historique* 124, no. 2 (2012): 141–60, https://doi.org/10.3917/adh.124.0141.

[29]Thomas Lacroix, *Les réseaux marocains du développement. Géographie du transnational et politiques du territorial* (Paris: Sciences Po University Press, 2012).

[30]Jean-Philippe Dedieu, 'L'internationalisme ouvrier à l'épreuve des migrations africaines en France', *Critique internationale* 50, no. 1 (2011): 145–67, https://doi.org/10.3917/crii.050.0145.

(Wagram concert hall) was covered by *Mosaïc,* and the news report aired on the show of 29 January. However, despite numerous attempts by journalist Djelloul Beloura to highlight immigrants' protests and political demands, the anchor, Jean-Michel Dhermay, essentially commented on the music, the number of artists, and the cheerful audience.[31]

Also in 1978, the movement to protest rising hostel rents took momentum. Some immigrant hostel residents had been able to emerge as spokespersons for the cause. The gap between the cause and the people representing them had eventually closed.[32]

After years of action, the movement united and connected 130 hostels and thirty thousand rent strikers. To give voice to their protest, a large meeting was organized in January 1978 that was labelled Africa Feast by the organizers (*Africa Fête*). African musicians, along with French singer-songwriters, came and supported the protest (e.g. Manu Dibango, Toure Kounda, François Béranger, Bernard Lavilliers and Claude Nougaro).[33]

The politics of contention, 1979–81

By 1979, the government decided to turn to forced-return migration by considerably restraining the renewal of residency permits and making illegal residence grounds for expulsion. Despite opposition from within the state apparatus itself, the government managed to pass the Bonnet law of 10 January 1980. It amended the 1945 decree on the conditions of entry and residence of foreigners for the first time in thirty-five years.[34] It was the first law to criminalize the illegal residence of foreigners in France. Until then, failure to comply with the rules meant prosecution, but no penalty, and certainly not actual deportation.

The passage of the 1979 Bonnet law represented the return of immigrant selection. In 1945, the passage of the ordinance relating to the conditions of entry and residence of foreign nationals was a victory of the principles of equality over attempts to introduce immigrant selection, based on ethno-national traits. However, supporters of immigrant selection had not completely

---

[31] *Mosaïc* (television programme), 29 January 1978. The discussion takes place five minutes into the program.
[32] Hmed, 'Challenging an Institution in the Case of an Unlikely Mobilization'.
[33] Hédia Yelles-Chaouche, 'Africa Fête, une lutte culturelle des travailleurs immigrés', *Hommes & migrations* 1330, no. 3 (2020): 73–5.
[34] Weil, *La France et ses étrangers*, 175.

disappeared. Already in the 1960s, when organizing immigrant reception, the considerable attention administrative officials allocated to the reception of Portuguese immigrants, perceived as 'more likely to assimilate', contrasted with the reluctance to facilitate the reception of Algerian immigrants and their families.[35] In preparation for the Bonnet law, the administration responsible for immigrants was planning not to renew 40 per cent of the one hundred thousand Algerian residence permits that expired each year. They anticipated that out of the fifty thousand deportations consequent to the non-renewal of their residency permit, thirty-five thousand would be Algerian adults.[36] The very fact that the administration detailed its plan of action by country of origin is indicative of its selective approach to immigration.

Even more telling is the governmental response to the arrival of 130,000 refugees from Vietnam, Cambodia and Laos who fled communist regimes and claimed asylum in France.[37] Despite being commonly called 'boat people', the refugees from former Indochina were brought to France by plane, granted welfare assistance and given specific access to employment or training. They began arriving by the 1975 fall of Saigon (now Ho Chi Minh City). However, their arrivals increased in 1979 with the Orderly Departure Program of the UN, which provided a legal emigration scheme for them to leave the Indochinese peninsula to seek refuge. Throughout the period from 1975 to 1985, the French office for asylum granted 90 per cent of its requests.[38]

Postcolonial ties do not fully explain the French welcoming approach to Southeast Asian refugees. Arguably, their fleeing communist regimes suited the anti-communist views of the right-wing government. They might be less likely to feel close to the far left, government officials thought, and therefore less likely to join the workers' strikes that were plaguing the country's economy at the time. However, the fact is that their presence in France reactivated stereotypes forged in the empire. People from the Indochinese peninsula were then described as 'docile' and 'hard working'. As a result, the arrival of Southeast Asians was seen as ideal to replace Algerian migrants who were increasingly being constructed as a 'problem'.

In fact, the French government tried and negotiated with the Algerian authorities to organize the return of Algerian nationals to Algeria, all through

---

[35]See previous chapter.

[36]Weil, *La France et ses étrangers*, 176.

[37]Karen Akoka, 'France: Boat People Brought by Plane', in *When Boat People Were Resettled, 1975–1983: A Comparative History of European and Israeli Responses to the South-East Asian Refugee Crisis*, ed. Becky Taylor et al. (Cham: Springer, 2021), 47–77, https://doi.org/10.1007/978–3 -030–64224–2_2.

[38]Karine Meslin, 'Les réfugiés cambodgiens, des ouvriers dociles? Genèse et modes de pérennisation d'un stéréotype en migration', *Revue européenne des migrations internationales* 27, no. 3 (2011): 83–101, https://doi.org/10.4000/remi.5646.

the year of 1979.[39] Algerian immigration was one of the largest, if not *the* largest, groups of foreigners living in France at the time.[40] The French authorities aimed for one hundred thousand returns per year, and they hoped to reach this objective by denying the renewal of Algerians' residency permits in France. This was, however, without fully taking into account the colonial ties forged between Algeria and France. Indeed, most Algerian immigrants might have been opting for French nationality after the independence of Algeria; their children born in France were French by birth by virtue of the principle of the *double jus soli*. Children born in France of foreign parents have the nationality of their parents until they reach eighteen, since 1927. However, in the case of children born in France of Algerian parents born in Algeria before 1962 (when Algeria was French), they were regarded as children born in France of parents themselves born in France. As a result, forcing the return of Algerian families to Algeria meant sending back mixed-status families composed of Algerian parents and French children.

The breach of the law – deporting its own nationals is illegal – made it impossible for French authorities to actually implement their policy of returning Algerian families to Algeria. However, the very fact that they thought about it, negotiated with the Algerian authorities and dedicated time to such a project is indicative of institutional hostility towards Algerian immigration. Moreover, it is revealing of a form of oblivion towards the consequences of colonization and the inextricable links between the two countries.[41] French authorities overlooked the fact that children of Algerian immigrants were actually French nationals.

This mixture of oblivion and enduring racism fuelled the continuing opposition to government politics in the early 1980s. The politics of immigration in the early 1980s were characterized by a growing confrontation between an increasingly restrictive government and the opposition that consisted of immigrant organizations, trade unions and the left. Nine hunger strikes took place from January to October 1980.[42]

Even the carefully staged show *Mosaïc* became the scene of a confrontation between state secretary for immigrant workers, Lionel Stoleru, and opponents. One particular show illustrates this point. On 4 June 1980, the production team recorded a debate with Lionel Stoleru. Things did not go as planned, however, and according to a journalist from the left-leaning newspaper

---

[39]Weil, *La France et ses étrangers*, 182–7.

[40]According to the French census, 709,785 Algerian nationals lived in France in 1975, second only to the Portuguese: 758,395. In 1982, 805,116 Algerians lived in France, more than Portuguese: 767,304.

[41]Benjamin Stora, *La gangrène et l'oubli: La mémoire de la guerre d'Algérie* (Paris: La Découverte, 1992).

[42]Siméant, *La cause des sans-papiers*, 434–6.

Libération who attended the show, the minister appeared rather unsettled. He had probably expected hand-picked speakers, instead of what he discovered: the representative from the organization of employers was not there; instead of which, only a representative of a trade union asked questions; the mayor of a city with many immigrants, supposed to give his opinion on their difficult insertion, was, in fact, a socialist and therefore a political opponent. Finally, even the representative of the Algerian Amicale, whom he thought would be on the side of the government, was in fact voicing the concerns of the families, along with the journalists of the Christian newspaper *La Croix* and the regular journalists from *Mosaïc*.[43]

The most heated moments of the debate that took place during the show *Mosaïc* were edited out under the supervision of the State Secretary Public Relations Service. However, Lionel Stoleru immediately wrote to the head of the office in charge of producing *Mosaïc*, asking why the journalist from the newspaper *Libération* was present, to which Francis Bouquillon answered that Jean-Louis Hurst had sneaked in and was seemingly attempting to discredit their action. Intended to be the vehicle *par excellence* for providing information and promoting immigrant cultures, *Mosaïc* had therefore become the official channel for government communication, just as much as it provided a possible arena for protest.

Eventually, the politics of immigration emerged transformed at the end of the 1970s. In this chapter, we saw that what had been a concern for some civil society organizations and a few administrative officials in the 1960s became a topic of political polarization at the end of the 1970s. On the one hand, there were right-wing government officials inclined to reduce the number of foreigners living in France, in response to the economic crisis, even if it meant introducing a dose of immigration selection and bypassing the principle of equal treatment. On the other hand, left-wing politicians, trade unionists, activists and civil society actors formed a political opposition that found a common denominator in the defence of immigrants as victims of capitalist and heartless policing. At the time, however, immigration was mainly an economic issue, and although the government had stumbled upon the fact that the children of Algerian immigrants were, in fact, French citizens by birth, the politics of immigration were still rather alien to the politics of citizenship – a discussion that was soon to change in the years that followed.

---

[43]Jean-Louis Hurst, 'Une bombe à *Mosaïque*', *Libération*, 7–8 June 1980.

6

The Right to Difference, 1981–8

On 10 May 1981, the socialist candidate, François Mitterrand, was elected president of the French Republic against Valéry Giscard d'Estaing. It was the first time since the beginning of the Fifth Republic that a left-wing politician was in power. Moreover, right after the presidential election, the electoral alliance that consisted of the Socialist Party and the French Communist Party won a comfortable majority in the National Assembly (329 seats out of 491). Socialist Pierre Mauroy became prime minister, forming a left-wing government of socialist, communist and centre-left ministers.

The political change of 1981 was a major one, and so were the hopes that came with it. Political work inside the Socialist Party, long negotiations with the Communist Party, and the efforts of many left-leaning activists led to the landslide victory. Once in office, the new government paid tribute to their determination. In the administration of immigration, Michel Perraudeau, a socialist, but also a member of a non-profit organization with a long-standing commitment to helping immigrants, was appointed head of the Social Action Funds. Moreover, several immigrant activists and intellectual figures (such as Algerian-born writer Assia Djebar) were appointed members of the executive board of the Social Action Funds. Secretary of state for immigrants François Autain and his team regularized 135,000 undocumented immigrant workers in the year that followed. Finally, the left-wing coalition had agreed to unite under a common programme that included two major legislative reforms for immigrants. The first reform was to grant foreigners the right to establish non-profit organizations and receive public funds. This was decided with a law on 9 October 1981. The second reform was to grant foreigners the right to vote. It was initially postponed but eventually abandoned.

Many changes that the left-wing electorate had hoped for, and activists had fought for, materialized in the first years of Mitterrand's presidency. By 1983, however, a change of government was on the cards, with Michel Rocard as prime minister and austerity measures on the agenda. The period was labelled 'The Austerity Turn' (*le tournant de la rigueur*). Finally, in the run-up to the 1986 legislative election, the right-wing party of Jacques Chirac resorted to an anti-immigrant stance in its campaign and won 286 seats, out of 577. Chirac became prime minister in 1986 and, for the first time since the beginning of the Fifth Republic, a left-wing president had to share power with a right-wing prime minister – a situation of divided government known as 'cohabitation' that only lasted two years. In 1988, Mitterrand was re-elected president, and the legislative elections that followed confirmed the left-wing majority in the National Assembly. The return of a left-wing government in 1988 did not bring the same stance on immigration as in 1981, as the meaning of the topic changed a great deal over a decade.

This chapter examines the change in what immigration meant throughout the 1980s and shows the ways in which the topic was articulated in relation to that of citizenship and national identity. First, it examines the consequences of the change in legislation for immigrant cultural life and how it illustrated the brief moment of *differentialism* that occurred after the election of François Mitterrand. Then it turns to the organization of the 1983 March for Equality and Racism, how it reached media and political attention, and also how it changed the narrative of immigration in France, from the classic narrative of low-paid workers who struggled to make ends meet to unemployed young people who experienced discrimination. What is remarkable is how most of the young people who organized the March were born in France. And yet their specific experience was related to immigration, because many of them were born to immigrant parents. This chapter examines this process, further illustrated by the organization of an art exhibition, entitled *Children of Immigration*, in the prestigious Georges Pompidou Centre. Finally, the chapter explains how both far-right and right-wing candidates attacked the Right to Difference in the run-up to the legislative election of 1986. With a rhetoric of cultural incompatibility and national preference, they solidified the link between immigration, citizenship and national identity.

Changing immigrants' lives, 1981

The joint programme of the Socialist and Communist Parties, which led them to victory, was entitled 'Changing Life' (*Changer la vie*). Even though immigration was not a highly politicized issue during the 1981 election campaign (much less than the economy and social welfare), the joint programme included a key proposal that was bound to, in fact, change the life of immigrants: freedom of association for non-nationals.

In 1901, the law affirming the principle of freedom of association enabled two or more people to create a non-profit organization. However, in the run-up to the Second World War, the government had introduced a specific provision that prohibited foreign nationals from establishing an organization, unless they obtained a special permission from the Interior Ministry (decree of 19 April 1939). This was meant as a surveillance of political activism among Eastern and Central European immigrants at the time.[1] However, after the end of the Second World War, the decree remained as such because of consistent suspicion towards foreigners.

The 1939 decree did not mean that foreign nationals could not form non-profit organizations at all. A case in point is the Moroccan group *Association des Marocains de France* that obtained such authorization in 1960.[2] By contrast, the *Amicale des Algériens en Europe* was less successful, and their 1966 application was rejected.[3] The *Amicale* was established nonetheless, yet could only receive funds from the Algerian government. Indeed, without permission to establish as an association under the 1901 law, non-profit organizations could not receive financial assistance from the French state.

Up until then, French charity organizations received funds and implemented social aid towards immigrants. As for immigrants who did not hold French nationality, if they wanted to improve the living conditions of their counterparts, they could either work for a French-run organization (many did) or engage in political activities without financial retribution.

The passing of the October 1981 law affirming the principle of freedom of association for foreigners allowed for many immigrant associations to form. It was therefore key for the immigrant movement and all the groups seeking to improve their living conditions. In this sense, it represented the culmination of the '70s demand for autonomy.

After 1981, numerous organizations formed. In some cases, they pre-existed the law, and registering them was mainly a formality to regularize the situation. In some other cases, they were brand new initiatives of several immigrants who decided to start an activity. In particular, numerous organizations were formed at the local level that aimed at organizing cultural activities and sought to apply for public funds to support their project. In particular, some of them applied for public funds from the French Ministry of Culture.

In 1981, the Socialist Party came to power with a programme that put culture at the forefront and an emblematic minister to embody it, Jack Lang. The budget of the Culture Ministry was doubled, and Lang introduced an extension of the scope of the ministry's funding to a wider array of artistic forms, such as rock 'n' roll, street art or comics. Moreover, Lang introduced the

---

[1] Janine Ponty, 'Les étrangers et le droit d'association au XXe siècle', *Matériaux pour l'histoire de notre temps* 69, no. 1 (2003): 24–5, https://doi.org/10.3406/mat.2003.402433.

[2] Lacroix, *Les réseaux marocains du développement. Géographie du transnational et politiques du territorial.*

[3] Archives of the Interior Ministry no. 1985 0087 box 37: Note au sujet de l'Amicale des Algériens en Europe du préfet de Police, Maurice Papon au ministre de l'Intérieur, 12 August 1966.

possibility for the Culture Ministry to financially support artistic productions by minority groups – a fundamental change in framing for the Ministry of Culture.

When the Ministry of Culture was created in 1959, it called for a project that excluded all amateurism and all group representation. The first minister of culture, famous French writer and long-time friend of General de Gaulle, André Malraux, did not support regionalism and the forms of folkloric expressions associated with it. France was still emerging from the Second World War, and the idea of guaranteeing the unity of the nation around common cultural values underpinned his idea.[4] Twenty years on, Socialist Minister Lang demonstrated that he was not afraid of dissolving France's cultural unity by encouraging the expression of regionalism and minority groups.

The change in framing within the Ministry of Culture paralleled a larger differential turn in governmental politics. During his campaign, François Mitterrand had advocated for a 'Right to Difference' (*droit à la* difference) that justified a major change in the relationship between citizens and the state. A year after the socialist government came into office, the Defferre law of 1982 engaged a process of transferring power from national to regional and local institutions, in an effort to bring political institutions closer to citizens and break the extreme centralization of power at the national level (e.g. in Paris). The 'Right to Difference' was a major change in the framing of French politics and national identity.[5] It made it possible to recognize the role of regions in the political decision process and French cultural pluralism.

All this is to say that both the increase in the budget of the Ministry of Culture and the new differential framing of governmental politics were not deliberately targeted towards immigrants and their demands. However, it was the opening of this new window of opportunity that made it possible for immigrant-based organizations to develop new projects and increase their participation in civil society.

The passing of the law in October 1981 gave a general sense of freedom, and many initiatives were launched as a result. A good example of this was the creation of numerous free radio stations. Paris-based Radio Beur hit the airwaves in November 1981; followed by Radio Aligre, also based in Paris; Radio Kaléidoscope, in Grenoble; Radio Gazelle, in Marseille; and Radio G 92, in Gennevilliers. All radio stations resulted from years of activism in defence of immigrant rights. For instance, founding members of Radio Beur had been active in the movement defending immigrant rights in the 1970s. They reported in the activist newspaper *Sans-frontières* (Without Borders). They

---

[4]Herman Lebovics, *Mona Lisa's Escort: Andre Malraux and the Reinvention of French Culture* (Ithaca, NY: Cornell University Press, 1999).

[5]Vincent Martigny, *Dire la France: Culture(s) et identités nationales 1981–1995* (Paris: Sciences Po University Press, 2016).

included medicine student Nacer Kettane, artist Mohand Amara and teacher Saliha Amara, who took part in the Kahina theatre group that featured in the festival for immigrant workers of 1978.

The choice of name for each radio station is revealing of the brief moment of *differentialism* that occurred after the election of François Mitterrand, both at the level of government and civil society. *Beur* is a term that was originally derogatory and that comes from the inversion of syllables in the word *arabe*. This form of slang, called *verlan,* was popular in the early 1980s. By labelling a channel of information intended to broadcast to French people of North African background, *Radio Beur,* the founding members purposely reversed the stigma. They reclaimed a name that resonated with their identity and specific experiences of being a minority. With a reference to a kaleidoscope, the founding members of the Grenoble radio addressed the distorted image of immigrants and the necessity to take into consideration the many dimensions of their experience. The name 'Radio Gazelle' referred explicitly to an animal characteristic of North Africa, praised for its beauty, intelligence and speed. As for Radio G and Radio Aligre, they anchored the experiences of immigrants in a specific place. G stands for the immigrant worker city of Genevilliers, outside Paris. Aligre was a lively immigrant-worker neighbourhood in the southwest of Paris, where the station studio was located.

When François Autain was appointed state secretary for immigrants, the greatest concern was not immigrant cultural life and expressions. According to him, it was rather the long-awaited regularizations of undocumented immigrants.[6] Indeed, the past years had been particularly damaging for the administrative status of many foreigners. The regularization programme that took place from 1981 to 1982 consisted in legalizing the situation of a vast majority of immigrant residents who had entered France legally but had not been able to renew their residency permits.[7]

The programme regularized 131,360 immigrants. The regularized workers were predominantly male, low-skilled workers who lived in the Paris region. They comprised 2 per cent of all workers in Paris and 1 per cent of all workers in France. Interestingly, later studies demonstrated how the 1981–2 regularization programme increased employment and wages for low-skill French or immigrant workers and raised French GDP by over 1 per cent. This was mainly because undocumented workers have limited power of wage negotiation and restricted economic opportunity. By alleviating this imperfection, a regularization programme can therefore move the market closer to a competitive equilibrium.

---

[6]Interview of the author with François Autain, 21 February 2007.

[7]George J. Borjas and Anthony Edo, 'Monopsony, Efficiency, and the Regularization of Undocumented Immigrants' (National Bureau of Economic Research, 2023), https://www.nber.org/papers/w31457.

Arguably, the economic consequences of immigration were higher on the political agenda of the state secretary. However, Autain did commission a report on immigrants' needs in terms of information and cultural expression to socialist deputy Françoise Gaspard. Gaspard had been engaged on issues related to immigrants as mayor of the working-class city of Dreux, outside Paris. In fact, what was really at stake here was the TV show *Mosaïc* that kept broadcasting every Sunday morning at the expense of the state secretary. In particular, the French public television company still charged broadcasting costs to the state secretary for immigrants because the programme was aimed at a specific audience, and not the French audience as a whole. However, despite long negotiations, the newly appointed head of television and radio broadcasting, left-leaning journalist Michèle Cotta, finally wrote to François Autain in November 1982 that 'specific television programmes need to be given specific funding'.[8]

The political change of 1981 was major, albeit not to the point that the living conditions of immigrants could make it into the mainstream of TV programmes. On this point, changing mentalities was probably more difficult than the new political majority was prepared to admit.

Racist crimes and police violence had not stopped following the elections of François Mitterrand in 1981. On the contrary, violence erupted in some working-class suburbs of Paris, Lyon and Marseille over the summer of 1981. It prompted the government to design a programme aimed at containing the kind of violence that could erupt during the long months of July and August. The causes of the unrest were essentially identified as economic and pertaining to the poor state of the neighbourhoods in which they lived. As a result, the government designed urban development programmes that consisted of cracking down on delinquency, sending young people to holiday camps when their parents could not afford to leave the city over the summer, and providing activities for those who stayed in the neighbourhood. However, by the summer of 1983, anti-racist organizations such as the Movement Against Racism and Antisemitism (MRAP) listed numerous crimes that could be attributed to anti-Arab racism.

The many youth activities and youth organizations that had emerged did not always succeed in maintaining dialogue with police forces, nor did they manage to prevent hate crimes. However, they managed to organize one of the most remarkable protests of the 1980s that propelled the anti-racist fight at the top of the media and political agenda, the March for Equality and Against Racism.

---

[8]Les 'émissions spécifiques doivent avoir un financement spécifique' (translated by the author). Letter from Michèle Cotta to François Autain, 12 November 1982. In Patrick Weil Papers (Fondation nationale des sciences politiques), box no. 48.

The March for Equality and Against Racism, 1983

On the night of 20 June 1983, a member of the youth organization *SOS Avenir Minguettes*, a working-class neighbourhood in the suburb of Lyon, was hurt during a police raid. Nineteen-year-old Toumi Djaïdja was injured and taken to the hospital, where, together with fellow *SOS Minguettes* members, he decided to organize a peaceful March across the country in protest against racist violence.[9] The decision did not come from nowhere. Active in the neighbourhood for a few years, Father Christian Delorme had already met with the youth organization and discussed the non-violent repertoire of action with them. The idea of the March stemmed from such protest culture as that of Gandhi and Martin Luther King. The idea of responding to violence through marching entertained a certain appeal to the Catholic priest. As for the young members of *SOS Minguettes*, the reference to Gandhi or Martin Luther King echoed their own fight against racism and against oppression. Together with Delorme, a group of young people from the Minguettes neighbourhood of the Lyon region set out to start a March from Marseille to Paris.

Over the summer, the future marchers announced their will to embark on such a journey and made contact with immigrant groups throughout the country who might be able to host them on their way. However, there were only thirty-two of them on the morning of 15 October 1983, in the neighbourhood of La Cayolle outside Marseille. They chose this neighbourhood because an attack claimed by the extreme right had taken place a few months earlier. On the day of their departure, Françoise Gaspard made the journey and represented political support from the socialist group of the National Assembly. Socialist deputy Gaspard had just lost the last municipal election in Dreux to the first-ever alliance of a right-wing candidate with the extreme right Jean-Pierre Stirbois of the National Front. She was therefore available and willing to show her support for an anti-racist March.

Nineteen men and women in their twenties, with or without immigrant parents, but all concerned by racist violence, formed the core of the 'Marchers'. They covered around thirty kilometres a day via Lyon, Dijon, Montbéliard, Strasbourg, Nancy, Metz, Lille and Paris, taking the train for some sections of the journey. However, it was nothing compared to the tens of thousands who marched with them two months later, from Bastille Square to Montparnasse, when they arrived in Paris on 3 December 1983. How can we account for such a success?

---

[9]Abdellali Hajjat, *La marche pour l'égalité et contre le racisme* (Paris: Amsterdam, 2013).

Social movement analysis pays extra attention to networks and organizations in explaining the dynamics of mobilizations – that is, the act of organizing a group of people for a purpose.[10] In the case of the March for Equality and Against Racism of 1983, the network of immigrant groups that had formed during the '70s, along with charity organizations and other non-profits described in the previous chapters, made it possible for the March to happen. In each city they reached by foot, marchers were able to find shelter with local organizations they had been in contact with.

However, it was another racist crime and the media coverage it received that truly made the March reach full momentum. On the night of 14 November 1983, 26-year-old Algerian Habib Grimzi, who was travelling back from Bordeaux to Marseille, where he planned to take a boat back to Algeria, where he lived, was stabbed to death and thrown out of the window to the Foreign Legion army by three French candidates. The absence of a reason for the attack – Grimzi was reportedly listening to music on a portable music player – the lack of reaction on the part of the dozens of train riders who heard him screaming, the violence of the assault, and the racist insults that were heard by train riders, made it the epitome of racist crime. A few years later, in 1986, the three Frenchmen were found guilty of the charge and sentenced to life in prison. A rare exception among the many unacknowledged racist crimes that are usually hard to prove.[11] The day after the Grimzi killing, the news gave unprecedented echo to the March for Equality and Racism. Governmental officials, anti-racist organizations and journalists immediately established a link between the brutality of Grimzi's death, the racist underpinning of the attack, the absence of reaction on the part of the other train riders and the March denouncing racism.[12]

As the Marchers approached Paris, it became clearer to government officials that they had to show their support for their action. The working papers of the state secretary for immigrants show that they received news of the project and shared the information during a board meeting as early as 23 September 1983. However, it was only after the Grimzi affair that government officials began arranging meetings with the Marchers. On 20 November, State Secretary for Immigrants Dufoix met them in Strasbourg;

---

[10]Aldon D. Morris, *Origins of the Civil Rights Movements* (New York: Free, 1986); Doug McAdam, Sidney Tarrow and Charles Tilly, *Dynamics of Contention*, Cambridge Studies in Contentious Politics (Cambridge: Cambridge University Press, 2001), https://doi.org/10.1017/CBO9780511805431.

[11]Save for when racist insults are clearly articulated by the perpetrator, racist crimes are often hard to prove as such. Rachida Brahim, *La Race tue deux fois: Une histoire des crimes racistes en France* (Paris: Syllepse, 2021).

[12]Céline Régnard, 'Le meurtre du Bordeaux-Vintimille', *Hommes & migrations. Revue française de référence sur les dynamiques migratoires*, no. 1313 (2016): 73–9, https://doi.org/10.4000 /hommesmigrations.3563.

on 29 November, Culture Minister Jack Lang walked with the Marchers for a few hundred metres in Mouy, a city outside Paris; and on 1 December, Social Affairs Minister Beregovoy met them in his Paris office.

Moreover, it was after a thousand walked with them from Nation to Bastille Square on the eve of 3 December 1983 that eight of them met with François Mitterrand in front of the cameras of French television. After which, Toumi Djaïdja stepped out of the president's office, announcing the ten-year residency permit (*la carte de dix ans*).

One immediate outcome of the March was indeed the passing of the Dufoix law of 17 July 1984, which instituted a ten-year residency permit for foreign residents in France, greatly facilitating their lives (e.g. no more tedious application and standing in line in front of administrative buildings every year). However, despite years of mobilization of the immigrant movement to obtain such a reform, the ten-year permit did not match the Marchers' demands in terms of anti-discrimination and equality. It is more likely that President François Mitterrand and his advisors thought it fitting to have the Marchers obtain *something* from their efforts, and that it was the project that was the most developed at that point.[13]

A less tangible, and yet key, outcome of the March was how it put second-generation immigrants on the map, and the specific issues they experienced under the gaze of media, politicians and even the arts. The Marchers resorted to a new form of protest culture that borrowed from the repertoire of non-violence advocated by Gandhi and Martin Luther King. Their journey was surrounded by a 'halo' of diverse forms of cultural expression: the music they listened to on portable music players, and the cartoonists who documented their journey throughout the country.[14]

The success of the March also highlighted the work of young artists and writers of immigrant background who were beginning to make a name for themselves – for instance, writer Mehdi Charef, who had just published *Tea in the Harem*, which told the story of Magid and his friend Pat idly spending their time in a working-class neighbourhood outside Paris.[15] Both Patrick and Magid go through different life experiences about love, friendship, family conflicts, unemployment and racist assaults. To his own admission, Charef did not take part in the March. However, through his writing, he did convey similar

---

[13]Daniel A. Gordon, 'A Victory for the March for Equality? Immigration, Policy, Protest and the Ten-Year Residency Permit of 1984', *French History* 37, no. 3 (2023): 294–316, https://doi.org/10.1093/fh/crac073.

[14]Angéline Escafré-Dublet, 'Art, Power and Protest. Immigrants' Artistic Production and Political Mobilisation in France', *New Diversities* 12, no. 1 (2010): 5–19.

[15]Mehdi Charef, *Tea in the Harem*, main edition (London: Serpent's Tail, 1989).

concerns about a generation of young people born in France to immigrant parents.

In the early 1980s, the emergence of a new generation of artists embodied a shift from associating immigrants with their country of origin to acknowledging their specific cultural identity in the host country. They addressed issues related to their experience of growing up with immigrant parents in France. Their relationship with cultural forms was less one of nostalgia towards their parents' country of origin than a search for creating something reflecting their specific experience as a minority in France. What was later to be referred to as the *Beur* movement stemmed from this political and artistic context of the early 1980s.[16]

The Lang Ministry of Culture was committed to a policy of supporting creation and took a keen interest in the work of this new generation of artists with an immigrant background. In 1984, under the joint sponsorship of Jack Lang and Georgina Dufoix, the prestigious Georges Pompidou Centre opened the *Children of Immigration* exhibition, featuring works by second-generation immigrants in France. They consisted of sculptures, paintings, videos, drawings, comic strips and theatre performances (as the exhibition space included an amphitheatre). The two curators, Veronique Baux and José Chapelle, sought to showcase the rich expression of young people with an immigrant background and created a space for artistic exchange between them.

However, the exhibition also revealed the complexity of the relationship between immigration, politics and the arts.[17] Two approaches came into conflict: on the one hand, the institutional approach, which consisted of showcasing the meeting of different immigrant cultures in French society; on the other hand, the artist's approach, which constructed his or her cultural identity through a mixing of experiences in the multicultural context of immigration.

Indeed, in these post-1981 years, 'children of immigration' easily claimed the culture, if not the citizenship, of their parents. Sending-country authorities, via their consulates, were eager to keep track of their nationals and the children of their nationals in France. This was particularly the case with the Algerian authorities. They would not miss an opportunity to remind French authorities that they had no say on the cultural life of the children of Algerian nationals. As a case in point, they criticized Jack Lang's meeting with the Marchers. On 3 November 1983, the president of the Algerian Republic issued the following statement in the TV show *Mosaïc*:

---

[16]Alec G. Hargreaves, *Immigration and Identity in Beur Fiction: Voices From the North African Community in France* (Oxford: Berg, 1991).

[17]Adèle Momméja, 'Les enfants de l'immigration au Centre Pompidou', *Hommes & migrations. Revue française de référence sur les dynamiques migratoires*, no. 1313 (2016): 97–102, https://doi.org/10.4000/hommesmigrations.3569.

I would like to ask our brothers who have emigrated to pay more attention to the younger generations, to remain faithful to our principles and above all to our Arab-Islamic civilization. I would like to stress this to the young people in particular, who should be proud to belong to this ancient civilization, to their homeland, Algeria and its revolution.[18]

In this political context, French authorities could not officially urge second-generation immigrants to reclaim their French citizenship. On the contrary, it was rather the case that immigrant parents did not want their children to become French – in particular, Algerian parents. In a scene taken from the movie adaptation of *Tea in the Harem,* a distressed Magid points out to his mother that he is unable to find employment because he does not have French citizenship – to which his mother answered, threatening him, 'Never, do you hear me, never do you take French papers!' (*jamais, tu m'entends, jamais tu ne prends les papiers français!*).

The scene between the immigrant mother and her son, born in France, is a good illustration of the relationship between immigration, citizenship and national identity in the early 1980s. Immigrants still considered themselves as non-nationals who could legitimately remain as such, even if they were eligible to acquire French citizenship. As a result, issues about immigration were articulated in anti-racist terms. As a case in point, student union activists who were close to the Socialist Party created *SOS Racisme,* in 1984, an organization designed to fight racism.[19] However, *SOS Racisme* members were rather estranged from the Marchers, who, for most of them, came back home and continued their activism in their own local organization.

The *differential turn* of the early 1980s was in its final hours, however. Not only was the Socialist rhetoric of the Right to Difference losing steam, but the extreme right had turned it on its head by proclaiming: 'the right to be different, yes, but at home'. And they were winning votes. In September 1983, the first alliance between a right-wing candidate and a far-right candidate in the municipal election of Dreux cost socialist deputy Françoise Gaspard her seat. In June 1984, the National Front won 10 per cent of the vote in the first

---

[18] 'Je voudrais demander aux frères émigrés de redoubler d'attention à l'égard des générations montantes, de demeurer fidèles à nos principes et surtout à notre appartenance civilisationnelle (sic) arabo-islamique. J'insiste, particulièrement auprès des jeunes qui se doivent d'être fiers d'appartenir à cette vieille civilisation, à leur patrie: l'Algérie et sa révolution' (translated by the author). Statement by the president of the Algerian Republic to Algerian emigrants in France for the television programme *Mosaïque,* set by telegram on 3 November 1983. Patrick Weil Papers (National Foundation of Political Science) box no. 40.

[19] Philippe Juhem, 'Entreprendre en politique. De l'extrême gauche au PS: La professionnalisation politique des fondateurs de SOS-Racisme', *Revue française de science politique* 51, no. 1–2 (2001): 131–53, https://doi.org/10.3917/rfsp. 511.0131.

European election. A big difference with the French election mode in general is that the European election is a proportional vote, said to favour minority parties. However, the signal was strong: with its anti-immigrant rhetoric, the National Front secured around 10 million votes in a national election – a dynamic that the traditional right-wing parties did not want to leave to the far-right in future elections.

Politicizing immigration, a winning ticket to power, 1986

In 1986, the Socialist Party had to acknowledge the counter-productive effect of asserting the Right to Difference: right-wing intellectuals and politicians used it to justify a discourse of exclusion against immigrants and, eventually, gain electoral votes.[20]

In an internal report of the Socialist Party on the issue of immigration, a group of politicians and intellectuals wrote the following: 'The ideological debate on the Right to Difference has its dangers. Right-wing parties and intellectuals use it for the promotion of their project of exclusion. . . . Pierre Chaunu, for example, continues to theorize about [it], citing supposedly intangible cultural and religious barriers'.[21] A historian of early modern Europe, Pierre Chaunu (1923–2009) was known for his political engagement against abortion rights in the 1970s alongside right-wing politicians. His approach to immigration was that of a historian of social and cultural ideas who believed that non-Europeans were incapable of assimilating into French society. He was close to extreme-right circles and a member of an intellectual society, *The Club de l'Horloge*.[22] The report also quoted Alain Griotteray, who published an essay entitled *Immigrants, the Shock* (*Immigrés, le choc*) in 1984. In his essay, Griotteray developed the idea that immigrants were actually here to stay, not to return home, since they had settled and formed families. As for Jacques Gallou, author of *Preferring the Nation: A Response to Immigration* (*La preference nationale: réponse à l'immigration*) and founding member of

---

[20]Pierre-Andre Taguieff, *The Force of Prejudice: On Racism and Its Doubles* (Minneapolis: University of Minnesota Press, 2001).

[21]'Le débat idéologique sur le droit à la différence montre ses dangers, la droite s'en sert pour son projet d'exclusion, . . . comme par exemple P. Chaunu qui continue à théoriser sur le droit à la différence et à s'appuyer sur de prétendues barrières culturelles et religieuses intangibles' (translated by the author). J.-M., Leguen, M.-P. de la Gontrie (de la), B. Stora, F. Terquem, 'Rapport sur l'immigration', décembre 1986. In: Patrick Weil Papers, National Foundation of Political Science, box no. 56.

[22]Sylvain Laurens, 'Le Club de l'horloge et la haute administration: promouvoir l'hostilité à l'immigration dans l'entre-soi mondain', *Agone* 54, no. 2 (2014): 73–94, https://doi.org/10.3917/agone.054.0073.

Club de l'Horloge, he advocated for politicians to pass measures that exclude foreigners from certain jobs and social allowances.

These arguments were part of a relatively common anti-immigrant discourse in France: cultural incompatibility, fear of demographic invasion and competition on the labour market. All these ideas had already been put forward at certain points in French political history. Competition on the labour market had been at the core of the Aigues-Mortes massacres of 1893, and the 1932 law introduced quotas for the number of foreigners per sector.[23] Cultural incompatibility and fear of demographic invasion were key to the project of immigrant selection after the Second World War. However, what was new in 1986 was the extent to which this rhetoric paid off, by the time the French legislative election came around.

In the run-up to the legislative election of 1986, immigration made its entrance in political debates. First and foremost, immigration was one of the main topics of discussion for the National Front. The party had managed to attract 10 per cent of the electorate in the European Elections of 1984, and even though that was far beyond the right-wing coalition under Simone Veil (43 per cent), this was still believed to be potential right-wing votes that were lost. Moreover, François Mitterrand ruled the 1986 legislative elections to be proportional, as a strategy to weaken the right-wing opposition. However, Mitterrand's strategy failed, and the right-wing coalition won the election. Even more so, Jacques Chirac and the right-wing coalition won a comfortable majority in the 1986 legislative elections with 290 seats out of 577 (44.84 per cent), against 212 seats for the Socialist Party (31 per cent). Finally, the shift to proportional elections marked the first entry of the National Front into the National Assembly, with thirty-five seats (9.25 per cent).

During the 1986 electoral campaign, there were divisions among right-wing politicians as to how they should approach National Front politicians and their ideas. Two distinct strategies can be identified. One was to adopt the ideas of the far right to keep the votes of right-wing voters. The other was to distance themselves from the ideas of the far right to push the National Front out of the race. The problem with the first strategy is that it tends to legitimize the ideas of the extreme right in the long run and reinforce voters in their choice to vote for the party that defends these ideas, right from the start. A route usually referred to as 'choosing the original version over the imitation' (*préferer l'original à la copie*).[24] However, it was the strategy that was the most common during the 1986 legislative election campaign. Some

---

[23]See previous chapters in this book.

[24]'Far Right: Voters Generally Prefer the Original to the Copy', 24 November 2023, https://www.lemonde.fr/en/opinion/article/2023/11/24/far-right-voters-generally-prefer-the-original-to-the-copy_6285464_23.html.

right-wing politicians emerged as strong advocates against immigrants. In particular, Charles Pasqua, a former Resistance fighter, long-time supporter of de Gaulle and close adviser to Jacques Chirac. Pasqua admitted sharing some common values with Jean-Marie Le Pen when it came to the topic of immigration. Once Chirac was in office as prime minister, Pasqua became the interior minister with an anti-immigrant agenda.

The politicization of immigration in the context of the 1986 general elections led to a restrictive turn in migration policy, both in terms of the residence of foreigners and the conditions for access to citizenship. In September 1986, the Interior Ministry passed the law on the conditions of entry and residence of foreign nationals in France. The so-called Pasqua law of 1986 restricted the list of foreign nationals who were automatically granted a residence permit and the list of foreign nationals protected against expulsion. It marked a major turning point in French migration policy, making it increasingly difficult for foreigners to obtain a visa, particularly non-Europeans from former colonial countries (such as Algerians). However, it was above all the government project to reform the nationality code that placed the issue of immigration at the centre of the debate on national identity. From then on, the politicization of immigration was systematically linked to a debate on national identity.

In November 1986, Justice Minister Albin Chalandon presented a bill to reform the nationality code. One of its aims was to amend Article 44, which allowed children born in France to foreign parents to automatically become French when they reached the age of majority. Calling this principle into question reflected the general distrust of young people from immigrant families. It was meant as a response to the emerging debate on immigration. The writings of the Club de l'Horloge were reportedly a source of inspiration for the project reform. The bill was finally withdrawn in a general context of protests against the government. However, in June 1987, the prime minister set up a Nationality Commission (*Commission de la Nationalité*), tasked with examining whether the nationality code was still appropriate. The commission was made up of fifteen members: five lawyers, three historians (including Pierre Chaunu), two sociologists, two senior civil servants, two doctors and one film-maker.[25] They worked under the chairmanship of senior civil servant, Marceau Long (1926–2016).

One of the most striking features of the Nationality Commission was that it consisted of hearings during eleven public sessions that were broadcast on television. As a result, from June to December 1987, close to a hundred members of NGOs, political parties, and also intellectuals and activists, one

---

[25]Hélène Carrère d'Encausse, Dominique Schnapper, Léon Boutbien Jean-Jacques de Bresson, Pierre Catala, Pierre Chaunu, Berthold Goldman, Salem Kacet, Pierre-Patrick Kaltenbach, Emmanuel Le Roy-Ladurie, Yvon Loussouarn, Jean Rivero, Alain Touraine, Jean-Marc Varaut and Henri Verneuil.

after the other, shared their experience of immigration and gave their views on the issue of nationality.

The debates during the time when the Nationality Commission hearings took place reflected a major change in perspective. In the past years, second-generation immigrants' automatic access to French citizenship was not welcomed positively. In particular, children of Algerians were reluctant to 'take French papers' as their parents had fought for Algerian independence.[26] In some cases, particularly for Algerians, the notion of 'betrayal' was put forward. Four years later, the situation had changed. For instance, on 6 October 1987, Christian Delorme, the Catholic priest from the Minguettes neighbourhood, outside Lyon, who took part in the March for Equality and Against Racism, gave the following speech in front of the Nationality Commission:

> Discovering that their children were French was very painful for many Algerian families. It took the years that have passed since 1979 for the Algerian community to be convinced that, in the end, it is not a bad thing for children born here to have French nationality, to have two nationalities, French and Algerian.[27]

With these words, Delorme recalled a development that he knew from his involvement in organizing the March in 1983. During the March, the articulation of political demands was framed in differential terms, such as calling for a pluricultural and pluri-ethnic France. The perspective had now shifted, and the Catholic priest was now seeking to defend the right of children from immigrant families to French citizenship. His words revealed a major change in the articulation between immigration, citizenship and national identity: the focus was now on demonstrating assimilation into French society and the will to be French.

Return of the Left, 1988

When new elections approached in 1988, and the possibility of François Mitterrand's re-election arose, the issue of immigration was no longer addressed in the same way by the left-wing parties as it had been in 1981. There was no

---

[26]Sayad and Bourdieu, *The Suffering of the Immigrant.*

[27]'La découverte [des jeunes qu'ils étaient français] fut très douloureusement ressentie par beaucoup de familles algériennes. . . . Et il a bien fallu les années qui se sont écoulées depuis 1979, pour que pénètre dans la communauté algérienne la conviction que, finalement avoir la nationalité française pour les enfants qui sont nés ici, avoir deux nationalités, la nationalité française et la nationalité algérienne, n'était pas une mauvaise chose' (translation by the author).

longer any desire to bring the demands of the immigrant movement – the Left was no longer a hotbed of opposition activists. In addition, the strategy of the right to be different had proved far too costly from an electoral point of view. François Mitterrand won the presidential elections against Prime Minister Chirac and became president of the Republic for a second seven-year term. As for the National Assembly, elections were called to renew its composition, this time on the basis of a two-round uninominal ballot. The Socialist Party won the majority of votes (275 seats) over Jacques Chirac's party (270). The change in the electoral system had the effect of reducing the FN's presence in the assembly from thirty-five seats to one. Yann Piat, the one FN deputy in 1988, ended up joining the centre-right a few months later after Jean-Marie Le Pen made some antisemitic comments. After that, there were no more representatives of the far-right National Front in the National Assembly.

However, the effective disappearance of the far right from the National Assembly in 1988 did not mean that the National Front was out of the game, and the issue of immigration would disappear from the debate. On the contrary, the succession of political events that had just unfolded profoundly altered the ways in which immigration issues were politicized from then on.

From improving the life of immigrants to asserting their will to become French nationals, this chapter showed how the 1980s were a time of rearticulation of the link between immigration, citizenship and national identity. It began with a brief moment of *differentialism* after the election of François Mitterrand in 1981 and the implementation of the concept of Right to Difference. The moment was short-lived, however, as the National Front reversed the rhetoric of the Right to Difference to an exclusive one in the following years. As a result, the Left gave up on the Right to Difference and made the choice *not* to deal with difference when back in office in 1988. Meanwhile, the role of colonization and decolonization, the politics of racism and antiracism lost their salience and fell into the realm of protest and resistance.

7

The global age, 1989–2004

On a global level, 1989 was the year of the dismantling of the Soviet Empire and the beginning of new population movements after the fall of the Berlin Wall. Migration flows became more global, and in Europe, the origins of immigrants became more diverse. However, for France, 1989 was also a moment to commemorate the 1789 revolution and the French Declaration of the Rights of Man and of the Citizen: a celebration specific to France's national history, but one to which President Mitterrand chose to give a global flavour. On 14 July 1989, a parade representing different peoples of the planet marched along the Champs-Élysées in front of a million spectators and hundreds of thousands of television viewers. However, the parade celebrated the global influence of the 1789 revolution rather than the cultural diversity of the French population. At that time, France's official discourse on difference stressed universalism over particularism.[1] The country entered the global age of migration moves, standing by its national values – exhuming them, redefining them and sometimes even reinventing them.

Moreover, the 1990s were a period of reorganization of migration flows with the creation of an intra-EU migration regime and subsequent strengthening of extra-EU border controls. The politics of immigration in France need to be understood within this new perspective. France was now just one of the many countries of immigration in the EU. As such, the French government began to actively commit to controlling migratory flows and asylum applications. With economic immigration put to a halt, those who might have travelled as workers in search of better economic prospects found themselves redirected to the 'asylum door'. This prompted a renewed concern to assess refugee's well-funded fear of persecution in their country of origin – a task for which intergovernmental cooperation could prove useful.

France, therefore, entered the global age of migration armed with a tradition of managing immigration, yet searching for new political tools to implement it.

---

[1] Angéline Escafré-Dublet, 'The Soundtrack of Immigration: A Look Back at the Exhibition "Paris–Londres: Music Migrations (1962–1989)" at the French National Museum of Immigration History', *French History*, 52, https://doi.org/10.1093/fh/crad052.

Asserting principles such as integration and secularism became central to the politics of immigration. Both proved to be essential compasses for navigating France's way into the twenty-first century.

The chapter locates the French case among its European counterparts in order to expose the common challenges versus the specific national response of countries of immigration. Its central argument is that governmental actors chose to reaffirm French secularism and define social integration as central elements of French national identity. In doing so, they further anchored the politics of immigration at the centre of national concerns. The chapter starts with the first headscarf affair of 1989 and situates France in the larger context of rising extremism in the world. It then turns to the emergence of the concept of integration in relation to the topic of immigration in France. It takes a public policy analysis perspective, in an attempt to disentangle the prescription ('a country of integration in theory') from the actual implementation of public action ('a country of integration in practice'). Finally, it analyses the media and political debate around the passing of new legislation related to immigration and the implementation of secularism in state-funded schools.

The first headscarf affair and a new framing for the politics of immigration, 1989

When, one fine morning in September 1989, three young girls arrived wearing Islamic headscarves at their secondary school in the town of Creil, north of Paris, their headmaster decided to expel them because they were in breach of the 1882 Ferry law on secularism in schools. In fact, when the law was passed at the beginning of the Third Republic, it referred mainly to teaching content and aimed at excluding religious dogma from the school curriculum – more specifically, Catholic dogma.[2] At the time, it had the further effect of casting out religious educators and establishing a network of state-funded schools, all around the country. So much so that in 1989, 86 per cent of the school population attended such schools. However, the school principal decided to refer to the principle of secularism (*laïcité*) not in reference to teaching or teachers as stated by the 1882 law but to pupils. He invoked the principle of secularism to reject the display of religious symbols by pupils – in this case, three girls who were wearing an Islamic veil.

---

[2] See Chapter 2.

Schoolgirls had been showing up at this school with headscarves already, without receiving such treatment. A brochure advertising the school's openness to diversity even featured a class photo with one schoolgirl wearing a headscarf.[3] When the principal decided to exclude the two school pupils at the beginning of the 1989/90 school year, he marked an important change in the interpretation of Islamic religious symbols in French state-funded schools, and in society at large. By invoking the principle of secularism, he was referring directly to the period of establishment of the Third Republic, at the end of the nineteenth century – an unusual reaction in relation to immigration issues, so far.

What is remarkable about the 1989 headscarf affair is the unexpected national coverage it received. At first, local NGOs condemned the exclusion. In particular, the local representations of the Human Rights League – an organization created around the time of the Dreyfus affair, whose main goal is to defend individual freedom. In this case, they condemned the way young pupils were prevented from receiving an education. The local Women's Rights Centre also condemned the exclusion, because female pupils were denied access to education. Finally, the Movement Against Racism (MRAP) condemned the exclusion because it targeted French girls of North African background. However, the issue went from being a local event to stirring a national debate on the wearing of the veil.[4]

The position of groups mobilized on the issue quickly evolved. In the weeks that followed, human rights organizations ended up opposing the wearing of the headscarf because it was infringing the principle of secularism in French state schools, that the headscarf was an expression of religious extremism and, finally, that it was a sign of women's oppression. One can observe the articulation of a counter position by no one else than the wife of the president of the Republic, Danielle Mitterrand. She based her position on religious freedom, that the exclusion of some was a threat to social cohesion.[5] Moreover, some feminist activists raised a concern that it might be patronizing to think of the Islamic veil as a sign of oppression and the Western understanding of women's

---

[3] Florence Rochefort, 'Foulard, genre et laïcité en 1989', *Vingtième Siècle. Revue d'histoire* 75, no. 3 (2002): 145–56, https://doi.org/10.3917/ving.075.0145.

[4] Although the number of girls wearing a headscarf in schools has never been determined, it could be estimated to be a few hundred. In 2005, a government report signalled three hundred cases of girls wearing a headscarf (Hanifa Chérifi, 'Application de la loi du 15 mars 2004', *Hommes & migrations* 1258, no. 1 (2005): 33–47, https://doi.org/10.3406/homig.2005.4391).

[5] See, for instance, the strong critique against the president's wife, Danielle Mitterrand, who wrote: 'If laïcité can not welcome all religions and all expression in France, then we are moving backward', *Le Monde*, 22–3 October 1989.

liberation as the right one.[6] However, their positioning was minor in comparison with most French feminists – and among them, notorious figures such as Elisabeth Badinter and Gisele Halimi – who firmly opposed the wearing of the Islamic veil.[7]

As for anti-racist organizations and immigrant groups, despite the initial reaction of the local branch of the Movement Against Racism (MRAP), they were not very vocal on the issue. One can observe the mobilization of the *Nana Beurs* collective, composed of women of North African descent, but they opposed the wearing of the Islamic veil by young girls because it was a symbol of oppression. At the time, the opposition to the headscarf was not interpreted as a rejection of Islam but rather as a rejection of an extremist form of Islam.

This is further illustrated by the fact that the most visible mobilization on the part of the Muslim community was a demonstration on 22 October, organized by the Islamic organization, Voices of Islam. It gathered only a few hundred Muslim people in Parisian streets, and the media coverage highlighted that the demonstrators were foreigners. They named them according to their country of origin: Pakistan, Iran, Lebanon – most notably, not the country of birth of the most numerous groups of foreigners in France (such as Algeria or Morocco).[8] Journalists also pointed to the participation of Mohamed Mouhajer as the leader in the demonstration. An Iranian activist, Mouhajer had earlier been linked to a series of planned terrorist attacks in 1986.[9] As a result, the demonstration was not perceived as representing the voice of Muslim people from France and supported the argument that schoolgirls wearing a veil were being manipulated by groups of foreign Muslims.

Finally, immigrant organizations were very limited in being mobilized on the grounds of their religious affiliation at the time. The difficulty of mobilizing on a Muslim identity in the French 1980s is reflected in the words of an activist who founded a Muslim Youth Union in 1986:

When it came to give a name to our collective, we labelled it Muslim Youth Union. We could have used the M for Maghreb [North Africa], this was much more accepted at the time, and we hesitated. But, we decided to

---

[6] Marie-Claire Boons and Françoise Collin, 'Le voile et la question de l'identité', *Les cahiers du GRIF* 43, no. 1 (1990): 197–201, https://doi.org/10.3406/grif.1990.2431.

[7] Elisabeth Badinter, Regis Debray, Alain Finkielkraut, Elisabeth de Fontenay, and Catherine Kintzler, 'Profs, ne capitulons pas!', *Nouvel Observateur*, 2–8 November 1989.

[8] 'Le défilé des "intouchables"', 24 October 1989, https://www.lemonde.fr/archives/article/1989/10/24/le-defile-des-intouchables_4126812_1819218.html. *Le Monde*.

[9] Didier Bigo, 'Les attentats de 1986 en France (Partie 2)', *Cultures & Conflits*, no. 4 (1991), https://doi.org/10.4000/conflits.750.

be provocative and go all the way through it and have the M stand for Muslim.[10]

Immigrant groups were much more commonly organized on cultural identity, such as the aforementioned *Nana Beurs*. As a result, there was no such thing as a Muslim voice or a Muslim representation to articulate a specific claim in reaction to the first headscarf affair in 1989.

Partly due to their lack of mobilization along religious lines and partly because of their perception that the issue was limited to only a few schoolgirls, immigrant organizations were not very vocal on the issue. By contrast, feminist and human rights organizations were much more active. They interpreted the wearing of an Islamic veil as a sign of extremism. As such, they considered the interdiction of the Islamic veil as the best bulwark against fanaticism and women's oppression.

At the governmental level, the first headscarf affair did not lead to the interdiction of the wearing of an Islamic veil in public schools. The State Council (*Conseil d'État*) ruled that the wearing of the headscarf was 'not contradictory to the values of secular French state school' provided students respected religious freedom and did not try to impose their views on others, nor did they contest teaching content.[11] Thus, public authorities left it to teachers and school directors to decide whether or not pupils were proselytes or contested teaching contents. As for the State Council, they stuck to the initial spirit of the 1882 Ferry law that aimed at excluding religious dogma from the school curriculum.

However, the understanding of the issue that emerged at the time inaugurated a rearticulation of the link between immigration, citizenship and national identity. Not only did immigrants and their children have to demonstrate their desire to be French, but now they also had to adhere to certain specific values, such as religious freedom and gender equality. The fact that Islam is a religion with which the French state had had a long relationship, dating back to the colonial period, was somehow lost in the process, and all that seemed to matter was that immigrant values should align.[12] It was in this context that the prime minister appointed a Higher Council of Integration to reflect and advise the government on the topic of the 'integration of foreign-born in France'.

---

[10]Interview with A.C., 27 January 2012, Collectif Against Racism and Islamophobia, former founder of Muslim Youth Union.

[11]State Council ruling of 27 November 1989. The State Counsil (*Conseil d'État*) is the highest administrative authority in charge of advising the French government. It is composed of 350 senior civil servants, among which eighty can be assigned outside the State Counsil to senior administrative positions.

[12]Davidson, *Only Muslim*.

A country of immigrant integration – in theory

Inaugurated by the Nationality Commission in 1987, the creation of a group tasked with reflecting on the principles that should guide immigration and integration policy was reintroduced in 1989 – this time permanently.[13] Still under the chairmanship of the senior civil servant, Marceau Long, Prime Minister Michel Rocard appointed a group of MPs, mayors and administrative officials to 'give their opinion and make any useful proposals on all issues relating to the integration of foreign residents or residents of foreign origin'.[14] The Higher Council of Integration included nine members, such as former director of the Office for Immigrant Cultural Advancement, Stéphane Hessel; the centre-right mayors of Roubaix and Deuil-la-Barre, two cities with large proportions of immigrants (André Diligent and Jean-Pierre Delalande) or Philippe Farine as a representative for non-profit organizations with a long-standing commitment to helping immigrants.[15] Only one of them was a woman, Marie-Thérèse Join-Lambert, who was a senior civil servant in the administration of social affairs, and none of them had an immigrant background, save for German-born Stéphane Hessel. The choice of members to sit on the High Council is revealing of who the people were deemed to be concerned with the fate of immigrants, or rather, the fate of immigrant policies: administrative officials, politicians and non-profit organizations that implemented public policy. No room was allocated to the experience of first and second-generation immigrants; only the experience of managing immigrants was considered.[16]

Like the 1987 Nationality Commission, the role of the Higher Council was to meet a series of resource people on immigration issues and issue reports to guide policymakers. The first report to be issued by the Higher Council was a proposal for a French model of integration. The report began by mentioning the fact that immigration to France was a long-standing phenomenon, dating back to the nineteenth century, and emphasized the

---

[13]The Higher Council lasted from 1989 to 2013, when it was transformed into a centre for the study of secularism (*Observatoire de la laïcité*).

[14]Decree no. 89-912, 6 December 1989, creating the Higher Council for Integration.

[15]Philippe Farine (1917–2006) was a lawyer and journalist, active in the Student Catholic Union (*Jeunesse étudiante catholique, JEC*) and director of the non-profit organization Catholic Committee Against Hunger and for Development (CCFD) from 1968 to 1977. In 1984 he was appointed head of the Immigrant National Commission a consultation body for immigrant associations.

[16]The Higher Council membership has evolved over the years to include people from immigrant backgrounds, such as businessman Yazid Chir, businesswoman Soumia Malinbaum, senior civil servant Nacer Medah and politician Salima Saa in 2009.

resulting intermingling of the French population. It, then, processed and defined integration as such:

> Without denying the differences, albeit without exalting them, it is on the similarities and convergences that a policy of integration lays the emphasis, to give everyone, regardless of their origin, the possibility of living in this society whose rules they have accepted, and of which they become a constituent part.[17]

The definition bore the stamp of the political context of the years that had just passed. In particular, the phrase 'take [differences] into account without exalting them' referred to the purported failure of differentialism in the early 1980s. In contrast, the report clearly established the need for integration policies to be colour-blind ('regardless of their origin') and for immigrants to conform to Republican values, even though secularism was not mentioned as such ('this society whose rules they have accepted').

The report then went on and quoted scientific studies on immigrants in the 1980s. However, the authors of the report mainly referred to academic work and statistical data that served to support preconceived ideas about immigrants and their settlement in France. For instance, contrasting with nineteenth-century immigration being an essential contribution to French demographic growth, the report quoted Fernand Braudel – famed historian of the early modern period – and his statement about a 'third wave' of immigrants in the 1970s, posing a 'colonial' problem within' France itself.[18] This way of contrasting immigration flows that were unproblematic in the past with the presence of immigrants that was problematic in the 1980s was more a reflection of the conceptions circulating in political circles at the time than what was emerging among historians. What's more, Fernand Braudel was famous for his economic and social approach to history, but he had passed away in 1985 and had only touched upon immigration history in his last book, *The Identity of France*, which was published posthumously.[19] There is no evidence that he would have endorsed this use of his work.

On the other hand, social historian Gérard Noiriel had just published *Le Creuset français*, which traced French immigration history and denounced

---

[17]'Sans nier les différences, mais sans les exalter, c'est sur les ressemblances et les convergences qu'une politique d'intégration met l'accent, afin de donner à chacun, quelle que soit son origine, la possibilité de vivre dans cette société dont il a accepté les règles et dont il devient un élément constituant'. Marceau Long et al., 'Pour un modèle français d'intégration' (Haut Conseil à l'intégration, 1991), 18.

[18]Long et al., 'Pour un modèle français d'intégration', 12.

[19]Fernand Braudel, *L'identité de la France, 3 tomes: Espace et histoire / Les hommes et les choses / Les hommes et les choses, tome 2* (Paris: Arthaud-Flammarion, 1986).

the lack of recognition of this part of French history.[20] As far as his work was concerned, the authors of the report only highlighted the 'strength of the "French model", compared with the "American model", which led to the emergence of "minority groups" of foreigners'.[21] Arguably, Noiriel compared immigration history in France and the United States in his book. However, the comparative perspective served to highlight the acknowledgement of the contribution of immigration to national history in the United States, compared to France. Not discussing which country had the best model. In fact, Noiriel's work took place against a backdrop of increasing anti-immigrant political discourse and aimed above all to raise awareness of the history of immigration in France. Moreover, the American model is also based on the incorporation of each individual into the nation. The emergence of group-based claims in the 1960s was a demand, not an achievement – the American Constitution recognizes primarily individual rights over group rights.

What this analysis of the report shows is that, for the authors of the report, what was key at that point was not historical accuracy but rather to assert a French specificity, in order to justify the imposition of French-style integration as a norm.

Finally, the authors of the report grounded their argument on census data collected by the National Institute of Statistics and Economic Studies and analysed by demographer Michèle Tribalat from the National Institute for Demographic Studies. The data came to support the idea of the intense intermingling of the French population so far. As of 1986, 18 per cent of the French population were either born abroad, or had a parent, or a grandparent born abroad (10 out of 57,86 million). However, the data were presented so as to reactivate the long-standing ideas that non-European immigrants were less desirable than European immigrants. Data analysis identified the share of European immigration flows 'bound to decrease' versus immigration flows coming from Maghreb, and overall sub-Saharan Africa and Asia bound to 'replace' them.[22]

As a result, the first report of the Higher Council for Integration reflected the political repositioning of the left-wing government on immigration issues. The text backtracked on attempts at differentialist policies to articulate a more traditional stance on immigrant selection and on the preference for European versus non-European immigrants, all formulated in terms of respect for

---

[20]Noiriel, *Le Creuset français*.
[21]Noiriel, *Le Creuset français*, 12.
[22]Noiriel, *Le Creuset français*, 32.

Republican values and the French legal tradition of assimilation.[23] A positioning that Patrick Weil coined the 'Republican synthesis'.[24]

The definition of French-style integration may have taken much political work, discussions and debates, but it ended up reinforcing already existing frames of reference, such as the preference for European immigrants and the necessity to manage immigrant integration.[25] However, these ideas had not been institutionalized as valid principles of immigration policies until then. On the contrary, back in 1945, the preference for European immigrants had encountered strong opposition.[26] What was different in 1991, when the report was published, was the need to fight far-right ideologists who took any claim for distinctiveness as evidence that immigrants should return to where they came from.[27] This justified taking a more restrictive stance on immigration issues. This point clearly illustrates how the politicization of immigration can affect immigration policies. The fact that right-wing politicians used the topic of immigration to take a political stance and win people's votes ended up limiting the options available to policymakers.

A country of immigrant integration – in practice

French-style integration was applied to public policies aimed at immigrant citizenship acquisition but also to social and cultural policies. In fact, it was not so different from what had been implemented until then: helping immigrants to settle and adapt to life in France, with the idea that some were more able to do so than others, according to their country of origin.[28] Except this time, it had the official justification that this approach was going against the progression of far-right ideas. Moreover, public policies would not apply to immigrants according to national origin groups, because of the principle of universalist egalitarian treatment. Yet, in return, immigrants should all embrace French Republican values – chief among them French secularism (*laïcité*).

The governmental agency that was the Social Action Fund kept on supporting organizations that helped immigrants, provided they aligned with

---

[23]Virginie Guiraudon, 'The Reaffirmation of the Republican Model of Integration: Ten Years of Identity Politics in France', *French Politics and Society* 14, no. 2 (1996): 47–57.

[24]Weil, *La France et ses étrangers*.

[25]Favell, *Philosophies of Integration*.

[26]See Chapter 3.

[27]Taguieff, *The Force of Prejudice*.

[28]See Chapter 4.

the new imperative of integration. Close attention to the work of non-profit organizations that developed cultural projects shows how their applications for financial support matched the new motto. The cultural projects that were sought, from then on, were those that promoted integration,[29] such as projects that organized the encounter between cultural forms of expression from different regions of the world (and not the promotion of a particular national culture – deemed, too separatist), or projects that promoted and gave equal access to the arts.

One privileged area of French-style colour-blind integration policies was urban development policies. Already in the early 1980s, the French government had initiated urban development programmes in order to improve the unfit housing stock and reduce social conflicts in poor neighbourhoods.[30] Even though it was seldom formally acknowledged as such, the politics of urban social development had the unofficial objective of targeting immigrants and their families.[31] A large proportion lived in deprived neighbourhoods (though not all of them), and targeting specific neighbourhoods was aligned with the universalist colour-blind approach of French public policies.[32] As such, the creation of the first minister dedicated to urban development in 1990 is usually regarded as particularly invested in managing the integration of immigrants.[33]

The creation of a minister dedicated to urban development and labelled Ministry for 'City Policy' is particularly revealing of the colour-blind principles underpinning French-style integration.[34] The decision to call this new category of state intervention 'City Policies' might somehow appear misleading. In fact, City Policies have nothing to do with municipal policies. They are designed at the national level. Moreover, they do not apply to all cities across the country. They target only a limited number of areas considered to be disadvantaged according to socioeconomic criteria (e.g. income level). However, it is a name that reflects the universalist framing of French urban development issues. City Policies consist of rebalancing territorial inequalities. The government taxes municipalities with the most

---

[29]Angéline Escafré-Dublet, 'The Whiteness of Cultural Boundaries in France', in *Whiteness and Nationalism* (London: Routledge, 2020).

[30]Hubert Dubedout, 'Ensemble, refaire la ville. Rapport au premier Ministre' (Paris: CNDSQ - Commission nationale pour le développement social des quartiers, 1982).

[31]Thomas Kirszbaum, 'Les immigrés dans les politiques de l'habitat. Variations locales sur le thème de la diversité', *Sociétés Contemporaines* 33, no. 1 (1999): 87–110, https://doi.org/10.3406 /socco.1999.1752.

[32]Sylvie Tissot, *L'Etat et les quartiers. Genèse d'une catégorie de l'action publique - Sylvie Tissot*, 2007, https://www.decitre.fr/livres/l-etat-et-les-quartiers-9782020914857.html.

[33]Damian Moore, *Ethnicité et politique de la ville: En France et en Grande-Bretagne* (Paris: L'Harmattan, 2002), 12.

[34]Escafré-Dublet and Lelévrier, 'Governing Diversity without Naming It'.

resources and allocates more resources to the areas in need. In other words, City Policies are redistributive policies.[35]

Moreover, urban development policies can be seen as a privileged area of French-style integration policies because they have an objective of social-mixing.[36] In France, social-mixing is based on the idea that the concentration of low-income inhabitants in one neighbourhood is an obstacle to social integration. Along this line, the concentration of immigrants of the same national origin is also regarded as an obstacle to their social integration. As a result, City Policies consisted of implementing social-mixing policies that unofficially targeted immigrants and their families.

The way urban development policies invested in hip hop in the 1990s is a good example of how the government relied on a subculture including music, dance and graffiti to solve issues related to violence, economic deprivation and discrimination. Hip hop emerged in the late 1970s in New York City and was soon transferred to Paris, where rap, in particular, met with great success in artistic *avant-garde* circles of the city centre.[37] However, it was mostly at the turn of the 1990s that it was particularly invested in by governmental policies and associated predominantly with disadvantaged neighbourhoods and French people with an immigrant background. Admittedly, hip hop originated from the African American community living in the Bronx, one of the poorest boroughs of New York City, which experienced severe urban decay throughout the 1960s and 1970s. As such, it has been a major vehicle to denounce poverty, discrimination and police brutality. As a result, it received a strong echo among young inhabitants of disadvantaged neighbourhoods with an immigrant background. However, the two main bands that became popular in the early 1990s, NTM and IAM, were respectively from the suburbs of Paris and Marseille, but not necessarily from disadvantaged neighbourhoods or with an immigrant background. While being from Saint-Denis, a working-class city outside of Paris, Didier Morville, a.k.a Joeystarr, and a member of NTM, mostly discovered rap music in downtown Paris. As for Philippe Fragione, a.k.a Akhenaton and singer of IAM, he grew up in a residential middle-class suburb of the nearby city of Marseille. He was able to discover hip hop culture, and rap music in particular, because he visited some family members in the United States. The association of rap music, hip hop dance and deprived

---

[35]Paola Salerni and Tito Marci, *Politique de la ville et aspects linguistiques de la France multiculturelle: histoire, évolution, contradictions* (Paris/Alberobello (Italy): L'Harmattan/AGA, 2023), 37.

[36]Sylvie Tissot, 'Une "discrimination informelle"?:Usages du concept de mixité sociale dans la gestion des attributions de logements HLM', *Actes de la recherche en sciences sociales* 159, no. 4 (2005): 54–69, https://doi.org/10.3917/arss.159.0054.

[37]Karim Hammou and Howard Saul Becker, *Une histoire du rap en France* (Paris: La Découverte, 2012), https://shs.cairn.info/une-histoire-du-rap-en-france-9782707181985?lang=fr.

neighbourhoods was, above all, the product of a media construct – a motif that politicians were quick to adopt.

Hip hop dance entered the French public agenda even though, in Europe and the United States, it existed mainly in the form of competitions that had nothing to do with public authorities.[38] In France, dance classes were developed in social and cultural centres in the suburbs; amateur dancers were encouraged to become professionals. All in the belief that hip hop dance would promote social integration, would open to other artistic forms and ultimately transmit ideas and values in line with the republican principle of universalism. This had to do with how the Lang Ministry of Culture had taken a keen interest in the work of a new generation of artists with an immigrant background in the 1980s. Except, this time around, the objective was not the artistic recognition of immigrant creation but rather the social integration of young people living in disadvantaged areas, with or without an immigrant background. The authorities thus contrasted hip hop dancers who participated in social centre programmes with others who did not. On the one hand, the hip hop dancers who participated in social centre programmes were considered respectful and open to other genres (e.g. contemporary dance, classical music and the visual arts). On the other hand, the hip hop dancers who did not participate in social centre programmes were regarded as confrontational and performance-oriented. In other words, authorities opposed the good citizens against the socially excluded, violent ones.

French public authorities' take on hip hop, particularly hip hop dance, did not prevent the development of a rich and varied hip hop scene, with the French rap scene being one of the most visible internationally.[39] The creation of festivals or the public support to artists and companies did contribute to giving a voice, a space and a career to many. At the local level, the promotion of hip hop culture led to the display of creative, multicultural cities, as in the case of the organization of a hip hop parade during the Lyon Dance Biennale.[40]

However, the institutional use of hip hop as an instrument of public action, and up to a certain extent, as an instrument of social control, explains some of the tensions surrounding the hip hop scene: the feeling of some artists to be instrumentalized, and the notion that hip hop is never really recognized as a legitimate form of art. Indeed, what became clear around that period was that when it came to artistic forms linked to immigration, art had to 'disguise itself

---

[38]Sylvia Faure and Marie-Carmen Garcia, 'Hip-Hop et politique de la ville', *Agora débats/jeunesses* 49, no. 3 (2008): 78–89, https://doi.org/10.3917/agora.049.0078.

[39]Hammou and Becker, *Une histoire du rap en France*.

[40]Lionel Arnaud, *Réinventer la ville: Artistes, minorités ethniques et militants au service des politiques de développement urbain. Une comparaison franco-britannique, Réinventer la ville: Artistes, minorités ethniques et militants au service des politiques de développement urbain. Une comparaison franco-britannique,* (Rennes: University of Rennes Press, 2012).

as social in its objectives' to convince and receive recognition.[41] Furthermore, this social and cultural approach to urban development did not address the socioeconomic issues plaguing deprived neighbourhoods, nor did it tackle ethno-racial discrimination that descendants of immigrants experienced in and outside those neighbourhoods.

At the turn of the 1990s, when movements of people and ideas were entering a new global dynamic (the circulation of hip hop music is a good example), France's response was to put its own spin on it: see it as a meeting of cultures, a new way of highlighting the universalist nature of art. However, this refocusing on Republican values, such as universalism, was soon to backfire on the Left. In the 1993 legislative elections, the Right, led by Jacques Chirac, won by an overwhelming majority (57 per cent of votes in the second round) thanks to an alliance with the centre-right party, UDF (*Union pour la démocratie françaize*). The second 'cohabitation' period began with right-wing Edouard Balladur as prime minister and left-wing François Mitterrand as president of the Republic.

Although the issue of immigration had not been at the heart of the political campaign, the new right-wing majority nonetheless brought to power a government that included Charles Pasqua as interior minister – a politician determined to pursue a restrictive policy towards foreigners. Refocusing on Republican values became useful when it came to asking second-generation immigrants to actively express their wish to become French citizens when they came of age. As a matter of fact, the 1889 French nationality code stated that immigrants' children born in France have the nationality of their parents until they come of age, at which point they automatically become French citizens. Moreover, interviews with people born in France of immigrant parents show that they are not always aware that they have not had French nationality up to that point.[42] In 1993, the Pasqua reform made it necessary for a child born in France to immigrant parents to make a declaration of intent (*manifestation de volonté*) to obtain French nationality. It was the first time this had happened since 1889, and was later abolished in 1998, when the Left came back to power (Guigou law).

The fact remains that, at the time, the law stirred up the idea that some children of immigrants did not want to be French citizens. This was not far from the far-right politicians' take on differentialism, who argued that immigrants who wanted to exert their Right to Difference should go back where they came

---

41According to artistic project manager Anne Golub: 'Le culturel est contraint de se travestir en social dans ses énoncés' in *Cultures en ville ou de l'art et du citadin*, ed. Jean Métral (La Tour d'Aigues: L'Aube, 2000), 85.

42Angéline Escafré-Dublet and Patrick Simon, 'Ce qu'il y a derrière l'identité nationale: l'appartenance face à l'altérisation', in *L'identité nationale: instruments et usages. Actes du colloque, Université de Picardie Jules Verne, 12–13 avril 2012 – Céline Husson-Rochcongar, Laurence Jourdain*, 2012, 63–80.

from. Except this time around, it was articulated in terms of intention to become French citizens. It corresponded to the terms of the definition of integration, which stipulated that everyone had to accept the rules of society, with their rights and obligations. However, applying the definition of integration to citizens born in France amounted to an unprecedented form of stigmatization.

However, a new issue stirred intense debate during the 1993 election campaign: the ratification of the Maastricht treaty and European construction. While it may have seemed far removed from the social integration of immigrants in France, it turned out to be directly related to the politics of immigration and the definition of France as a country of immigration among others.

Towards the end of border control and the creation of Fortress Europe

In the political campaign leading to the ratification of the Maastricht treaty, most of the discussion dealt with sovereignty and the leverage of the French state in future economic regulations. Creating a space for the movement of goods and people was at the centre of the European project. As for the politics of nationality and citizenship, they were destined to remain the preserve of each member state. However, with the creation of an intra-EU migration regime came the strengthening of Europe's outside borders. Already in 1990, European countries had signed the Dublin Convention that stipulated that the asylum seeker can only apply in one country and may not restart the process in another country after receiving acceptance or rejection. The aim was to avoid multiplying the procedural costs of examining asylum applications for each European state. It marked the beginning of European cooperation on asylum policy. With the preparation of the Maastricht treaty, cooperation increased. Not only were the Dublin provisions incorporated, but, in addition, the Maastricht treaty introduced the principle of burden-sharing aimed at balancing the number of refugees each country received in 1993.

European cooperation on asylum policy is not something that had been part of the plan, originally. When EU member states agreed to gradually remove border controls and to introduce freedom of movement in 1985, they mainly discussed the free circulation of European citizens and goods across those countries.[43] Road transport companies had complained about the time lost at border crossings. The reduction in border controls was therefore aimed above all at maximizing the movement of goods. Moreover, non-European migratory

---

[43]Virginie Guiraudon, 'Les effets de l'européanisation des politiques d'immigration et d'asile', *Politique européenne* 31, no. 2 (2010): 7–32, https://doi.org/10.3917/poeu.031.0007.

flows were relatively stable and rather low, at that time. This changed drastically after the collapse of communism and the fall of the Berlin Wall, in 1989. Eastern Europeans, with more freedom to travel, began to join the thousands of people fleeing conflict elsewhere in the world and sought asylum in Western Europe. In 1989, the French Office for the Protection of Refugees and Statelesss persons (OFPRA) registered sixty thousand demands, even though the office only granted an average of ten thousand refugee status per year.[44] When the end of border controls went into effect in 1995, member states embarked on increasingly intense intergovernmental cooperation to control extra-EU migratory flows. It consisted in coordinating asylum applications but also tightening controls at the European Union's external borders and fighting illegal immigration.

Illegal immigration was high on the European media and political agenda throughout the 1990s. It stirred much debate in France, where the plight of the *sans papiers* polarized opinion. The *sans papiers* movement – the movement in defence of undocumented immigrants – started in 1973 when the government passed the first law restricting migrant flows. However, it reached momentum in the 1990s after the 1993 Pasqua laws tightened the conditions for obtaining entry visas for foreign travellers from the former colonial empire, such as Algeria, Senegal, Mali, the Ivory Coast and Cameroon. Just as in the 1970s, the common image of foreigners passing the border illegally was not representative of the vast majority of undocumented migrants who had entered the country legally but were unable to renew their residency permit. However, the right-wing government of the time persisted in restricting foreigners' residence in France, because opinion polls were in favour of a tough approach to immigration. Conversely, left-wing circles, and in particular artistic circles, came to the defence of undocumented migrants. All through the 1990s, the defence of *sans papiers* became characteristic of left-wing people who identified with humanitarian values.

For instance, in 1996, a group of undocumented immigrants occupied Saint Bernard Church in the northeastern part of Paris in an attempt to raise awareness about their difficult situation. A group of Malian undocumented workers had already occupied a church in the southwestern part of Paris earlier in the year but had quickly been expelled. This time around, the group included women, men and children, and received the support of the Catholic priest of the Saint Bernard Church. Father Henri Coindé did not call for their expulsion on the grounds that it was the right of the church to bring shelter. All through the summer of 1996, the group of undocumented immigrants occupied the church that kept on and celebrated masses, weddings and funerals. Ten of the undocumented migrants began a hunger strike.

---

[44]Blanchard, *Histoire de l'immigration algérienne en France*, 86.

The occupation of the Saint Bernard Church over the summer of 1996 was also a shifting moment for the French immigration movement. Existing networks of solidarity supported the undocumented migrants, such as the Human Rights League or the leftist union, CGT. However, new figures also emerged. Senegalese-born Madjiguène Cissé is one of them.[45] A German language teacher from Dakar and mother of three, Cissé had travelled to Paris on a tourist visa, to visit one of her daughters studying there. She was one of those undocumented migrants who had overstayed a tourist visa and found a job willing to employ her without a work permit. With a background in union activism in Senegal, she soon joined the movement to help other undocumented men and women. In her memoir, she describes a bulk of women who had travelled from rural Mali to join a husband on a tourist visa, and found themselves undocumented after a few months, either because the husband's residency permit had expired, or because they were the second wife and could not legally benefit from family reunification. She was a rare female figure to emerge from the French immigrant movement, and she was able to articulate a specific claim for undocumented women. She took the floor in public meetings, otherwise mainly held by men.

Occupation of buildings, particularly churches, and hunger strikes dated back to the first mobilizations of undocumented migrants in 1973. They had been successful in bringing their plight to public attention and in obtaining a favourable response from the government. This time around, the government proved difficult to convince, but the occupation and the media coverage it received did bring attention to the cause. On the morning of 23 August 1996, the police entered and evacuated the Saint Bernard Church. French national television aired live and filmed the exit of the *sans papiers*. They received support from artists, in particular Emmanuelle Béart, who was seen exiting the church with them. Béart had just taken part in the Tom Cruise blockbuster movie *Mission: Impossible* (1996) and was very famous. This might explain why she was the one to be on the news that day to talk about the eviction. She lost her contract with the luxury brand Dior for appearing on screen wearing no make-up.[46] However, it is also a testimony of the little agency given by the media to the undocumented migrant activists, despite spokespersons such as Madjiguène Cissé.

The violence of the police intervention and the media coverage it received changed the public perception of immigration and also revealed the increasing

---

[45]Madjigène Cissé, *Parole de sans-papiers* (Paris: La Dispute, 1999).

[46]'Emmanuelle Béart's advertising contract with Dior will not be renewed. The fashion house has no intention of criticizing the actress for her commitment to humanitarian causes, but by appearing in public alongside the underprivileged, without make-up and without having her hair done, the star "no longer corresponds to the chic image of the brand"'. *Le Monde*, 3 April 1997.

racialization of immigrants.[47] The figure of the male undocumented worker from a sub-Saharan country emerged, despite the small proportion of nationals from sub-Saharan countries among the undocumented population, in general. Indeed, sub-Saharan African immigrants only accounted for 30 per cent of the illegal immigrants who later applied for a regularization procedure between 1999 and 2006 (30 per cent: North Africa, 16 per cent: Asia and 12.3 per cent: America).[48] However, on the morning of 23 August 1996, the police separated occupants of the church into groups of Black and white, with the whites being allowed to go free whilst the Blacks were arrested. This meant that white undocumented migrants were not arrested, but many of those Black immigrants who were arrested did actually hold residence papers.

In 1997, the newly appointed interior minister, Jean-Louis Debré, announced his project to pass even more restrictive measures targeting not only undocumented migrants but also those coming to their rescue. The law proposal included the creation of a file of people accommodating undocumented foreign nationals in their homes. Partly because it criminalized the very act of helping people in difficulty, and also because it was aimed directly at nationals, the prospect of this measure aroused indignation and mobilization. A group of filmmakers, including Patrice Chéreau, Arnaud Desplechin, Mathieu Kassovitz, Bertrand Tavernier and Sandrine Veysset, launched the following call to protest:

> We, French film-makers, hereby declare that each and every one of us is guilty of having recently – for personal or professional reasons – provided accommodation for illegal immigrants.

The group of filmmakers followed in the footsteps of their illustrious predecessors who published their manifesto in the left-wing weekly newspaper *Nouvel Observateur:* the 121 intellectuals and artists declaring their right to insubordination, in opposition to the Algerian War in 1960 (including Jean-Paul Sartre, Simone de Beauvoir, André Breton and Marguerite Duras); the 343 women declaring that they had had an abortion when it was illegal in 1973 (including Simone de Beauvoir, Catherine Deneuve and Jeanne Moreau). This time, they published simultaneously in the daily newspapers *Le Monde* and *Libération*, as well as in the monthly cultural magazine *Les Inrockuptibles.*

---

47 Jane Freedman, 'The French "Sans-Papiers" Movement: An Unfinished Struggle', in *Migration and Activism in Europe since 1945*, ed. W. Pojmann (New York: Palgrave Macmillan, 2008), 81–96.
48 Cris Beauchemin and David Lessault, 'Migration from Sub-Saharan Africa to Europe: Still a Limited Trend', *Population and Societies*, no. 452 (2009): 4.

Left support for undocumented migrants revealed a new stage in the politicization of immigration issues. Notably, accommodation certificates had already been requested since the early 1980s following a measure passed by the socialist government.[49] Moreover, Socialist Prime Minister Rocard famously stated that France could not host 'all the misery of the world' back in 1988. However, left-wing circles saw in this decision the paroxysm of right-wing anti-humanism. The right-wing government's involvement in recent conflicts in African countries with which France had historical ties (such as Rwanda in 1994) and its reluctance to grant asylum to those coming to seek refuge in France contributed to the perception that right-wing politicians were racist and unable to accept the consequences of their actions.

The media and political interest in the plight of undocumented migrants was short-lived, however. In April 1997, President Jacques Chirac called snap elections on the basis of opinion polls that favoured the Right. Yet, it was a left-wing majority that won the elections, and a third *cohabitation* ensued with left-wing Lionel Jospin as prime minister and right-wing Jacques Chirac as president. With the return of the Left to government, the fight for the undocumented migrants was no longer necessary to mark the political divide between the two camps. The left-wing government launched a regularization campaign, but Interior Minister Jean-Pierre Chevènement also made clear his intention to remain 'firm' on immigration issues.[50] This is what Patrick Weil coined a 'Republican Synthesis' – that is, the fact that left-wing government officials settled on the necessity to restrict immigration flows but tacitly decided not to officially admit it.[51] The number of undocumented migrants did not drop, but their plight received less political and media attention afterwards.

The relative silence in which the cause of undocumented migrants fell after the Left came back to power in 1997 derived from the politicization of immigration issues. Political parties used the topic of immigration in order to take a political stand – for the Left, the defence of vulnerable people as proof of their humanitarian concern; for the Right, the defence of national identity as a way to attract far-right voters. Yet, in practice, it did not drastically change the way they implemented immigration policies. Both concurred on the necessity to restrict immigration flows, while abiding by certain international standards, such as the rights to asylum and family reunification.

French governmental officials had indeed made progress in their European cooperation on the issue of controlling migratory flows. In 1999, the European treaty signed in Amsterdam came into effect. It provided for the creation of

---

[49]Siméant, *La cause des sans-papiers*, 212.
[50]87,000 regularizations took place out of 135,000 applications, which was way less than in 1981–2 (131,360).
[51]Weil, *La France et ses étrangers*, 271.

an area of Freedom, Security and Justice, tasked with the mission to ensure security at the external borders of Europe. Member States remained fairly autonomous in their decisions to accept immigrants and asylum seekers. The idea that the European Union was forcing member states to accept a certain number of immigrants was largely unfounded. In fact, the European Union could only impose figures on which all member states unanimously agreed. Either way, the whole point of coordinating immigration policies was that member states could cooperate in border management and the fight against illegal immigration.

As an instance of this, the French government supported the construction of a Red Cross camp on the banks of the Channel, in the village of Sangatte, in 1999. Designed to host a maximum of six hundred refugees on their way to seek asylum in the United Kingdom, it ended up hosting thousands of people from Kosovo, Iraq and later Afghanistan. A humanitarian gesture – refugees were found lingering in the villages around Calais in the prospect of illegally passing the border – the camp was a direct consequence of European cooperation on asylum and immigration. One of the reasons why asylum seekers kept a low profile is that they wanted to apply for asylum in the UK and, in accordance with the Dublin Convention, could not risk being identified in France. Otherwise, they would have had to apply for asylum in France, and not in the UK. Moreover, when the United Kingdom engaged in the war in Iraq in 2003, it agreed to receive more asylum seekers from these regions (in compliance with the principle of burden-sharing). For this reason, many asylum seekers from Central Asia (such as Iraq and Afghanistan) aimed to apply for asylum in the United Kingdom.

What began as cooperation between governments to save time and reduce transport costs became the creation of an intra-EU migration regime and subsequent European cooperation on immigration and asylum policy. The latter consisted of coordinating the conditions of entry for non-EU citizens and tightening controls at EU external borders. In other words, the creation of Fortress Europe. In order to coordinate their efforts, member states created Frontex in 2004, an agency tasked with the coordination of border control with each member states border and coastal guards.

The demographic fact of superdiversity

The increase in global movement following the fall of communism and conflicts around the world resulted in an intense diversification of immigrants all around Europe. American sociologist Steve Vertovec forged the concept of 'superdiversity' to refer to the continuous diversification of immigrants living in European cities, in terms of origin country, as well as socioeconomic status, migratory paths and attitudes towards ethnicity and religion.[52] Even though Vertovec's analysis stems from his work on Britain, some of his remarks fit well with the French context. In particular, it provides an opportunity to reflect on the diversity of experiences related to immigration. At the turn of the twenty-first century, the picture of the (male) immigrant worker coming to France from Southern Europe or North Africa had greatly complexified.

First, the 1990s were synonymous with the diversification of migratory flows in terms of countries of origin. 'More people were migrating from more places', to quote Vertovec. From 1990 to 1999, immigration from Asia and Africa increased by 35 per cent and 37 per cent, respectively. Southern Europeans and North Africans were still the most numerous (see Table 4). Yet, they were joined by other immigrants from a greater number of countries, with or without colonial ties with France, such as immigrants from Turkey; Southern European refugees from ex-Yugoslavia fleeing conflicts in the Balkan region; African immigrants from Ivory Coast, Cameroon and Congo fleeing the social and economic crisis that this former French colonial countries were going through; South East Asian immigrants from former French colonies of Indochina: Cambodia, Laos and Vietnam; South Asian immigrants from Sri Lanka, fleeing governmental repression against the Tamil minority. Moreover, they settled mostly in the regions around Paris, Lyon and Marseille, the Paris region being the most diversified and where most Asian and African immigrants concentrated.

Second, during the 1990s, the most common immigration routes experienced a slowdown. Still the largest group of foreigners, the Portuguese were less numerous in 1999 (553,663) than in 1990 (649,714). As for Algerians, they were the second-largest group in 1999 (477,482), yet not as numerous as a decade earlier (614,207). For the Portuguese, even if immigration to France continued to represent a major prospect for economic development, their country's entry into the European Union in 1974 helped to improve the economic situation and made immigration to other European countries possible.[53] In the case of Algerians, it is above all the acquisition of French nationality that may explain their decreasing number among foreigners (see Table 5). By contrast, Algerians were the largest group of immigrants in 1999 – that is, the group that includes foreign-born who have become French citizens (575,740). Algerians were followed closely by Moroccan-born, with a total of 521,000, in 1999, of which 17,000 had become French.

---

[52]Steven Vertovec, 'Super-diversity and Its Implications', *Ethnic and Racial Studies* 30, no. 6 (2007): 1024–54, https://doi.org/10.1080/01419870701599465.
[53]Irène Dos Santos and Sónia Ferreira, *Les Portugais en France: une immigration invisible: XXe-XXIe siècles* (Paris: Cavalier Bleu, 2024).

TABLE 4 Number of Immigrants by Country of Birth, in 1999

Europe	Germany	125,227	Africa	Algeria	575,740
	Italy	380,798		Cameroun	26,890
	Poland	98,566		Congo	35,318
	Portugal	570,243		Congo (Dem. Rep. of)	23,727
	Spain	316,544		Ivory Coast	29,879
	United Kingdom	74,683		Madagascar	28,272
Asia	Cambodia	50,526		Mali	35,978
	China (Peo. Rep. of)	30,418		Mauritius	27,806
	Laos	36,708		Morocco	521,059
	Lebanon	28,169		Senegal	53,859
	Sri Lanka	24,113		Tunisia	21,700
	Turkey	175,987	America	USA	29,381
	Vietnam	72,318	Other countries of the five continents		734,618

Source: INSEE, French Census

As of 1995, the French census recorded the number of foreigners and immigrants. Up until that date, foreign-born individuals who had acquired French nationality technically 'disappeared' from census data and were registered as French. The census did not record their nationality of origin, even if they were bi-nationals. The only foreign nationals to appear in the census record were those who did not hold French nationality and only held a foreign nationality. As such, the introduction of the category revealed the extent to which foreign nationals became French citizens: 36 per cent of immigrants were French citizens in 1999.

The introduction of the immigrant category in 1995 followed similar practices in other immigration countries, particularly EU countries. It introduced a dose of comparability between EU member states and goes hand in hand with the process of becoming a country of immigration, among others. However, this did not happen without debate. Politicians, but also social scientists, contended that this did not follow the principle of Republican colour-blindness, since foreigners were 'tracked down' even after they had completed full assimilation by becoming French citizens. This was, in a way, admitting that the French melting pot did not really work after all and that French nationals did not really share a common identity anymore. On the one hand, opponents to the introduction of the immigrant category argued that recording the origin country of French citizens born abroad was a way of denying them full assimilation into French nationality. On the other hand, advocates maintained that counting immigrants allowed for a better knowledge of the dynamics of immigration and integration in France.

Even though supporters of a focus on Republican values may have been more numerous among right-wing politicians and intellectuals, the political positioning on the issue of recording immigrants by nationality of birth was not that clear. For many advocates of a progressive approach to immigration and integration, pointing to French citizens' foreign background may have resulted in denying their ability to assimilate into French society. They condemned the excessive 'ethnicization' of society, to refer to the culturalist argument that consisted in attributing irrevocable differences to individuals, based on their ethnic or racial background. All this is to say that counting foreign-born and recording their country of birth was as specific as the French census could get in terms of describing the demographic fact of superdiversity. As for collecting census data on ethnic and racial background, even based on self-identification, as in the United States or the United Kingdom, it remained out of question. The ethno-racial dimension of France's superdiversity was therefore mostly approached through the *proxy* of nationality and the nationality of origin of immigrants. As a result, referring to French citizens as 'having an immigrant background' (*avoir des origines immigrées*) went as far as the everyday French language could go in referring to composite identities. Hyphenated identities such as African-America or British-Indian never took off. As for third-generation

TABLE 5 Most Represented Nationalities Among Foreign Residents in France (1962–99)

	Spaniards	Italians	Portuguese	Algerians	Moroccans	Tunisians	Other	Total Foreigners	Foreigners per cent	Total Population
1962	441,478	623,156	49,930	350,224	33,260	26,529	638,248	2,162,825	4.67	46,282,816
1968	605,624	565,024	295,508	473,252	79,176	60,688	524,056	2,603,328	5.27	49,444,776
1975	496,155	457,215	758,395	709,785	245,900	138,245	609,670	3,415,365	6.52	52,380,365
1982	327,156	340,308	767,304	805,116	441,308	190,800	842,208	3,714,200	6.84	54,295,612
1990	216,047	252,759	649,714	614,207	572,652	206,336	1,084,887	3,596,602	6.35	56,651,955
1999	161,762	201,670	553,663	477,482	504,096	154,356	1,210,157	3,263,186	5.58	58,520,688

Source: INSEE, French Census

TABLE 6 Foreigners and Immigrants, by Country of Birth in 1999

Country of birth	Algeria	Morocco	Portugal	Spain	Rest of the world	Total	Per cent	Total Population
Foreigners	477,482	504,096	553,663	144,039	1,583,906	3,263,186	5.58	58,520,688
Immigrants	575,740	521,000	570,250	316,544	2,326,466	4,310,000	7.36	

Source: INSEE, French Census

immigrants or afro-descendants from the French overseas (Antilles, Guyana, Martinique and Reunion), there are no official means to reflect their number in the French population.

Interestingly, France's 1998 FIFA World Cup final win brought about new attempts to describe the multicultural character of the French national soccer team. Following the win, the phrase '*Black, Blanc, Beur*' emerged to describe the ethno-racial diversity of the French soccer players. *Black* could refer to soccer players born in an African country (such as Marcel Desailly, born in Ghana) or born in France of afro-descendants parents from the French overseas (such as Thierry Henry, born in France of parents born in the West Indies; Lilian Thuram, born in Guadeloupe; and, Christian Karembeu, born in the French oversea territory of New Caledonia). *Blanc* could refer to soccer players born in France with a European immigrant background (e.g. Yuri Djorkaeff, whose grandfather was from Russia, and mother from Armenia). *Beur* could refer to soccer players born in France to parents born in North Africa (Zinedine Zidane, born in France, whose parents were born in Algeria). The phrase, however, does not account for all the diversity of origins in France (it does not include any term to refer to Asian immigration) and remains vague. It could not accurately reflect the ethno-racial dimension of France's superdiversity.

Third, a distinctive feature of Vertovec's definition of 'superdiversity' is the way it points to the various socioeconomic and legal statuses immigrants may have. Indeed, the number of educated and skilled migrants had increased since public authorities had put a halt to free economic migrations. The number of university-educated migrants rose from 1974 to 1999, along with the number of skilled immigrants in the field of health, education and information technology. The number of men and women was now comparable (2.16 million men and 2.14 million women). As such, the composition of each origin group had to be considered in light of the variability of all those dimensions. For instance, there might be a high number of Moroccan immigrants who arrived and looked for a job as industry workers, but there were also many university-educated young male and female Moroccan immigrants who came and took a job in the business or service industry. Moreover, when the Algerian Islamist Group (GIA) challenged the official Algerian authority and launched a series of terrorist attacks in Algeria, a number of political and media elites from Algeria sought asylum in France. Even though they came from the same country – Algeria – these new arrivals added to the already complex picture of Algerian immigration in France.

Finally, the National Institute for Demographic Studies issued the first major survey on immigrants since the 1950s.[54] Based on a representative sample of

---

[54]Michèle Tribalat, Patrick Simon and Benoît Riandey, *De l'immigration à l'assimilation: enquête sur les populations d'origine étrangère en France* (Paris: National Institute for Demographic Studies Press, 1996).

17,500 interviewees, the Geographical Mobility and Social Inclusion survey (MGIS) analysed the migratory path of foreign-born from Algeria, Cambodia, Laos, Mali, Morocco, Portugal, Senegal, Spain, Turkey and Vietnam. It included a representative sample of second-generation immigrants of at least one parent born in either Algeria, Portugal or Spain. The survey highlighted the high rates of intermarriage and citizenship acquisition, but also language acquisition, with 87 per cent of French people with at least one parent born in Algeria declaring that French was their first language. As for attitudes toward religion, 63 per cent of them declared no religious practice, despite some commitment to the Ramadan fast. However, the question of religious diversity came high on the political agenda, at the turn of the twenty-first century, at both international and national levels.

France's response to religious diversity

When September 11 happened in New York City in 2001, France had already experienced Islamist attacks back in 1995. On 25 July, a bomb exploded in the central train station of Saint Michel, killing eight and injuring 117 people. The attack was claimed by the Algerian Islamist Group (GIA), a political organization challenging the official Algerian authority. Because of its strong and long-standing links with Algeria, France experienced the consequences of the Algerian Civil War and Islamic terrorism on its own soil. However, after September 11 and the subsequent Global War on Terror initiated by the United States, the suspicion and hostility directed towards people identified as Muslims reached a new level. As argued by British sociologist Tariq Modood, there was an 'anti-Muslim wind' blowing across Europe, yet the landscape was not 'uniform'.[55]

In France, the landscape was a state that had long had a complex relationship with Islam. Dating back to the colonial period, Islam as a religious identity had been associated with the irreducible difference of the natives. Referring to Algerians as French Muslims was part of the process of racializing their specific identity and inability to fully become French citizens. The reaction to the first headscarf affair of 1989 can be understood in this perspective and was a reiteration of the incompatibility between Islamic signs and French citizenship. Moreover, Islam as an organization had long been seen as something to control. Back in 1905, when France passed the law separating Church and State, it was not implemented in Algeria, for the French Republic sought to keep control over the Muslims of Algeria through the Oulema organization. As such, attempts at

---

[55]Tariq Modood, 'Muslims and the Politics of Difference', *Political Quarterly* 74, no. 1 (2003): 100–15, https://doi.org/10.1111/j.1467–923X.2003.00584.x.

organizing Muslims on metropolitan soil had multiplied in the decade prior to September 11. In 1994, the Interior Ministry recognized the Council of Muslims of France. Finally, Muslims as a group were not identified in the census due to a legal impediment to officially recording religion. However, the Muslim group appeared as heterogeneous in terms of country of origin (North Africa and sub-Saharan Africa) and attitudes towards religious practice with some devout Muslims and a large proportion of first- or second-generation immigrants being identified as Muslims based on their name or country of origin, but not declaring any religious practice apart from doing Ramadan, at times (e.g. 63 per cent of French people with at least one parent born in Algeria declared no religious practice, apart from occasionally doing Ramadan).

Partly because of this long and troubled relationship with Islam, and partly because of the new global context of war on terrorism and subsequent suspicion towards Muslims, when a second headscarf affair arose, the governmental reaction was less hesitant than the first time, in 1989. In March 2003, sixteen-year-old Alma and eighteen-year-old Lila Levy-Omari began wearing a veil covering their hair and neck while going to their high school in Aubervilliers (north of Paris). Though the State Council had not formally stated that the Islamic veil was forbidden in high school and had left it to school directors to decide whether or not pupils were disturbing school activities, the centre-right education minister François Bayrou had issued a more explicit circular asking secondary and high school directors to forbid any conspicuous display of religious signs in 1994. The circular left it to the school director to decide whether or not the religious signs were 'conspicuous'. In the case of the Levy-Omari sisters, the school director decided as such after months of discussion with them, and they were expelled on 10 October 2003. Compared to the first case in 1989, the sisters expressed attachment to religious practice. However, they were well aware of the circular, did not proselytize, and were not the only ones wearing a veil in their high school. Their father was a lawyer, and together with the anti-racist organization MRAP, they protested the decision. Following the second headscarf affair, President Chirac called for the creation of a specific commission to reflect on the implementation of secularism in French schools and beyond, under the tutelage of centre-right politician and long-time anti-racist advocate Bernard Stasi.

The Stasi Commission of 2003 consisted of administrative officials and social scientists who specialized in issues related to immigration and secularism in France (such as Jean Baubérot and Patrick Weil).[56] It made a series of suggestions to secularize French schools, such as the adaptation of the school holiday calendar (such as giving the opportunity for Muslim and Jewish

---

[56] Jean Baubérot, *Histoire de la laïcité en France* (Paris: Universities of France Press, 2000).

students to miss class on the day of important religious celebrations such as Yom Kippur and Eid El Kebir). However, President Chirac mostly followed the recommendation to ban ostentatious religious signs when issuing the law.

The decision to go further and pass a law banning religious signs in schools can be understood in the context of the intense politicization of immigration in relation to Islam and *laïcité*. President Chirac had been re-elected in 2002 following an eventful election. For the first time since the beginning of the Fifth Republic, the major contender in the second round was not a left-wing candidate, but a far-right candidate, National Front leader Jean-Marie Le Pen. In a massive electoral mobilization against the far-right vote, Chirac was elected with 82.21 per cent of the vote with a record rate of 79 per cent participation. Following this, the president-elect articulated a discourse that emphasized Republican values to distance itself from the far right. The adoption of such a law was therefore part of this political positioning. Moreover, *laïcité* had been a core value of the Left in opposition to the Catholic right-wing electorate all throughout the twentieth century. By championing secularism, the right-wing president was asserting this value and re-articulating the left-right divide in French politics. A 2003 survey showed that people who recognized *laïcité* as an important value for them were indeed people who declared anti-immigrant feelings and positioned themselves on the right side of the political spectrum.[57] This indicated a major change in the understanding of *laïcité* and revealed how the politicization of immigration can transform a historical principle dating back to the end of the nineteenth century.

The law banning religious signs in public schools was passed on 15 March 2004 and took effect with the new school year of 2004/5. Surveys showed that public opinion was supportive of the law. To the statement 'Some young girls want to keep their veil in class', 20 per cent of the respondents chose 'this should be accepted because all religions should be respected' versus 80 per cent who selected 'this should be forbidden because in a secular (*laic*) school there should be no religious signs'.[58] Arguably, for school directors who had to make the decision to exclude or not a student who was wearing an Islamic veil, the law solved the issue. As stated by a principal:

---

[57]Martine Barthélemy and Guy Michelat, 'Dimensions de la laïcité dans la France d'aujourd'hui', *Revue française de science politique* 57, no. 5 (2007): 649–98, https://doi.org/10.3917/rfsp.575.0649.

[58]Sylvain Brouard and Vincent Tiberj, *As French as Everyone Else?: A Survey of French Citizens of Maghrebin, African, and Turkish Origin* (Philadelphia: Temple University Press, 2011).

After the passing of the law, it is clear that we enjoyed a blissful peace. Before, you had to deal with the pupil, the family and even some religious associations. You had to negotiate. After the law, no more of that. . . . [59]

Principals established different arrangements with students wearing Islamic veils outside school, sometimes arranging for a changing room inside the school, sometimes asking students to take off their veils before entering the school.

However, the passing of the 2004 law banning religious signs in public schools raised debates and polarized civil society. On the one hand, proponents of the law saw the reaffirmation of the principle of *laïcité* justified in light of previous pressures that religious groups had put on French public schools (mainly Catholic groups). French authorities feared that 'fundamentalist groups' would use schools as a battleground and would impose the wearing of the scarf upon others.[60] Moreover, some feminist activists argued that the Islamic veil represented the domination of men over women in the Islamic religion. However, other organizations, such as the Human Rights League, argued that the principle of *laïcité* was already in French law and that, with regard to schools, it mainly applied to teaching and teachers, not pupils. New groups formed that criticized the law for stigmatizing Islam (such as *Collectif Contre l'Islamophobie en France*) and/or contended that the Islamic veil was not necessarily an instrument of domination of men over women (such as *Collectif une Ecole pour Tout-Es*). Moreover, they expressed concern that the law might discourage the schooling of girls practicing Islam. One year later, a report stated that there were only forty-seven exclusions of pupils among the 639 religious signs that were listed by school directors and that among the students who did not want to remove the Islamic veil or Sikh turban, half of them ended up registering for distance learning.[61] Some families reported their disappointment when they heard that by 'dialogue' the law did not mean the possibility of negotiation, and some cases appeared unexpected, as in the case of the law preventing the schooling of Sikh pupils. Moreover, teachers reported students complaining of the disproportionate room allocated to Catholicism in the academic calendar. They pointed out that Catholic holidays were still the rule (Christmas and Easter notably) and were left with the impression that *laïcité*, in practice, was a two-tier concept: it banned the expression of religious symbols that pertain to Islam, but it allowed for the expression of Catholicism. The Stasi Commission had highlighted this

---

[59]Interview of the author with a high school director in the Paris Region, on 5 May 2011.
[60]Patrick Weil, 'Lifting the Veil', *French Politics, Culture & Society* 22, no. 3 (2004): 142–9.
[61]Chérifi, 'Application de la loi du 15 mars 2004'.

limit to the implementation of secularism. However, it was not followed by policymakers.

As a way to deal with religious diversity, the passing of the law banning religious display in French schools might have simplified the job of school directors and given French authorities the impression that they were fighting fundamentalist groups – it was first and foremost a reaffirmation of French Republican values.[62] From the first headscarf affair of 1989 to the passing of the 2004 law, France's response to religious diversity was to reaffirm the principle of secularism.

At the turn of the twenty-first century, France emerged as a country of immigration among others. The French government took part in the negotiation of immigration policies at the EU level, and very much like its European counterparts, French authorities dealt with an unprecedented diversification of immigration flows. In its attempt to define a commonness in the face of the demographic fact of superdiversity, we saw in this chapter that French government officials chose to reaffirm a definition of its identity around civic values. This was not uncommon in other European member states. Commentators have observed a turn to civic measures (such as civic tests in the process of citizenship acquisition) as deemed more suitable for the objectives of social and cultural integration of immigrants.[63] In France, it took the shape of reaffirming French secularism and defining integration as central to national identity.

[62]Joan W. Scott, 'Symptomatic Politics: The Banning of Islamic Head Scarves in French Public Schools', *French Politics, Culture & Society* 23, no. 3 (2005): 106–27.
[63]Nasar Meer et al., 'Examining 'Postmulticultural' and Civic Turns in the Netherlands, Britain, Germany, and Denmark', *American Behavioral Scientist* 59, no. 6 (2015): 702–26, https://doi.org/10.1177/0002764214566496.

8

From riots to attacks, 2005–15

On the evening of 27 October 2005, two teenagers aged fifteen and seventeen were killed in an electrical shed while trying to escape a police check. What began as a tragic incident in the remote Parisian suburb of Clichy-Sous-Bois turned into a particularly violent sequence of urban riots across the country. The riots involved the youth, who set fire to local buildings, garbage cans and private vehicles. By 7 November, conflict had spread to almost three hundred cities nationwide, and it was not until 17 November that the authorities considered the riots were over.[1] Many interrogations arose as to where this civil unrest came from, and what it signified. One frame of interpretation attributed the riots to a perceived failure to incorporate second-generation immigrant youth in France.[2] Fifteen-year-old Bouna Traoré was born in France to parents born in Mali. As for seventeen-year-old Zyed Benna, his parents were born in Tunisia, to where they have since returned. However, it can also be seen as a consequence of the mistrust that had grown up towards police forces; the lack of opportunities for a section of the youth living in the most disadvantaged areas of the country and, finally, the few opportunities they had to make their demands heard through typical political channels. In other words, it is possible to analyse this violent episode in relation to the consequences of immigration and the ways in which they cut across the economic, social and political dimensions of French society.

Following the 2005 riots, a new cycle of protest emerged with claims against police violence and for a greater recognition of the plight of French citizens with an immigrant background. Indeed, the meaning of French citizenship was transformed between 2005 and 2015. On the one hand, research highlighted the discrimination experienced by the descendants of immigrants from North and sub-Saharan Africa. On the other hand, the

---

[1] David Waddington, Fabien Jobard and Mike King, *Rioting in the UK and France: A Comparative Analysis* (Cullompton: Willan, 2009).

[2] David Snow, Rens Vliegenthart and Catherine Corrigall-Brown, 'Framing the French Riots: A Comparative Study of Frame Variation', *Social Forces* 86 (2007): 385–415, https://doi.org/10.1353/sof.2008.0004.

political authorities were increasingly focusing on the issues of immigration and national identity, in order to change the legislation governing the entry and residence of foreigners. The politicization of immigration became one of the main themes of the election campaign and a constant subject of media attention.

This chapter looks at the 2005 riots and explains how they led to greater recognition of the discrimination faced by the descendants of immigrants from North and sub-Saharan Africa. It then discusses the intense politicization of immigration that followed the creation of a Ministry of Immigration and National Identity (2007–10). It argues that the successive decisions on the control of migration flows and religious diversity increased the polarization of public opinion on the topic of immigration. As a result, when the terrorist attacks of 2015 took place, governmental discourse of inclusion struggled to prevent an increase in anti-Muslim attacks.

The 2005 riots and the changing meaning of citizenship in France

Violence had already erupted following racist crimes and police violence in the previous decades, and in this sense, the riots of 2005 were part of a rather long tradition.[3] Located in deprived urban areas outside Paris, Lyon or Marseille, riots (*émeutes*) involved young male inhabitants confronting police forces and causing various damages (such as setting cars on fire). Most rioters had a North African or sub-Saharan immigrant background, for much of the discontent stemmed from accusations of racism following violent encounters with the police. All through the 1990s, such unrest erupted in the outer suburbs of Paris (Mantes-la-Jolie in 1991; Sartrouville in 1992, Melun in 1993, Dammarie-lès-Lys in 1997), Toulouse in 1998 and Lille in 2001. Most of these urban riots consisted of confrontations between the youth and the police or any representative of public services (e.g. bus drivers, firefighters). They also entailed fights between youth groups or gangs, yet in fewer proportions (one out of three). The riots that erupted in Clichy-Sous-Bois in October 2005 therefore followed an established pattern of violent reactions to deadly encounters with the police.

However, the 2005 riots stood out for their duration and scale. The twenty-two-day period of disorder did not result in any casualties, but 201 policemen

---

[3]Fabien Jobard, 'An Overview of French Riots: 1981–2004,' in *Rioting in the UK and France: A Comparative Analysis*, ed. David Waddington, Fabien Jobard and Mike King (Cullompton: Willan, 2009), 27–38. See also Chapter 6.

and 26 firefighters were injured, 10,000 private vehicles were deliberately ignited, and 250 public buildings were damaged, at a total cost of an estimated €200 million. The young age of the victims and the fact that they were simply returning home after playing football at the time of the events might have added to the anger. Bouna Traoré and Zyed Benna had visibly run from the police because they anticipated a heavy-handed police check. Their death revealed a deep distrust of the police. A change in police enforcement had indeed culminated in this tragic event.

As of 1993, the centre-right government implemented a tougher policy on juvenile delinquency – a development that Nicolas Sarkozy took to a whole new level when he was appointed interior minister in 2002. In 2003, he pronounced the end of neighbourhood policing – that is, sending teams of police officers to prevent crime and improve feelings of security, which resulted in the increased militarization of local police forces. This was amplified by his discourse on the issue. A few months prior to the events of October 2005, he had claimed to 'cleanse' a neighbourhood with a high-pressure hose (*Kärsher*), in La Courneuve (north of Paris), and a few days before, he had stated that he would rid the inhabitants of Argenteuil of the riff-raff (*racaille*), there. The 2005 riots could therefore be seen as the culmination of a long-term process and the tragic events of Clichy-Sous-Bois, as the final straw.

Moreover, the return of a right-wing government in 2002 had put an end to economic development programmes aimed at young unemployed people. Urban development policies that had originally been aimed at improving the unfit housing stock as well as social development were now exclusively dedicated to urban renewal, that is, the destruction and reconstruction of buildings. No more state-sustained jobs for the youth who experienced difficulties securing jobs. In fact, a 1999 survey demonstrated that second-generation immigrants faced major difficulties entering the labour market.[4] In addition to being overexposed to unemployment, they were more precariously employed and more dependent on subsidized jobs. The survey data exposed the existence of ethno-racial discrimination in employment, which mainly affected the descendants of North African, African and Turkish immigrants. It showed that they were two times more likely to be unemployed. Hence, the riots could also be attributed to economic conditions and associated with the high level of unemployment, or limited opportunities among the residents of disadvantaged areas.[5]

---

[4]Patrick Simon, Dominique Meurs and Ariane Pailhé, 'Persistance des inégalités entre générations liées à l'immigration: l'accès à l'emploi des immigrés et de leurs descendants en France', *Population* 61, no. 5–6 (2006): 763–801, https://doi.org/10.3917/popu.605.0763.
[5]Snow, Vliegenthart, and Corrigall-Brown, 'Framing the French Riots'.

The lack of opportunities and experience of discrimination gave way to a widespread feeling of second-class citizenship among the descendants of immigrants from North and sub-Saharan Africa. A few months before the events in Clichy-Sous-Bois, an anti-racist group had formed on similar premises, arguing that descendants of immigrants were treated as *quasi-colonial* subjects. The Party of the Indigenous of the Republic (*Parti des indigènes de la République, PIR*) reclaimed the term 'indigenous' to point at the state's unequal treatment of French youth with a Caribbean, North African or sub-Saharan African background. Moreover, since the passing of the 2001 Taubira Law recognizing the trade of enslaved people as a crime against humanity, there has been a discussion over the appropriate recognition and possible reparation of slavery and colonialism in France.[6] As such, despite the widespread criticism that the riots were senseless acts of violence, they were actually followed by a new wave of political mobilization and the articulation of new claims, such as the recognition of ethno-racial discrimination and the political participation of French people with an immigrant background.

Following the 2005 riots, a series of activist groups formed in defence of inhabitants from disadvantaged areas. For instance, in Clichy-Sous-Bois, the organization AC-le feu (*Collective Association for Freedom, Equality, Fraternity – Together, United*) gathered social workers with residents and toured around France to gather the grievances of people living in disadvantaged areas and present them to the National Assembly, a year later, in October 2006. The organization did not emerge from a vacuum. There had been groups active since the 1980s in many of these neighbourhoods: local groups with social or cultural projects (e.g. radio) and youth organizations that focused on the fight against police violence.[7] Moreover, many of these organizations around France were in contact with each other through a network movement called MIB (*Mouvement des immigrés de banlieue*).[8]

However, there was a new wave of group mobilization that articulated claims against discrimination and for recognition. The organization Duties of Remembrances (*Devoirs de mémoires*) is one of them, for it voiced an open recognition of France's colonial past. The expression *duty of remembrance* refers to the duty to remember historical events such as the Second World War and the Holocaust. Putting it in plural – *duties of remembrances*, the organization called for pluralizing the recognition of founding events to include

---

[6]Crystal Marie Fleming, *Resurrecting Slavery: Racial Legacies and White Supremacy in France* (Philadelphia: Temple University Press, 2017).
[7]See Chapter 6.
[8]Camille Hamidi, 'Riots and Protest Cycles: Immigrant Mobilization in France, 1968–2008', in *Rioting in the UK and France: A Comparative Analysis*, ed. David Waddington, Fabien Jobard and Mike King (Cullompton: Willan, 2009), 135–46.

slavery and colonization. In this sense, it was a new type of claim-making. The organization gathered activists who canvassed urban areas and urged young people to register and vote. Although the movement benefited from the involvement of famous figures (such as musician Joey Star and comedian Jamel Debbouze), members were met with a mixed reception when they came to Clichy-Sous-Bois. They were confronted by local leaders on their opportunism. Yet, some inhabitants did go to the town hall and registered to vote. Eventually, observers estimated a general increase in registration rates across the country.[9]

Finally, the call for a better participation of French people with an immigrant background in politics inevitably raised the question of who to vote for. In the run-up to the presidential election of 2007, there was a mobilization for a better representation of French people with an immigrant background, with the slogan of ensuring better representation of 'diversity' in politics. Around the mid-2000s, policymakers began to use the term diversity for all issues pertaining to the consequences of immigration and the formation of ethno-racial minorities.[10] First formalized in the business world to meet the need to combat discrimination in employment, the term was taken up by the political elite to demand better career prospects for its members. For instance, in 2004, Rachida Dati and Hakim El-Karoui founded Club 21st Century – a social club that organized gatherings with CEOs and politicians for the promotion of French people with an immigrant background to key positions in the public and private sectors. In 2006, the club issued a Diversity Charter for Politics that called for mainstream parties to include more candidates with an immigrant background in the run-up to the legislative election. Yet, they only had it signed by Socialist candidate, Ségolène Royal and the club was more successful in networking and securing key positions in the public and private sectors. For instance, Dati did not run for the legislative election of 2007, but President Sarkozy appointed her justice minister a few days after his election, and she served from 2007 to 2009.[11]

The call for greater representation of diversity in politics was not confined *to* the national level of government, however. From 2005 to 2007, calls emerged

---

[9]Christophe Jakubyszyn, 'Les jeunes des banlieues veulent devenir électeurs', *Le Monde*, 28 December 2005.

[10]Laure Bereni and Alexandre Jaunait, 'Usages de la diversité', *Raisons politiques* 35, no. 3 (2009): 5–9, https://doi.org/10.3917/rai.035.0005.

[11]Article 8 of the Fifth Republic states that the president of the Republic appoints ministers on the recommendation of the prime minister. Ministers do not have to be elected representatives. Even though it is a practice to select government members from the members of the National Assembly, it is not an obligation.

on both sides of the political spectrum.[12] Left-wing parties (such as the Socialist Party and the Green Party) had been the ones to include the highest number of members with an immigrant background due to their connections with antiracist organizations. Yet, twenty years after the 1983 March that was supposed to mark their entry onto the political scene, left-wing elected representatives were only a limited number in French political bodies.[13]

Arguably, party politics are competitive, and places are hard to get. However, there were several reasons that political parties had often been reluctant to present minority candidates in elections. A common justification had been the purported fear of alienating the mainstream electorate and thereby advantaging far-right parties.[14] As such, the idea that minority politicians would only represent communal interest had been the main argument for avoiding the inclusion of activists who had spent sufficient time in the party to apply for an electoral mandate. This did not mean that, at the local level, politicians had stayed away from patronage and clientelism. On the contrary, minority politicians described instances of being assigned to specific neighbourhoods because of their surname or purported origin. However, this was rarely an opportunity for them to make their way through the top electoral positions.

The story of Hamida, born in France to parents born in Algeria, indicates this difficulty in breaking the glass ceiling of political representation in a suburban city outside Paris.[15] In 1995, Hamida was active in an anti-racist organization when she met the mayor, who gave her a job in the city council and assigned her the responsibility of urban development and women's issues. He also wanted to include her on his electoral list for the next city election. Yet, at the time, she was not eligible, for she did not have French citizenship. Six years later, however, she had finally acquired French citizenship and wanted to be on the list, except this time it was a definite no. This was because, in the meantime, she had worked, and people had started getting to know her. According to her, there were people of North African descent who did not necessarily like her, and French people who liked her. So that did not fit in with the mayor's strategy to reach out to the North African community as a whole anymore. When she saw that he had not included her on the list, she recalled being in 'a shock'. She added, 'I really felt that I was *not white*'. She did try to run on the Socialist list, later on, but Socialist Party members found another

---

[12]Patrick Simon and Angéline Escafré-Dublet, 'Représenter la diversité en politique: une reformulation de la dialectique de la différence et de l'égalité par la doxa républicaine', *Raisons politiques* 35, no. 3 (2009): 125–41, https://doi.org/10.3917/rai.035.0125.

[13]Vincent Geisser and El Yamine Soum, *Discriminer pour mieux régner. Enquête sur la diversité dans les partis politiques* (Ivry-sur-Seine: Atelier, 2008).

[14]Romain Garbaye, *Getting into Local Power: The Politics of Ethnic Minorities in Brittish and French Cities* (Malden, MA: Wiley-Blackwell, 2005).

[15]Interview with the author, 29 August 2008.

woman who had only been in the Party for a few months. After which, she decided to leave.

Hamida was confronted with the phenomenon of tokenism. When a North African-sounding name seemed fitting to win a district, she was welcome to run for elections, regardless of her lack of experience in politics. When her name began to be associated with her work, she was no longer that token individual who could create the impression of social inclusiveness and diversity. While the phenomenon is generic to most multicultural societies, it is interesting to note that the French universalist context was not immune to it.

Partly because of the post-2005 mobilization and partly because they thought a diverse candidate might bring more votes, right-wing parties also engaged in diversifying their candidates for the legislative election of 2007. Within Sarkozy's right-wing party, the Circle for Republican Diversity supported right-wing minority candidates. According to the Circle's chair, Dogoui, a businessman born in the Ivory Coast, 'A party that does not change in the same way as society changes loses votes!'.[16] The cost-benefit approach to electoral votes mirrored a similar development in the business sector at the time.

The passing of the European directive prohibiting discrimination in the workplace in 2000 had indeed initiated a substantial change in the sector. The law no longer only punished racist comments made by isolated individuals (the Pleven law of 1972); it was now possible to take a company to court after demonstrating that a refusal of recruitment or career progression was discriminatory. The stakes were high for business operators, and initiatives flourished to prevent discrimination in the workplace: organizations began to sign diversity charters and commit to promoting diversity and equal opportunities to their staff.[17] They elaborated a discourse that made diversity a business opportunity; one of the chief arguments being that, for companies, discriminating meant losing talent.

Moreover, the introduction of diversity policies in the workplace had the unexpected effect of moving anti-discrimination from the left to the right of the political spectrum.[18] In particular, Interior Minister Sarkozy used it to differentiate himself from other right-wing contenders, such as former Prime Minister Villepin, in the run-up to the presidential election. Combined with the values of individual and economic success, diversity, and the fight against discrimination, it could indeed shine a new light on the main right-wing party. It enabled Sarkozy to present himself as a pragmatic right-winger with a good

---

[16]Interview with the author, 18 September 2008.

[17]Laure Bereni, *Le management de la vertu: La diversité en entreprize à New York et à Paris* (Paris: Sciences Po University Press, 2023).

[18]Patrick Simon, 'Comment la lutte contre les discriminations est passée à droite', *Mouvements* 52, no. 4 (2007): 153–63, https://doi.org/10.3917/mouv.052.0153.

grasp on the business world, while capitalizing on voters with an immigrant background – a section of the electorate that had hitherto been relatively left wing.[19]

The openness to issues of diversity and the fight against discrimination should not, however, leave any doubt as to the increasingly restrictive turn taken by the politics of immigration in the late 2000s. More so, the period marked a decoupling of immigration issues. On the one hand, anti-discrimination was meant to rectify the obstacles that had disrupted the upward trajectory of deserving descendants of immigrants. On the other hand, immigration as a topic was increasingly invested with notions such as security and the preservation of national identity.

The creation of a Ministry of Immigration and National Identity in 2007

On 17 May 2007, Nicolas Sarkozy succeeded Jacques Chirac as president of the Republic after a second round against Socialist candidate Ségolène Royal. The announcement of the creation of a ministry dedicated to immigration and national identity in March 2007 had pushed him up a few points in the polls. And so it was. Two days after taking office, President Sarkozy appointed Brice Hortefeux, minister of immigration, integration and national identity. Immigration had already had its own ministry when Valéry Giscard d'Estaing created a state secretary for immigrant workers in 1974. However, it was attached to the Labour Ministry and had no say on the politics of citizenship acquisition. This time around, the Ministry of Immigration gathered prerogatives from the Interior, Labour and Foreign Affairs Ministries. It was competent in the areas of citizenship acquisition, border control, and foreign nationals exercising a professional activity in France.

The creation of a Ministry of Immigration and National Identity marked a turning point in the politicization of immigration in France. It was the first time that a restrictive stance on immigration significantly increased a candidate's chances of winning an election. The politics of immigration hit the top of the political agenda in the months that followed the presidential election, with Hortefeux claiming that France had had 'no immigration policy so far' and proposing a law introducing limitations to family reunification, quotas per professional branch and a change in the nationality code. The creation of the ministry institutionalized the link between immigration and the politics of citizenship acquisition. As such, it marked the culmination of a process

---

[19] *Brouard and Tiberj, As French as Everyone Else?*

begun in the mid-1980s, which had consisted in making citizenship acquisition a means to regulate immigration.

The creation of the ministry and the subsequent legislative proposals have not failed to provoke debate in the political, media and academic spheres. On the announcement of the creation of a Ministry of Immigration and National Identity, all the academics involved in the project to create a national museum for the history of immigration resigned. The project to create a memorial (*Lieu de mémoire*) to immigration in France had been simmering for a long time in activist and academic circles.[20] In the end, however, it was a right-wing government that had launched the project in 2002. President Chirac's team and his prime minister, Jean-Pierre Raffarin, saw it as a way of making a gesture to the left-wing electorate that had rallied so massively for his re-election against Le Pen. The project was headed by Jacques Toubon, former minister of culture in Edouard Balladur's right-wing government (1993–5). The theme of the memory of immigration, therefore, seemed to cut across the political divide. Moreover, the Ministry of Immigration was responsible for the policy of remembrance, and the museum was to be under its supervision, as well as that of the Ministry of Culture and the Ministry of Education.

Academics resigned because the museum was supposed to 'take account of the diversity of individual and collective histories and memories' while being placed under the supervision of the Ministry of Immigration and National Identity. They highlighted the issues involved in associating the terms 'immigration' and 'national identity' in the title of the same ministry. In their view, it was not 'the role of a democratic state to define identity'. Therefore, equating 'immigration' with 'national identity' was 'part of a discourse that [stigmatized] immigration and [was] part of the tradition of a nationalism based on mistrust and hostility to foreigners in times of crisis'.[21] They were referring to the period of rising xenophobia between the wars, during which the government of the Third Republic had helped to institutionalize xenophobia by passing protectionist measures on labour.[22] This period in French history gave credence to racist discourse and paved the way for the fall of democracy and the advent of the authoritarian Vichy regime (1940–4).[23]

---

[20]Nancy L. Green, 'A French Ellis Island? Museums, Memory and History in France and the United States', *History Workshop Journal* 63, no. 1 (2007): 239–53.

[21]'Associer immigration et "identité nationale" s'inscrit dans la trame d'un discours stigmatizant l'immigration et dans la tradition d'un nationalisme fondé sur la méfiance et l'hostilité aux étrangers, dans les moments de crise'. Marie-Claude Blanc-Chaléard et al., 'Un amalgame inacceptable !', *Le Monde*, 21 May 2007.

[22]See Chapter 2. Law of 10 August 1932 regulating salaried labour and introducing quotas for the number of foreigners in each business sector or region.

[23]Gérard Noiriel, *Les origines républicaines de Vichy* (Paris: Hachette, 1999).

However, the government maintained its position, and President Sarkozy did not attend the museum's inauguration when it opened in October 2007. It was not until 2012, when Socialist François Hollande became president of the Republic, that the museum was officially inaugurated.

The creation of a Ministry of Immigration and National Identity was followed by a law proposal that stirred much debate. In particular, one provision conditioned family reunification on a DNA test in order to avoid fraudulent claims. Arguably, family reunification had become the only means of entry on French territory for non-nationals who could not secure a working visa in advance, nor could they claim to be persecuted in their home country. However, the number of people granted the right of entry on the ground of family reunification was not that high and concerned mainly French nationals marrying a foreign national (therefore not eligible for a paternity or maternity test). All in all, the DNA test would have applied to a few cases. Moreover, there was a risk of violating privacy and discovering an adulterous child, since 80 per cent of family reunification applications are submitted by fathers.

The DNA test proposal made the headlines and created a debate for months. Immigrant rights organizations took the case to the anti-discrimination authority to demonstrate the discriminatory nature of the provision.[24] In its decision of 17 December 2007, the French Equal Opportunities and Anti-Discrimination Commission ruled in their favour on the grounds that the measure strongly stigmatized applicants for family reunification, which is a fundamental human right (HALDE Deliberation 2007-370). Moreover, politicians on both sides of the political divide also attacked the very principle of using genetic tools. On the one hand, from an ethical point of view, genetic testing should be limited to medicine. On the other hand, the use of genetics is highly symbolic and a parallel was drawn with its use by the Nazi regime during the Second World War.

Eventually, the proposal passed but was never fully implemented as such. It was made optional and only for mothers. However, it is a good example of the excessive politicization of immigration and its consequences. With such a highly publicized proposal, the Sarkozy government contributed to forging a narrative of problematic immigrants. It spread the idea that immigrants were people who would go so far as pretending they were the father or the mother of individuals they were not. It consolidated a picture of immigrants originating from countries with divergent family norms and where having many children with various partners was common. In terms of immigration

---

[24]Groupe d'information et de soutien des immigrés (Gisti) and Ligue des droits de l'homme (LDH), *Lettre à la Haute autorité de lutte contre les discriminations et pour l'égalité*, 2 July 2007 (http://www.gisti.org/IMG/pdf/halde_20070702_lettre-gisti-ldh.pdf).

policy, the proposal was pointless. It covered only a few cases and was not implemented. In terms of the politicization of immigration, however, it was effective. It kept the subject on the agenda and under media spotlight. It forged an alarming image of prospective immigrants and increased the legitimacy of the government in its attempt to restrict their entrance on French soil.

Finally, major decisions were taken as part of the law of 20 November 2007 on immigration control, integration and asylum. They did not receive similar media coverage, even though they ended up changing the French immigration context in a more lasting way. In particular, the 2007 Hortefeux law further criminalized illegal immigrants. It made it more difficult to provide emergency accommodation for people in need and made it easier to deport people at the border. While this was a general evolution taking place at the EU level, it did mark a change in context for undocumented migrants living in France, when the immigration minister set a target of twenty-five thousand evictions by the end of 2007. In sharp contrast, the law benefited employers of illegal labour by allowing them to regularize their employees if they were working in a sector with a short labour supply.

Last but not least, the 2007 immigration law tackled the procedure for accessing French citizenship. It made it compulsory for foreigners legally arrived in France to sign a contract stipulating their commitment to respect the laws of the republic and to learn French (Contrat d'accueil et d'intégration).[25] Arguably, the provision prepared the way for the procedure for acquiring French citizenship, which includes an assimilation criterion assessed based on the level of French. However, this was first and foremost a way for the government to require foreigners to commit to integrating into French society, understood as accepting Republican values and knowing French.[26] Eventually, this was also a way of placing responsibility for the success of citizenship acquisition on the individual rather than on the state.[27]

The creation of a ministry that brought together immigration and nationality policies had effectively linked the definition of nationality to immigration. From then on, French nationality was defined as the culmination of a process of integration that included both civic (respect for Republican values) and linguistic (mastery of the French language) dimensions. This shift was felt, even in the procedure for acquiring citizenship. Although the applicants were

---

[25]The Contrat d'accueil et d'intégration became the Contrat d'intégration républicaine, in 2016.
[26]Myriam Hachimi-Alaoui and Janie Pélabay, 'Contrats d'intégration et "valeurs de la République": un "tournant civique" à la française?', Revue européenne des migrations internationales 36, no. 4 (2020): 13–33, https://doi.org/10.4000/remi.17069.
[27]Meer et al., 'Examining "Postmulticultural" and Civic Turns in the Netherlands, Britain, Germany, and Denmark'.

often people who had been in France for a long time, they were treated as newcomers who had to prove whether or not they deserved to be French.[28]

A 2007 ministerial circular made it compulsory to hold ceremonies to welcome new French citizens. In the United States and Canada, these kinds of ceremonies have existed for a long time. They consist of taking an oath under a flag and singing the national anthem. However, in Europe, there are more recent ones. Some German cities began organizing such ceremonies when the nationality law opened to foreign nationals in 1999. Great Britain and the Netherlands followed in 2004 and 2006, respectively. In France, ceremonies consist of a speech by a state representative (such as a mayor), followed by the national anthem, *La Marseillaise*, and a moment when successful applicants receive a naturalization decree, an identity card and a voting card (provided all these papers are ready). Each town hall or state administration is free to add any other information such as a presentation on French history or famous French figures with an immigrant background (such as the Nobel Prize winner Marie Curie-Slobodowska, born in Poland; singer Serge Reggiani, born in Italy; Actress Isabelle Adjani whose father was born in Algeria and mother in Germany; and footballer Zinedine Zidane, whose parents were born in Algeria).[29]

Eventually, the intensification of the focus on national identity contributed to the stiffening of the official discourse on religious diversity in general, and the Muslim religion in particular. After the passing of the 2004 law banning the conspicuous display of religious signs in French public schools, any manifestation of the Muslim religion in the public space would increasingly be framed as an attack requiring a 'reaffirmation' of the principle of secularism. In March 2007, it came to the attention of antiracist organizations in the Paris and Lille regions that heads of primary schools banned mothers wearing a veil from taking part in school outings.[30] As in 1989, school headmasters extended the scope of application of secularism in schools even further. More precisely, in 1989, the secondary school headmaster extended the scope of the application of the 1882 Ferry law from teachers to pupils; in 2007, school headmasters extended the scope of application of the 2004 law from pupils to parents – more precisely, mothers.

Arguably, banning some mothers from accompanying school outings because they wore an Islamic headscarf did not have the same impact as banning pupils from state schools. It cannot be attacked as preventing young girls' access to education. However, in some neighbourhoods, this

---

[28]Sarah Mazouz, *La republique et ses autres. Politiques de l'altérité dans la France* (Lyon: Ens Lyon, 2017).

[29]Fassin and Mazouz, 'Qu'est-ce que devenir français?'

[30]Stéphanie Le Bars, 'Des mères d'élèves portant le foulard islamique sont interdites de sorties scolaires dans l'académie de Créteil', *Le Monde*, 26 March 2007.

was tantamount to depriving teachers of the opportunity to take their pupils on school outings.[31] Moreover, it revealed a systematic tendency to invoke respect for secularism to restrict any manifestation of the Muslim religion. This was also the case when extreme right-wing organizations protested against the practice of praying in the street.[32] This tended to happen when mosques were too small to accommodate all the worshippers on certain Fridays. After far-right organizations pointed it out, Interior Minister Claude Guéant invoked the principle of secularism to ban them.

Finally, the government passed the 2010 law banning the concealment of the face in public space. Even though the argument of the law is a security one and it does not formerly refer to secularism. It was explicitly coined the burqa-ban, and multiple references to secularism (*laïcité*) were made during the political and media debate that preceded the debates in the National Assembly.

The systematic reference to French secularism (*laïcité*) in all circumstances about Islam in France had the effect of giving it a very negative perception among the Muslim community. According to a Muslim activist, they considered that it was 'something opposed to Islam' and interpreted any attempt at reaffirming the enforcement of *laïcité* as targeting Muslim people.[33] However, a growing mobilization took place to oppose the increased stigmatization of Islam in all these circumstances. Even though the Muslim community was usually divided according to immigrants' country of origin, the common experience of discrimination built a sense of commonality. The creation of such an organization as the Collective against Islamophobia in France was remarkable from this point of view, as it departed from the usual group representation of Islam and gathered French people who experienced discrimination as Muslims (whether when they applied for a job or in their interaction with schools).[34]

Eventually, the government put an end to the Ministry of Immigration and National Identity in November 2010. The core of its prerogatives (issuing work visas, controlling illegal immigration, processing asylum applications and supervising the process of acquiring citizenship) went to the Interior Ministry. So, in the end, the creation of the Ministry of Immigration had the long-lasting effect of shifting responsibilities from Foreign Affairs (asylum policy) and

---

[31]Samir Hadj Belgacem and Hanane Karimi, 'Politization du voile et mobilization des accompagnatrices scolaires contre la circulaire Chatel: Le cas du collectif Sorties scolaires: avec nous !', *Sociétés contemporaines* 127, no. 3 (2022): 95–119, https://doi.org/10.3917/soco.127.0095.

[32]Fatima Khemilat, 'La construction des prières de rue comme problème public', *Confluences Méditerranée* 106, no. 3 (2018): 81–94, https://doi.org/10.3917/come.106.0081.

[33]Interview with the author, 17 February 2012.

[34]The Collective against Islamophobia in France (*Collectif contre l'islamophobie en France*, CCIF) was created in 2013 with the aim to collect information, help victims and publish reports. The Interior ministry announced it had dissolved the collective in December 2020.

Labour (work visas) to the one and only Interior Ministry (already in charge of border control and citizenship acquisition). This was the real outcome of those three years of relentless debates on immigration: the Interior Ministry taking over immigration in all its economic, social and international dimensions. As a case in point, the responsibility of the French Office for the Protection of Refugees shifted from Foreign Affairs to Interior on 25 November 2010.

As for anti-discrimination, the government also put an end to the French Equal Opportunities and Anti-Discrimination Commission (*Haute autorité de lutte contre les discriminations et pour l'égalité, HALDE*) in 2011. The commission was created in 2004, following the recommendation of the European Commission against Racism and Intolerance, to monitor the implementation of anti-discrimination in France.[35] An intense debate followed its creation on the possibility of recording ethno-racial data.[36] On the one hand, academics and policymakers argued for the collection of ethno-racial data to measure discrimination. On the other hand, other academics and antiracist organizations opposed the decision because it was going against the French universalist principle of equal treatment. In the end, the latter position prevailed. From 2004 to 2011, the commission mostly set up a hotline to register complaints, provided tools to support victims and published reports to inform policymakers.

No matter how compliant with French universalism the anti-discrimination commission may have been, it was still the *bête noire* of the Right. At the national level, it recorded a growing number of complaints that incriminated large corporations.[37] Moreover, the commission limited the executive branch's power when it opposed the introduction of the DNA test in the 2007 immigration law. Finally, the institutionalization of the fight against discrimination opened up new possibilities at the local level. Despite the difficulty of getting used to the framing of anti-discrimination, long-standing anti-racist activists, politicians and new generations of citizens seized the opportunity to get involved in new types of initiatives to combat ethno-racial discrimination.[38] In sum, the commission and everything it stood for was too much trouble. The government therefore shifted the anti-discrimination policy

---

[35]Angéline Escafré-Dublet and Patrick Simon, '9 Ethnic Statistics in Europe: The Paradox of Colourblindness'.

[36]Patrick Simon, 'The Choice of Ignorance: The Debate on Ethnic and Racial Statistics in France', *French Politics, Culture & Society* 26 (2008): 7–31, https://doi.org/10.3167/fpcs.2008.260102.

[37]'La Halde perd sa tête, avant de disparaître?', 17 November 2010, https://www.lemonde.fr/politique/article/2010/11/17/la-halde-perd-sa-tete-avant-de-disparaitre_1440889_823448.html.

[38]Angéline Escafré-Dublet, Virginie Guiraudon, and Julien Talpin, eds, *Fighting Discrimination in a Hostile Political Environment: The Case of 'Colour-Blind' France* (London: Routledge, 2023), https://doi.org/10.4324/9781003441489.

to the already existing Human Rights Defenders, which included the defence of children's rights and public service users.

In the run-up to the 2012 presidential elections, President Sarkozy abandoned his proactive attitude towards diversity and affirmative action that had marked his 2007 campaign and fully embraced a security approach to immigration issues. After the launching of an 'official debate' on national identity in 2009, the government launched an 'official debate' on *laïcité,* in 2011.[39] So-called 'official debates' were essentially communication initiatives that consisted of inviting politicians, administrative officials and a selection of civil society representatives to present and discuss said issues, in fact, occupy the space for debate. However, this time around, the strategy that consisted of adopting a restrictive stance on immigration did not pay as much, and Sarkozy lost the 2012 presidential election to Socialist François Hollande.

Tightening Republican values – the Socialist version

When François Hollande became president, it was twenty-four years since a left-wing candidate had won the presidential election (President François Mitterrand in 1988) but only ten years since France was last governed by a left-wing coalition (Prime Minister Lionel Jospin from 1997 to 2002). Compared to 1981, the politicians who came into government were already accustomed to power. What's more, the context had changed, and the politicization of immigration issues had increased. All that is to say, that during the campaign, Hollande may have resurrected some of the old-time demand of the immigrant movement to extend the right to vote to all legally resident foreigners. However, when in office, the reshuffling of immigration policies simply did not happen.

The tone with which immigration issues were tackled softened when Hollande became president. He went and officially inaugurated the National Museum for Immigration History, for instance. However, when it came to deciding which department would be responsible for immigration, it remained the prerogative of the Interior Ministry. More precisely, the ministry's main task with regard to immigration was to monitor the Reception and Integration Contract (i.e. providing language classes and overseeing the process to acquire citizenship). As for anti-discrimination, it ended up under the umbrella of an interministerial unit in charge of fighting racism and antisemitism (*Délégation interministérielle à la lutte contre le racisme et l'antisémitisme, DILCRA*).

---

[39]'Laïcité: trois heures de débat pour clore deux mois de polémiques', *Le Monde,* 5 April 2011.

During the 2012 presidential campaign, Hollande announced the introduction of measures to limit the use of racial profiling during police checks.[40] The demand came from the movement against police violence that emerged at the time of the 1983 March, and regained momentum in the aftermath of the 2005 riots. Advocates asked that police officers deliver a receipt to any individual they stopped. Receipts would serve as evidence to monitor police stops. It would allow for a better understanding of the frequency with which racialized individuals were subjected to stop-and-frisks. So far, lawyers had complained that they had no evidence to demonstrate the systematic arrest of people based on racial profiling.[41] However, when in office, Interior Minister Manuel Valls abandoned the project.

After the presidential election of 2012, all happened as if the Left wanted to close the period during which the recognition of ethno-racial discrimination was seen as an appropriate response to inequalities and their discontent. One can observe a further tightening around Republican values, such as colour-blindness, universalism and secularism.

First, President Hollande reaffirmed the principle of colour-blindness when he proposed the removal of the word 'race' in the constitution. The term indeed appeared in Article 1 as follows: 'France ensures the equality of all citizens before the law, regardless of origin, race or religion'.[42] Although preceded by the negative 'regardless of', it was considered to give credit to racial distinction by several antiracist organizations and politicians. For instance, the anti-racist organization LICRA praised the proposal that would belie the existence of institutional racism within the state itself. They further argued that it would suppress the word in the name of which millions of victims were killed during the Second World War. Along the same lines, Justice Minister Christiane Taubira praised a noble and necessary gesture.

While it is true that UNESCO recommended the suppression of the word race in 1950, the whole project was deemed irrelevant by many in 2012. Suppressing the word 'race' had not suppressed 'racism' precisely because 'race' as a category is a social construction that permeates societies and creates inequalities.[43] The proposal did not go through. However, it reveals a context of reaffirmation of Republican values.

---

[40]Emmanuel Blanchard, 'Contrôle au faciès: une cérémonie de dégradation', *Plein droit* 103, no. 4 (2014): 11–15, https://doi.org/10.3917/pld.103.0011.

[41]Jérémie Gauthier and Fabien Jobard, *Police: questions sensibles* (Paris: Universities of France Press, 2018).

[42]'La France est une République indivisible, laïque, démocratique et sociale. Elle assure l'égalité devant la loi de tous les citoyens sans distinction d'origine, de race ou de religion. Elle respecte toutes les croyances'.

[43]Brun and Cosquer, *Sociologie de la race*.

Second, universalist equality policies replaced the equal opportunity programmes that targeted first- and second-generation immigrants. A good example is urban development policies that have been developed as part of the Equal Opportunity Agency since 2006 (*Agence nationale pour la cohésion sociale et l'égalité des chances, ACSE*). In 2014, the Agency was replaced by a Committee for Territorial Equality (*Commissariat général à l'égalité des territoires, CGET*). Although ACSE was specifically in charge of immigrant families and responsible for addressing the social difficulties they encountered, CGET was not. It was mostly in charge of urban development and approached inequalities from a territorial point of view.

As a case in point for the return of universalist equality policies, the urban renewal law of 2014 defined disadvantaged neighbourhoods based on the income of their inhabitants. Moreover, the 2014 law introduced a person's address as a criterion for discrimination. In other words, the law made it possible to prove that someone had been discriminated against because they lived in a certain area (a disadvantaged area in particular). This was tantamount to asserting the primacy of economic and social criteria at the root of inequalities over ethno-racial affiliation. Moreover, it followed in the tradition of the urban renewal policies of the 1980s, which exemplified French-style integration.[44]

Third, Socialist Education Minister Vincent Peillon issued a Charter of Secularism (*Charte de la laïcité*) to be pinned in all state-sponsored schools. Arguably, the Socialist government did not follow up on the Right's project to prevent headscarf-wearing mothers from accompanying school outings. However, the government chose to reassess French secularism, instead of addressing rising Islamophobia in society.

From 2004 to 2012, the Interior Ministry recorded a rise from 123 to 155 of anti-Muslim acts. Interior only records acts or comments deemed anti-Muslim from a criminal point of view. According to the Collective against Islamophobia in France, these numbers could be reassessed to a rise from 182 to 298, provided all victim statements were recorded.[45] Moreover, a 2008 survey demonstrated that nearly one out of two French people who identify as Muslim declared they experienced discrimination (47 per cent), even though they rarely ascribed it to religious motives (5 per cent).[46] Those latter figures

---

[44]See Chapter 7.

[45]Houda Asal and Marwan Mohammed, 'Islamophobie en France: formes, définitions et mesures', in *Migrations et mutations de la société française* (Paris: La Découverte, 2014), 316–23, https://doi .org/10.3917/dec.poins.2014.01.0316.

[46]Yaël Brinbaum, Mirna Safi and Patrick Simon, 'Les discriminations en France: entre perception et expérience', in *Trajectoires et origines. Enquête sur la diversité des populations en France* (Paris: INED, 2015), 413–42, https://www.ined.fr/fr/publications/editions/document-travail/discriminations -france-perception-experience/.

tend to support the hypothesis of a racist construction of Islam in France, since it is not the practice of the Muslim religion that seems to be at stake there but rather the stereotypes associated with Muslim identity. This was not going to get any better after the brutal attack against the satirical weekly magazine, *Charlie Hebdo* on 7 January 2015.

'Je suis Charlie' or 'Je suis Ahmed'? Being French and Muslim in 2015

Charlie Hebdo was a leftist, anti-militarist and anti-clerical newspaper created in the wake of May '68. In 2006, the newspaper published a series of cartoons from a Danish newspaper depicting the Prophet Mohammed. Although it was not the only media outlet to publish these cartoons – the daily *France-Soir* had done the same a few days earlier, *Charlie Hebdo* preceded the publication of the cartoons inside the magazine with a drawing depicting the prophet holding his head in his hands and exclaiming: 'hard to be loved by idiots'. Accused of treating all Muslims as 'idiots', *Charlie Hebdo* was on trial in 2007. The trial resulted in the acquittal, for the insult was deemed only aimed at extremists, and not all Muslims. As for the Danish cartoons, it was considered that their publication fell within the scope of press freedom. *Charlie Hebdo* team further argued that they had made numerous more aggressive attacks on the Catholic religion, without receiving such reactions.

Already in 2006, the Danish newspaper cartoonists had received death threats by Islamic extremists, following the publication of their cartoons. As for *Charlie Hebdo*, they had already experienced a criminal fire in 2011 and had relocated their offices to the 11th arrondissement of Paris. This is where, on 7 January 2015, Saïd and Chérif Kouachi, brothers born in France to Algerian parents who had ties to Islamic extremism, attacked and killed twelve people, including five cartoonists (Cabu, Charb, Honoré, Tignous and Wolinski), four journalists (Elsa Cayat, Bernard Maris, Mustapha Ourrad and Michel Renaud) and three security guards (Frédéric Boisseau, police officer Franck Brinsolaro and police officer Ahmed Merabet). Both Chérif and Saïd Kouachi claimed they were acting on behalf of the terrorist organization Al Qaïda in Yemen. They died two days later after they had taken refuge in a printing shop and were surrounded by the police.

On the evening of the attack, hundreds of thousands gathered at the Place de la République and President Hollande declared a national day of mourning on 8 January 2015. Moreover, on 9 January 2015, there was a hostage situation in a Hyper Cacher supermarket near Paris in which another French man, Amedy Coulibaly, born of Malian immigrant parents and who had ties to Islamic extremism, killed four people. On 10 and 11 January, more than a million French people marched across the country to protest the attacks and mourn the deaths, to the phrase *Je suis Charlie*.

When President François Hollande addressed the country on 9 January 2015, he made sure to be inclusive of all, regardless of one's belief and distinguish between terrorism and Islam: 'The perpetrators of these acts, these terrorists, these madmen, these fanatics, have nothing to do with the Muslim religion'.[47] The president and his team were indeed worried about the possible violence that may arise and were aware of the rising stigmatization of Islam in society.[48] An advisor to the president wrote that 'some harsh comments' were already circulating on social networks by the evening of 8 January 2015. At the funeral of slain police officer Ahmed Merabet, the phrase '*Je suis Ahmed*' could be seen. It revealed the difficulty for French people with Muslim-sounding names to feel included in this collective moment of mourning.[49] As a matter of fact, both the French National Observatory against Islamophobia and the Collective against Islamophobia in France reported a hundred Islamophobic attacks in the three weeks following the attacks. They included attacks on mosques and on headscarf-wearing women.

Similar to the rise in Islamic terrorism, the rise in Islamophobia is not a phenomenon restricted to France.[50] Though the term first appeared in French, in reference to the situation of Islam in the colonial empire (1991), it was mostly developed in English following the publication of a report by the British anti-racist organization the Runnymede Trust (1997). In *Islamophobia: A Challenge for Us All*, the Runnymede Commission on British Muslims admitted that the term was not 'ideal', but that it was necessary to refer to 'unfounded hostility towards Islam' and 'the practical consequences of such hostility in unfair discrimination against Muslim individuals and communities'.[51] As such, it became an important concept to refer to the expression of anti-Muslim feelings, at the level of the European Union and the United Nations. In 2004, UN General Secretary Kofi Annan addressed the General Assembly with these words: 'But when the world is compelled to coin a new term to take account

---

[47]'Ceux qui ont commis ces actes, ces terroristes, ces illuminés, ces fanatiques, n'ont rien à voir avec la religion musulmane'. Presidential address, 9 January 2015 (https://www.vie-publique.fr /discours/193497-declaration-de-m-francois-hollande-president-de-la-republique-sur-la)

[48]Laurie Boussaguet and Florence Faucher, 'La construction des discours présidentiels post-attentats à l'épreuve du temps', *Mots. Les langages du politique*, no. 118 (2018): 95–115, https://doi .org/10.4000/mots.23867.

[49]Jean Beaman, 'France's Ahmeds and Muslim Others: The Entanglement of Racism and Islamophobia', *French Cultural Studies* 32, no. 3 (2021): 269–79, https://doi.org/10.1177/09571558211009370.

[50]Erik Bleich, 'What Is Islamophobia and How Much Is There? Theorizing and Measuring an Emerging Comparative Concept', *American Behavioral Scientist* 55, no. 12 (décembre 2011): 1581–600, https://doi.org/10.1177/0002764211409387.

[51]Bleich, 'What Is Islamophobia and How Much Is There?', 4.

of increasingly widespread bigotry, that is a sad and troubling development. Such is the case with Islamophobia'.

The use of the term Islamophobia remained contentious in France.[52] The fact that President Hollande's advisor used the term 'stigmatization of Islam' to refer to hate speech circulating on the internet the day after the attack on *Charlie Hebdo* is no coincidence in this regard. The contested nature of the term has to do with freedom of thought and the French understanding of secularism. According to these principles, criticizing religion should be possible, whether it is the Catholic or the Muslim religion. This line of argument fits very much with *Charlie Hebdo*'s defence in the 2007 trial following the publication of the 'hard to be loved by idiots' cartoon. However, it assumes both religions are treated equally, which is not the case. The construction of Islam as problematic dates back to the colonial period.[53] Therefore, it contrasts sharply with the power that the Catholic Church has exercised over French society for many years. Most authors who use the term Islamophobia analyse it as a phenomenon more akin to cultural racism than religious intolerance. They use it to describe the processes of racialization that define a group by the religious marker, in the same way as antisemitism.

Moreover, in 2015, the arrival of hundreds of thousands of people from the Middle East, and Syria in particular, profoundly changed the European migration context. The uprisings that followed the Arab Spring and the outbreak of civil war in Syria led many citizens of countries around the Mediterranean to seek refuge in Europe by land and sea. However, this increase in arrivals tested the European Union and the solidarity of its member states. Member States situated on the land border (Hungary, in particular) were reluctant to assume their proportionate share of the burden. As for those on the maritime border (Greece and Italy, in particular), they were confronted with a series of maritime disasters and requested the establishment of processing centres on the most advanced islands to handle the influx of applications (such as Lesbos, Chios, Samos, Kos and Leros in Greece, Lampedusa and Pozzallo in Italy).

France played its part in welcoming migrants, though its involvement did not exceed its capacities. By contrast, Germany took in the most, following the formula launched by Chancellor Merkel, 'We can do this' (*wir schaffen das*). By 2020, Germany had accepted seventeen times more Syrian applications for asylum than France (645,420 versus 36,680).[54] However, the Right and the extreme right opposed this flood of migrants, against a background of

---

[52]Houda Asal, 'Islamophobie'.

[53]Abdellali Hajjat and Marwan Mohammed, *Islamophobie: Comment les élites françaizes fabriquent le 'problème musulman'* (Paris: La Découverte, 2013).

[54]François Heran, *Immigration: le grand déni* (Paris: Seuil, 2023), 42.

Islamophobia. As 'the most generous country in Europe', France was threatened with 'submersion', said Marine Le Pen on the radio (4 September 2015).

The series of terrorist attacks continued. On 13 November 2015, 130 people were killed after a group of Islamic terrorists opened fire in a concert venue (*Bataclan*) and several other cafés and restaurant terraces. This time, the perpetrators were associated with the Islamic State organization operating in Iraq and Syria, and François Hollande mentioned a 'state of war' in his presidential address.[55] It was no longer a question of unity so much as avoiding confrontation and division. In these circumstances, it was once again Republican values that were invoked in the president's words. However, the stress was on the imperative to remain united in the fight against religious fanaticism, rather than the need to avoid conflating Islam with terrorism.

In the years that followed, the politics of anti-discrimination shifted from fighting the ethno-racial structure of inequalities to tolerance education and the fight against prejudice. The Interministerial Delegation for Combating Racism and Anti-Semitism (DILCRA) funded anti-discrimination plans in disadvantaged neighbourhoods. However, it served the promotion of intercultural dialogue and combating prejudices, rather than addressing unequal access to employment and ethno-racial discrimination.[56]

In this chapter, we saw that, from 2005 to 2015, French citizenship was deeply challenged in its civic and universal foundations. The riots of 2005 highlighted the ethno-racial structure of inequalities in France. They challenged the Republican promise of equal treatment regardless of race, origin or religion. Moreover, the political response to the crisis was one of security and reaffirmation of national identity. It could be noted that there was an opening to issues of equal opportunity and visible minorities, but it was quickly shattered when the Anti-Discrimination Commission (HALDE) was merged into the Human Rights Defender in 2011. Finally, the difficulty in reconciling Islam with French identity was visible in the reaction to the terrorist attacks of January and even more so in November 2015. No matter how inclusive and universalist the politicians' discourse was, Muslim identity appeared suspicious, as evidenced by the rise in anti-Muslim acts.

---

[55]Boussaguet and Faucher, 'La construction des discours présidentiels post-attentats à l'épreuve du temps'.

[56]Angéline Escafré-Dublet and Camille Hamidi, 'From Victims to Culprits? The Reshaping of Local Antidiscrimination Policy in France', *Ethnic and Racial Studies* 46, no. 4 (2023): 727–48.

Conclusion

Immigration, a French identity

From the seventeenth to the twenty-first centuries, France underwent a significant transition, from a colonial empire to a country of immigration. This profoundly transformed French identity, and this book unpacked some of the key developments underpinning this change. This final chapter highlights three of them. First, the colonial dimension of immigration. It explains why the word immigration is often used to refer to issues pertaining to race relations and implies going back to the period of the colonial conquest. As a result, it disrupts the conventional timeline of French immigration history, which usually began in the nineteenth century with the emergence of the nation-state. Second, immigration policies. They follow a different timeline, with a few milestones reached in the 1930s, and an intensification of regulations in the post-war period. The book adopted a social approach to political history in order to highlight some of the key reasons behind decisions, such as the definition of a labour migration regime and management of immigrant reception. Third, the politicization of immigration. The book showed how and why the word 'immigration' was used to discuss issues that have nothing to do with actual immigration politics, but with discrimination, religious diversity and the French model of citizenship. In this chapter, we further argue that the politicization of immigration resulted in a negative connotation of the term, which makes it all the more complex to introduce oneself in relation to immigration. The chapter ends with an analysis of a series of oral history interviews. The analysis highlights the ways in which immigration, as a topic, affects people's life and their sense of belonging. It shows the necessity to tell a political history of immigration in France in order to understand the complex relationship between immigration and French identity.

Disrupting the conventional timeline of French immigration history

The book adopted a long historical arc in order to grasp the differential treatment of people outside Europe and how this impacted the politics of immigration when non-Europeans settled in France. These two worlds – France and the colonial empire – were indeed never meant to collide. As explained by going back to the period of the conquest in the seventeenth century, the ways in which French rulers exerted authority over territories and people stood in sharp contrast with what was happening in Europe. As such, the unexpected presence of enslaved people, who came to France with their masters, created a situation that the king did not want. As a result, he ordered their deportation. Nevertheless, some of them stayed, and this explains the continued presence of a Black community in France since the eighteenth century.

Turning a blind eye to an unsettling situation proved counterproductive, as this situation was meant to repeat itself. First, when the government appealed for the help of colonial soldiers in the First World War. Despite the administration's repeated attempts at sending them back home, after the end of the conflict, some of them stayed and formed a first group of colonial migrants in the interwar period (e.g. the census counted 102,000 North Africans in 1931). Second, when the government of the Fourth Republic granted colonial population free circulation after the Second World War and hundreds of thousands of Muslim French citizens from Algeria arrived in France (e.g. the census counted 208,540 Muslim French citizens from Algeria in 1954). Last but not least, the French government negotiated the 1962 Evian agreements that put an end to colonial rule in Algeria. Government officials did not expect the continuing Algerian immigration to France (e.g. the census counted 473,252 Algerian nationals in 1968 and 805,116 in 1982). Algerians came as foreign nationals and – for some of them – became French citizens. In all these circumstances, what had been planned to stay in the colonies did not stay in the colonies.

The successive arrival of enslaved people, colonial soldiers, colonial migrants and postcolonial immigrants deeply challenged the great divide between France and the empire, which colonial ruling had carefully established through the centuries. In particular, the post-war arrival of colonial migrants played a crucial role in the emergence of French immigration policies.

A social approach to the political history of immigration policies

As the book showed, France is an old country of immigration, with significant entry rates dating back to the mid-nineteenth century (e.g. the census counted 381,000 foreigners – that is, 0.3 per cent of the total population in 1851). However, up until the mid-twentieth century, the essential regulation to govern the entrance and settlement of foreign nationals was the French code of nationality, inherited from the French Revolution of 1789. As a result, foreigners were able to live, work and become French after a five-year stay. Already during the interwar period, policymakers made a few attempts at regulating the stay of foreigners in France. In 1927, they created the identity card in order to identify and locate all foreigners residing in France. In 1932, the government passed a law restricting their access to specific jobs in order to protect the French workforce. However, it was really only the post-war need for foreign labour combined with the unexpected arrival of numerous colonial migrants that prompted the emergence of concerted immigration policies.

The book adopted a social approach to political history to highlight the power relations between governmental actors and the circulation of ideas in the making of immigration policies. It showed how colonial migrants from North Africa and labour migration from Southern European countries were the targets of two different types of policies. On the one hand, the presence of colonial migrants was unexpected, and administrative officials were essentially concerned with their adaptation to life in France, which they assumed to be particularly challenging. This led them to rely on a series of non-governmental organizations that formed a network of welfare services specialized in providing aid to colonial migrants. On the other hand, the need for labour force and demographic recovery prompted the government to actively recruit workers abroad and to issue the ordinances of 1945.

This deep dive into immigration policymaking highlighted the extent to which policymakers apprehended European labour immigration differently from colonial immigration. These two issues were not even handled by the same services in the administration. The recruitment of foreign workers was the responsibility of the Ministry of Labour, while colonial workers were the responsibility of the Ministry of the Interior. It was only because decolonization happened, and colonial migrants ended up staying, that policymakers brought those two distinct issues together and developed the management of immigrant reception. Within this new field of political intervention, however, policymakers kept apprehending European immigrants differently from postcolonial immigrants. This was further illustrated by the role of experts and non-governmental actors, who produced and circulated ideas about the immigrant's ability to assimilate into French society, or not.

Finally, a political history of immigration cannot be restricted to a history of top-down immigration policies. The book examined the role of immigrant activism and the politics of protest in changing the landscape of immigration in France. From the 1970s, when immigrants formed a movement in defence of their rights, to the 1980s, when young people of immigrant parents mobilized for equality and against discrimination and changed the narrative of immigration in France. However, their wide-ranging demands, from housing, working conditions, religious practice and equal opportunities, have all been grouped under the term 'immigration' in the political debate. This can explain why the word immigration became such a catch-all phrase to refer to a wide range of issues, ranging from race relations to secularism and the French model of citizenship.

Immigration, the only legitimate marker of identity in France

The book highlighted the gradual politicization of immigration in France. Its origins can be traced back to the 1973 oil crisis, when the government imposed a halt to labour migration as a solution to the crisis. However, it was really in the 1980s that the topic of immigration began playing an increasing role in political campaigns. In the run-up to the 1986 legislative elections, right-wing candidates adopted an anti-immigrant discourse so as not to lose too many votes to the far-right party of Jean-Marie Le Pen. As a response to rising anti-immigrant discourse, successive governments adopted a strategy to reaffirm Republican values, such as universalism – the principle of colour-blind egalitarian treatment – and *laïcité* – the French understanding of secularism that confines all expression of religious faith to the private sphere. As a case in point, governments of the 1980s and the 1990s developed social development policies, in particular urban development policies, that did not officially target immigrants even though it was their unofficial objective. This specific context helps in understanding why colour-blindness is so deeply entrenched in policy implementation.

Another consequence of the rise in anti-immigrant discourse is that it shattered any attempt at articulating a group-based identity. In the early 1980s, the beginning of a differentialist turn made it possible for the articulation of specific identities. After the passing of the October 1981 law affirming the principle of freedom of association for foreigners, several free radio stations emerged, with names referring to specific identities (such as *Radio Beurs*). During the March for Equality and Against Racism, phrases such as pluri-ethnic or pluricultural France emerged. However, after the 1986 electoral victory of the Right and the subsequent appointment of a Nationality Commission, this discourse quickly ceased. As illustrated by Christian Delorme's speech in front of the commission, 'it had not always been like that, but now, immigrants were eager to be French nationals'. Dual nationality remains possible in French law, but any attempt at claiming a hyphenated identity is suspected of cultural separatism (*communautarisme*). Only referring to one's immigrant background or 'origin' is legitimate, as if anything that was not French had to go back to a long-gone past, like the moment of migration. There have been attempts at alternative formulations, such as at the time of the football team's victory in 1998, when people spoke of '*black, blanc, beur France*'. However, this remained fragmented and failed to describe the full complexity of French identities.

The vocabulary of immigration and origin became the norm for describing identities in France, in everyday and scientific language. Even though, as the book clearly showed, immigration covers a large number of very different situations in France, and for some individuals, immigration goes back several generations. But more problematically, the intense politicization of immigration has also resulted in a negative connotation of the term. As a result, the only terminology available to describe identities in France has negative connotations, which makes the issue of self-presentation and self-identification particularly complex. In the following, we shall see how all this plays out at the individual level.

Personal history, identity and sense of belonging

The methodology of oral history – the collection of historical information from people, families and everyday lives – has proved particularly important for examining the histories of migrant groups.[1] Specifically, it has been crucial in bridging the gap in archival records for ill-documented and hidden histories of migration. However, it has raised the important concern of the reliability of memory as a historical source. Historians have therefore adopted strategies

---

[1] Alistair Thomson, 'Moving Stories: Oral History and Migration Studies', *Oral History* 27, no. 1 (1999): 24–37.

to ensure the validity of people's memories, such as checking with other people's accounts and corroborating with other (printed) material.

However, historians have also argued that unreliable memories are a resource and not a problem, for there is meaning in the forms in which life stories are narrated. More precisely, there is value in the way people conceptualize the past because it is revealing of how they respond to their social environment. With this in mind, the collection of interviews with French people born in France of parents born abroad appears as a valuable insight into the experience of being French with ties to immigration (i.e. one in four French people under the age of sixty in 2022).[2]

In the following, I explore the story of Stéphane, Fouad, Christophe and Laurence, who are all born in France, of parents born abroad, and their relationship to immigration.[3] Their statements about immigration, and the way it relates to their family history, reveal a way of identifying as French with (or without) an immigrant background.

When I met with Stéphane, after he came back from work on a September evening of 2010, he was eager to discuss the story of his family, how it was complex and how he liked to say, he had 'foreign origins' (*des origines étrangères*). Stéphane was white and had a French-sounding family name. However, he explained to me that his father was born in Cameroon because Stéphane's grandfather was a French soldier posted there, back when it was part of the colonial empire. Stéphane's grandfather married a French woman from the French West Indies whose family also lived in French colonial Cameroon. It was, in fact, a distinctive feature of the imperial economy to send French citizens from the West Indies to work in other parts of the colonial empire. Stéphane's grandparents' encounter is therefore a reflection of the story of the French colonial empire. Stéphane was still very much influenced by his Black grandmother, who cultivated in him the taste for Cameroonian

---

[2]'La diversité des origines et la mixité des unions progressent au fil des générations - Insee Première - 1910', accessed 26 December 2025, https://www.insee.fr/fr/statistiques/6468640.

[3]The extracts come from a series of semi-direct interviews I conducted, together with Patrick Simon, as part of a research project on nationality acquisition in 2010 (*Enquête Trajectoires et origines en 2008*, INSEE-INED). All interviewees were randomly selected among respondents of the survey who had declared at least one parent born abroad. They all had agreed to be contacted for an interview. I received permission to contact and meet with them, two years after the end of the data collection process. Questions ranged from their knowledge on the process of citizenship acquisition in France, their representation about immigration and colonial history, and their sense of belonging. Depending on their own family story, but also depending on how society view them, they had various ways of relating to French immigration history. The series of interviews took place in 2010, when the Ministry of Immigration and National Identity existed (2007–10). All first names were changed, while maintaining their general ethnic attributes. For more information on the research: Escafré-Dublet and Simon, 'Ce qu'il y a derrière l'identité nationale: l'appartenance face à l'altérisation'.

food, even though she later lived in France, where she raised Stéphane's father.

Stéphane was part of the survey's sample because his mother was born in Spain to left-wing activist parents who opposed the Spanish military dictatorship (1937–78) and immigrated to France for political protection. Yet, it was the heritage on his father's side, and more specifically, his Black grandmother, that he was the most eager to talk about. As such, Stéphane identified as having 'foreign origins' for political purposes:

> People cannot know that I have foreign origins if I don't tell them. I like to say that I have foreign origins. It is also a way of distinguishing myself from people for whom the notion of 'native French' is paramount. It is a way of saying that I'm French while at the same time affirming my open-mindedness towards other cultures.[4]

For Stéphane, identifying himself as having 'foreign origins' was a way to make a political statement. He identified a clear division between those concerned with being 'native French' and those open to other cultures. He thus exemplified the politicization of immigration that occurred in the 2010s, when it became a defining issue of the right–left divide.[5]

However, Stéphane admitted that he could say he had 'foreign origins' because they were not visible. 'People cannot know that I have foreign origins unless I tell them', he explained. He therefore acknowledged the stigmatization and discrimination of visible minorities in France. As such, his take on the issue stands in stark contrast to the one expressed by Fouad.

French by birth since he was born in France of a French mother, and his father was born in Algeria when it was a French colony, Fouad made sure to differentiate himself from people with an immigrant background, when I met him in March 2010:

> I'm not from an immigrant background, because my father was born French, my mother is French, and I was born French. People with an immigrant background are people who have come to France, who have applied for

---

[4]'Les gens ne peuvent pas savoir que j'ai des origines étrangères si je ne leur dis pas. J'aime bien dire que j'ai des origines étrangères. C'est aussi une manière de me distinguer des gens qui sont complètement rivés sur l'idée d'être Français de souche. C'est une manière de dire que je suis Français mais j'ai une certaine approche des autres cultures'. Interview with the author, 23 September 2010.

[5]Sylvain Brouard, Emiliano Grossman, and Isabelle Guinaudeau, 'La compétition partizane française au prisme des priorités électorales: Compétition sur enjeux et appropriations thématiques', *Revue française de science politique* 62, no. 2 (2012): 255–76, https://doi.org/10.3917/rfsp. 622.0255.

nationality, who are residents, who have had children and who have the right of the soil. They don't have the right of blood.[6]

Fouad has a North African family name and mentioned over the course of the interview that he did not like being asked for his birth certificate to prove he was French, when he had his identity card renewed at the prefecture: 'It's got me worried' (*ça m'a chiffoné*). Although he was able to obtain his identity card without any problems after presenting his birth certificate, he was nonetheless shaken by the fact that his nationality had been questioned. He explained that he had secured his papers against the risk of theft or fire, because it is important to be 'careful' and to be able to 'prove that you are who you say you are' (*prouver qu'on est bien nous-même*). His cautious attitude showed that he did not take for granted the fact that he was seen as French. This explained why he was afraid of being confused with people 'from an immigrant background'.

Moreover, Fouad's family history reflected the long and troubled relationship between Algeria and France. His father was born in 1921 in Kabylie (Algeria) and was recruited as a colonial soldier during the Second World War. He took part in liberating France in the southeast. Indeed, Marseille and Toulon were liberated by Algerian riflemen under the command of General de Lattre de Tassigny. At the end of the war, Fouad's father stayed in France and began working as a miner in the North of France. There was, in fact, a large concentration of colonial migrants from Algeria who contributed to the post-war reconstruction, some of whom worked in the mines in the northern part of the country.

According to Fouad, his father contributed to the fight for Algeria's independence by donating part of his wages to the FLN organization. This was indeed how the organization received most of its financial support. Finally, his father became Algerian after the independence of Algeria to preserve his right to inherit his ancestors' property but also with regard to his family (*il s'est dit, la famille, comment on va me voir?*). According to Fouad, it was an 'inner conflict' (*un conflit interieur*).

In *The Suffering of the Immigrant*, sociologist Abdelmalek Sayad described the tension between the hard-won independence of the Algerians and the fact that many of them continued to live in or move to France.[7] The tension manifested itself particularly over the issue of papers and nationality, as illustrated by the fact that Fouad's father had French citizenship without knowing

---

[6]'Je suis pas issu de l'immigration, parce que mon père est né français, ma mère est française, je suis né français. Les gens qui sont issus de l'immigration, c'est des gens qui sont venus, qui ont demandé la nationalité, qui sont résidents, et qui ont eu des enfants, qui ont le droit du sol. Le droit du sang, ils l'ont pas'. Interview with the author, 12 March 2010.
[7]Sayad and Bourdieu, *The Suffering of the Immigrant*.

it. More precisely, Fouad explained that he and his sister found out that their father was listed as a French national on his disability card. As a miner, he had had a serious accident at work and had received disability status subsequently. According to Fouad, his father did not know he had French citizenship, because when he and his sister asked him, he replied that he did not know. 'I don't think he said that because he didn't want to tell us', explained Fouad. 'But really, he probably didn't know. It was often the foremen in the mines who did the paperwork for people like him who hadn't been to school'. And he added, 'But he certainly didn't take any steps to say, I want to remain French'.[8] Fouad's father had therefore never intentionally asked to hold French citizenship despite his veteran status and continuous stay in France, where he lived until he passed away in 1997. He epitomized the generation of Algerian immigrants at the time of independence, as described by Abdelmalek Sayad: torn between their allegiance to their country of origin and the reality that they had built their lives on French soil.

As for Fouad, he encountered the difficulty of French society in acknowledging the inextricable links between the histories of France and Algeria.[9] After all, he was right to say that he was not of 'immigrant background'; in fact, he was the perfect example of a Franco-Algerian. He was born in France to a French mother and an Algerian father and was sent to Algeria to complete part of his schooling. Fouad spoke Arabic and had married an Algerian woman, with whom he was living when I met with him for the interview. The hiatus derived more from the reality that French society tends to regard the descendants of Algerians as immigrants, without taking into account the shared history between France and Algeria.

Fouad's story is therefore an example of how the term 'immigrant background' plays a key role in the process of othering in France, denying Frenchness to certain groups. In fact, a face-to-face survey conducted by the French National Consultative Commission on Human Rights showed that 43 per cent of respondents expressed the view that children of immigrants born in France were 'not really French' (November 2023).

Finally, a global perspective is necessary when considering French history in general and the history of French immigration in particular. Centuries of population movement and French colonial rule have resulted in a complex web of statuses and specific cases. When I met Christophe, a 22-year-old Frenchman living with his parents outside Paris, all I knew was that he had a

---

[8]'Je ne pense pas qu'il disait ça parce qu'il ne voulait pas nous le dire. Mais véritablement, il ne le savait probablement pas. C'était souvent les chefs d'équipe des mines qui faisaient les démarches administratives des gens comme lui qui n'étaient pas allés à l'école. . . . En tous les cas, lui, il n'avait fait aucune démarche pour rester français'.
[9]Stora, *La gangrène et l'oubli*.

Muslim-sounding family name and that both his parents were born in Vietnam. When the door opened, and his mother let me in, there was a Buddhist altar, and Christophe briefly spoke Vietnamese with his mother. He later explained to me that his parents came to France in 1973 during the great Boat People migration. However, his mother had French nationality and was able to take a plane, he said.

Christophe's mother holds French nationality thanks to her father. Christophe's grandfather was born in the French colonial settlement of Pondicherry in India, where he was able to claim French citizenship after India gained independence.[10] Moreover, he explained to me that his grandfather on his father's side was also from India and from a Muslim family, which explained his Muslim-sounding family name. As a result, Christophe's background was a blend of French colonial presence in India (Pondicherry) and Southeast Asia (Vietnam). Moreover, he lived in France in a household infused with Vietnamese culture and religion, despite having a Muslim-sounding family name.

Later during the interview, Christophe explained that his family experienced difficulties with this Muslim-sounding family name. He gave the example of his father, who had to receive a recommendation from a friend to secure his current job. Finally, Christophe recalled an encounter with the police during which he was accused of holding false identity papers. The police officers took him to the station because they thought his documents were fake. They could not believe an Asian looking French boy could have a Muslim-sounding family name. This latter incident demonstrates how family names in France serve as markers of identity, leaving little room for the nuances and complexities of French history.

The need for a more global approach to French history is also apparent in Laurence's comments. Born in France to a mother repatriated from Algeria. She was part of the sample because her father was born in Benin. When we discussed her representation of French history, the thirty-year-old stated, 'I do not know where my ancestors were during the 1789 revolution, but I guess that they were not in France'. Yet, Laurence is French, and her family history is another reflection of France's complex history, from colonial, to global, and back.

Research interviews reveal a desire to situate one's family history within a broader narrative. However, there are contrasting views on the topic of immigration, which is plagued by intense politicization and negative framing. The politics of immigration are therefore crucial not only to understanding the political and media debate but, even more significantly, the dynamics of identity in France.

---

[10] Simone Massicot, 'Effets sur la nationalité française de l'accession à l'indépendance de territoires ayant été sous la souveraineté française', *Population (French Edition)* 41, no. 3 (1986): 533–46, https://doi.org/10.2307/1532807.

Afterword

On colonial sillage and the politics of immigration in France

Hana Qugana

'I choose my vehicle, and I can cross any bridge'.[1] Guided by this conviction in the dying days of Les Halles in Paris in the 1970s, a young Filipino man named Kidlat Tahimik took one of the market's ageing vendors for a drive in his automobile. Initially, the atmosphere was exuberant: 'Today, I got my first French kiss', he announced proudly – the first of seven from his passenger, a local French purveyor of double-yoked eggs whom he affectionally called *lola*, a word for 'grandmother' in his country of origin. With its distinctively boxy, elongated and colourfully painted body, Kidlat's vehicle was equally a sight to behold. The old, retrofitted United States Army jeep or *jeepney* had accompanied him halfway around the world, from the peripheries of one colonial empire to the centre of another, only to cruise the storied city's streets mostly vacant, as if intended by the cosmos just for Lola to ride it, much to her delight. The ebullience of the moment, however, turned out to be fleeting. 'Lola was worried', observed Kidlat, as she climbed in. 'She spoke of a bad dream'. 'I fear it is my last season', she confided, to which he replied later, 'Do not worry, Lola. We'll fight all the egg phantoms together'.

The above vignette does not appear in *A Political History of Immigration in France*, yet it immediately came to mind when asked to write this Afterword.

---

[1] Kidlat Tahimik in *Perfumed Nightmare*, directed by Kidlat Tahimik (San Francisco: Zoetrope Studios, 1977), 00:02:35.

While navigating the labyrinth of French laws that have governed 'the foreign', Angéline Escafré-Dublet's book never neglects a simple truth: Along every border drawn by the state, there is a human poised, defiantly, to cross it. But rarely do they cross it alone. It is not just the bonds a nation's Others forge among themselves, but with its citizens, especially those likewise on the margins of society, that sustain and nourish resistance to the scintillating allure of capitalism, xenophobia and other colonial vestiges inherited by the modern nation-state. At the heart of the present volume, for me, a historian of the Global South, is the struggle between these otherwise disparate subalterns and an institution whose logic has no obvious language to describe the bridges of amity built between them, viewing people only through categories of 'citizenship', 'origin' and 'utility'.

Unfortunately for both migrant and native, on this occasion, the fighting promise made by the *tsuper* (jeepney driver) turned out to be as empty as his metallic steed. Unable to stem the spectral tide of 'progress', Lola's nightmare would come to pass, both in her lived experience and in the 1977 film in which this moment was imaginatively re-enacted. Four years before the real Kidlat Tahimik[2] released the semi-autobiographical *Mababangong Bangungot* (*Perfumed Nightmare*) to international critical acclaim,[3] Les Halles' remaining vendors had already been relocated from the 1st arrondissement to Rungis near Paris-Orly Airport, and all but one of its iconic iron structures unceremoniously demolished to make way for the Centre Pompidou, or in the film, simply *the supermarché* (the supermarket).[4]

From the vantage of postcolonial studies, scholars and critics often cite this definitive displacement of the *marchands des quatre-saisons* (merchants of the four seasons) as a watershed for Kidlat, as he grapples with the consequences of globalization for both postcolony and metropole.[5] As a young

---

[2]The real-life Kidlat Tahimik will henceforth be referred to as 'Tahimik'. His film persona will continue to be distinguished as 'Kidlat'.

[3]Aside from praise received from Werner Herzog and Francis Ford Coppola, Susan Sontag has often been cited as saying *Perfumed Nightmare* 'makes one forget months of dreary moviegoing, for it reminds one that invention, insolence, enchantment, even innocence, are still available to film'; e.g. Charles Fairbanks, 'Tahimik, Kidlat', *Senses of Cinema* 100 (January 2022). It is worth noting, however, that this may be an apocryphal quotation. Although widely circulated in numerous commentaries about the film, I have not been able to locate its original source.

[4]'Les Halles Dead at 200, A Victim of Progress', *New York Times*, 13 January 1973.

[5]See e.g. Fredric Jameson, '"Art Naïf" and the Admixture of Worlds', in *The Geopolitical Aesthetic: Cinema and Space in the World System* (Bloomington: Indiana University Press and the British Film Institute, 1992), 186–213; E. San Juan Jr, 'Kidlat Tahimik's Cinema of the Naïve Subaltern', in *After Postcolonialism: Remapping Philippines-United States Confrontations* (Lanham: Rowman and Littlefield, 2000), 143–62; more recently, Fairbanks, 'Tahimik, Kidlat', and Portia Placino, 'History Through the Bamboo Camera', *ArtAsiaPacific* 127 (Mar/Apr 2022): 53–9. To read about the wider Philippine context in which this film sits, see Rolando B. Tolentino, ed., *Geopolitics of the Visible: Essays on Philippine Film Cultures* (Quezon City: Ateneo de Manila University, 2000).

man growing up in Balian, a *barangay* (village, suburb or neighbourhood) in southern Luzon, he had dreamed of travelling to the New World: 'Because in America, I could become an astronaut'. Instead, he finds himself waylaid in the Old World of Europe, where he witnesses first-hand how (in E. San Juan Jr's words) 'machines and efficient technology destroy certain values necessary for human freedom and happiness'.[6] As the focus turns to his personal odyssey, decolonizing space and time, Lola disappears from view altogether.

It is unclear by the end of this *Perfumed Nightmare* whether the pair ever reunites. (And perhaps that is beside the point, given the comparative lack of scholarly attention to this plotline.) Nevertheless, as a diasporic Filipina living in Europe for nearly twenty years, I find myself captivated by Kidlat's enigmatic attachment to Lola – now more than ever, given its broader implications for the global turn in French history to which this Bloomsbury book series is a response.[7] She, the white French *marchande*, and he, the exoticized *tsuper* from the Philippines, Lola and Kidlat form the unlikeliest of friendships: a genuine, unmediated human connection that somehow manages to thrive amidst the racial tensions of post-1945 France. Their story, as such, does not merely play out in front of, but is emmeshed within shifting conceptions of French identity and citizenship in the period of rapid decolonization and economic change following the World Wars. It relies on this context for its form and narrative, and its improbability in a time of growing support for *le seuil de tolérance* ('the threshold of tolerance').[8]

While galvanized by the apocalyptic rise of the *supermarché*, Kidlat and Lola's relationship is not defined by it. If they were a superhero duo, *tsuper-merchande* would have made a fitting portmanteau, gesturing to a distinctively French configuration of the foreign and the familiar also enveloping them in this moment. Equally salient for this reason is how it is not Kidlat's experiences in the Philippines or even the US, but in France specifically, and the rapport he develops with Lola and other white Europeans over the course of the film that strengthen his resolve to 'declare [him]self independent from those who would build bridges to the stars'. *A Political History of Immigration in France*, moreover, provides an intriguing opportunity to consider these often-overlooked, latent qualities of immigration as a global consequence of empire, experienced viscerally, while being policed locally through ideas, culture, rhetoric, policy and law.

---

[6] E. San Juan Jr, 'On the Cinematic Art of KIDLAT TAHIMIK', *THE PHILIPPINES MATRIX PROJECT* (blog), 6 August 2008, https://philcsc.wordpress.com/2008/08/06/on-the-cinematic-art-of-kidlat-tahimik/.

[7] For a recent appraisal of the transnational and global turns in French history, see Jessica Lynne Pearson, 'Globalizing the History of French Decolonization', *French Politics, Culture and Society* 38, no. 2 (2020): 1–8.

[8] The following article is credited with this concept's inception: Alain Girard, Yves Charbit and Marie-Laurence Lamy, 'Attitudes des Français à l'égard de l'immigration étrangère: Nouvelle enquête d'opinion', *Population* 29, no. 6 (1974): 1015–69.

Bringing both the particularities and wider synergies of the French case meticulously laid out in the preceding chapters to bear on Tahimik's beloved masterpiece of Third Worldist or, simply, Third Cinema, this essay represents Kidlat and Lola's kinship as a form of vernacular humanism that endures despite the grand political and economic narratives of the state, while nonetheless remaining susceptible to their magnetism. Coexisting alongside established appraisals of the film as a universalist critique of an amorphous and abstract 'colonialism' is another interpretation, which explores lived and embodied possibilities of mutual aid among migrants and natives in Europe. Reimagined as a story of argotic worlds, embryonic solidarities and persistent cross-imperial hang-ups, *Perfumed Nightmare*, in turn, offers a contrapuntal commentary on Escafré-Dublet's insightful history, accentuating the long colonial sillage left by the French state's historical attempts to control and manage varied populations, and that still threatens the very possibility of human connection today. Distinctions so often taken for granted between background and foreground, logic and affect become muddled as a result. We are compelled to reinscribe the distances between the local, the national and the global differently. This resonates with the migrant-historian, reconciled, like Kidlat/Tahimik, to losing and finding different selves with the seasons, when making border crossings in strange vehicles, far from home.

Confluent vernaculars and the vernacular migrant

'I choose my vehicle, and I can cross all bridges'.[9] Kidlat modifies this refrain continuously throughout *Perfumed Nightmare* to suit the shifting terrain of his journey. It serves as a metonym for the migrant's adaptability. Correspondingly, Arjun Appadurai writes of how the meanings of things like cars and crossings are 'inscribed' not only in their 'forms', but in their 'uses' and their 'trajectories': how 'even though from a *theoretical* point of view human actors encode things with significance, from a *methodological* point of view it is the things-in-motion that illuminate their human and social context'.[10] They have lives of their own, he asserts, over which they develop, shift and intersect with others. Here, we follow the coalescing journeys of some such things, to find out about the human migrant who so assuredly chooses his faithful *jeepney* to cross all the bridges he encounters, seemingly, all at once.

---

[9]Kidlat in *Perfumed Nightmare*, 00:03:50.

[10]Arjun Appadurai, 'Introduction: Commodities and the Politics of Value', in *The Social Life of Things: Commodities in Cultural Perspective*, ed. Arjun Appadurai (Cambridge: Cambridge University Press, 1986), 3–63, 5.

The bridge connecting Kidlat and Lola to each other, in friendship and solidarity, is one of several of significance in *Perfumed Nightmare*. Some, evidently, are crossed. Some are not and simply marvelled at like the travelators of Paris-Charles de Gaulle Airport. Sometimes they are traversed simultaneously and out of chronological order in ethereal montage. Together, these bridges form a multiversal vernacular of refusal through which the filmmaker, Tahimik, and his alter ego, Kidlat, resist the singular linearity dictating how much of the Global North understands time, space, history, and ultimately, themselves.

The film begins with the *tsuper*, at first, progressing steadily forward, then abruptly reversing his *jeepney* back across a literal bridge to give way to oncoming traffic, against the tropical backdrop of *probinsiyal* Laguna, due east of Manila. Although never revealing itself to the viewer, the opposing vehicle's presence is still felt, the imperial wraith hovering just beyond the frame. Kidlat begins narrating in Tagalog, before being abruptly interrupted by the English voiceover, also provided, disorientatingly, by himself: '*Ito ay ang tulay ng aming bayan. Ito ay ang isang daan papasok sa Balian* – this is the bridge to our village. It is the only way into Balian'. After a brief pause, he continues speaking over his native self, 'And it is the only way out; *at ito ang iisang daan palabas*'. The Tagalog grows fainter until the odorous, technocratic language of the archipelago's most recent colonizers takes over nearly completely:

> Our bridge is 3 meters wide and 10 meters long. It is our bridge of life. The Spanish soldiers built the bridge after destroying the original bamboo bridge built by my grandfather. Then the US army engineers wanted to widen it for the military convoys, but they failed because of the strong winds of Amok Mountain nearby. The bridge is used by everybody. It is used by those who make big profits and it is also used by those who make small profits.[11]

In the absence of any official record of note, this bridge serves Kidlat's barangay not as a mere thoroughfare, but a dynamic historical text, memorializing in real time successive and overlapping imperial projects built upon indigenous ruins. It dictates passage, a border used by those with power and those without. Analogously, *A Political History of Immigration in France* asserts that the legal and physical infrastructures of the professedly modern world are built upon the foundations of empire, creating a shared, if deeply unequal, history that continues to shape the politics of immigration and belonging in France, Britain, and other parts of Europe, and their past and present possessions overseas.

After Kidlat leaves for France, the bridge in Balian comes to embody the migrant's condition, or what Ranajit Guha once articulated as 'temporal maladjustment': the constant navigation of clashing and confluent temporalities,

---

[11] Kidlat in *Perfumed Nightmare*, 00:01:00.

where one's past feels like 'nostalgia' and one's future, 'alien'.[12] Interspersed throughout the footage of the tsuper's time abroad are scenes taking place in the Philippines, with narrations where the Tagalog vernacular is spoken over by the colonial English; the latter become direct sonic representations of this disjuncture. Just as his analogous Filipino self seems set to dissipate, it never does entirely. It continually reasserts itself in various volumes and registers, not just by breaking with the common convention of fully dubbing or subtitling 'foreign' films to cater for 'international' audiences and to be considered for awards by 'the academy'.[13] It resists presenting through one essentializing 'native' language in the first place (the other one in the film being Arabic, audible in Moro communities on the Philippine islands of Mindanao, Palawan and the Sulu Archipelago).[14] In this manner, the village bridge facilitates interdimensional travel, as a sort of wormhole between worlds, one consisting symbolically of resilient (Philippine) bamboo, the other, fleeting (French) perfume.

Once a migrant himself living, first, in France, then in Germany (from 1968 to 1979),[15] Tahimik would later affirm the intentional 'provincializing' of Europe[16] behind these and other creative choices in *Perfumed Nightmare*. After leaving definitely in the 1980s, he insisted on the necessity of the unhurried pace, or (as another famous Filipino emigrant to Europe, José Rizal, sardonically put it) the 'indolent' manner[17] in which these choices were made – provincialising-as-method in its own right:

It takes a sort of discipline to resist the emperor's-new-clothes perception that time is an adversary always to be contended with (i.e., finish as many artworks as you can in your lifetime).

---

[12] Ranajit Guha, 'The Migrant's Time', *Postcolonial Studies* 1, no. 2 (1998): 155–60.

[13] The inequity between English and non-English language films on the world stage is perhaps best encapsulated by the longstanding controversy over the US-based Academy of Motion Picture Arts and Sciences (AMPAS) award category known (prior to 2020) as Best Foreign Language Film. For an introduction to the politics of this award, see Sam McMillan, Xinyi Yuan, and Mingshu Wang, 'An Academy of Nations? The Enduring Eurocentrism of the Best International Feature Film Award', *Environment and Planning B* (2025): 1–3; Nate Jones, 'The 2020 Oscars Get Their First Self-inflicted Controversy', *Vulture*, 5 November 2019; Peter Debruge, 'The Oscars' International Feature Film Category Needs a Total Overhaul. Here's a Simple Fix', *Variety*, 2 November 2022.

[14] An oral and aural analysis of *Perfumed Nightmare* that does justice to the ethnic diversity of the Philippines is sorely needed, but beyond the scope of this essay.

[15] Tahimik has discussed the biographical details of his life in various interviews, e.g. Tobias Hering and Tilman Baumgärtel, '"I trust the cosmos". Interview with Kidlat Tahimik', *Plaridel* 16, no. 1 (2019): 165–216.

[16] Dipesh Chakrabarty, *Provincializing Europe: Postcolonial Thought and Historical Difference* (Princeton, NJ: Princeton University Press, 2000).

[17] José Rizal, 'Sobre la Indolencia de los Filipinos' ('The Indolence of the Filipinos'), *La Solidaridad*, nos. 35–8, 15 July –31 August 1890, as reproduced (in the original Spanish and English translation) in *La Solidaridad*, vol. 2, Guadalupe Forés-Ganzon, trans. (Quezon City: University of the Philippines, 1973), 450–597.

My film being made now [*Takedera Mon Amour*] might just be an extension of a 'film' I lived in some previous life, or just a transitional sequence to a 'film' I will experience in my next life. So why rush this life's scenario?[18]

In this viewpoint, he shares with the early twentieth-century German-Jewish intellectual, Walter Benjamin, who saw his own life not as an essentialist identity, but as one (borrowing from Catherine Russell) 'thoroughly grounded in experience and observation', and (from Susan Buck-Morss) an evolving 'allegory for social reality'.[19]

Tahimik's sense of self has never been a static identity, carried with him from the Philippines. Born Eric Oteyza de Guia, the auteur chose his stage name – his vehicle, if you will – in direct response to his experiences in Europe: *kidlat tahimik* (in Tagalog, lightning that is quiet or dormant) being a reference to the Kidlat Club formed by Rizal and other Philippine emigrés living abroad to tour the 1889 *Exposition Universelle* in Paris, where they witnessed the ghastly spectacle of human zoos. Tahimik interrogates this historical phenomenon from the perspective of the subaltern in Werner Herzog's 1974 philosophical fable *Jeder Für Sich Und Gott Gegen Alle* (English title: *The Enigma of Kaspar Hauser*),[20] where he plays *ein indianischer Wilder aus dem neuspanischen Sonnenreich* (an Indian savage from the New Spanish Empire of the Sun). Introduced as 'Hombrecito',[21] he is displayed, tellingly, alongside people with biological abnormalities in one such freakshow travelling the picturesque, nineteenth-century German countryside.[22]

Formative moments like these, when migrants experience the 'failure of one culture to slot smoothly' in tempo with another, are the lifeblood of migration stories, including my own. A dual Philippine and American citizen by birth, and British by 'naturalization', I inhabit multiple positions within Guha's migrant paradigm, always 're-evaluating [my] temporality' amid each new iteration of 'conflicts and convergences'.[23] Compelled as a migrant (in Shyam Patel and Saba Alvi's words) to 'refract',[24] I anchor my reading of Escafré-Dublet's book

---

[18]Kidlat Tahimik, 'Cups-of-Gas Filmmaking vs. Full Tank-cum-Credit Card Fillmaking', *Discourse* 11, no. 2 (1989): 80–6.

[19]Catherine Russell, *Experimental Ethnography: The Work of Film in the Age of Video* (Durham: Duke University Press, 1999), 275; and Susan Buck-Morss, *The Dialects of Seeing: Walter Benjamin and the Arcades Project* (Cambridge, MA: MIT Press, 1989), 32.

[20]The original German title translates literally as *Every Man for Himself and God Against All*.

[21]In its diminutive form, *hombre* (man) has infantilizing, patronizing connotations; it is often used in Spanish affectionately to address a young boy – which the Philippine filmmaker certainly was not.

[22]See e.g. Craig Geoffrey Scharlin, 'A Filmmaker and His Film', *Cinema Review* 12, no. 3 (1980): 30–2. His first screen credit using the name 'Kidlat Tahimik' was for *The Enigma of Kaspar Hauser*, directed by Werner Herzog (West Germany: Filmproduktion, 1974).

[23]Ranajit Guha, 'The migrant's time', *Postcolonial Studies* 1, no. 2 (1998): 155–60.

[24]Shyam Patel and Saba Alvi, 'We Do Not Let History Shroud Us: The Body as Curriculum and Its Refractive Possibilities', *Journal of the Canadian Association for Curriculum Studies* 21, no. 1 (2024).

to the confluences between France's migrative vernacular and those of other formerly colonizing states.

A relative realization came to me years ago in a final-year colloquial French course at a high school in California. What we were studying, of course, was never called colloquial, informal or even conversational French (all instinctively neutral terms), but that of the *banlieue* and *'la rue'*, *l'argot* and *verlan*,[25] as if the place and manner of utterance alone somehow rendered it a lesser tongue.[26] Instead, films by Mathieu Kassovitz and *le rap* of MC Solaar revealed a far more complex, riveting engagement with language, held together by the classist, racialized threads of France's colonial past. *Le rebeu, le feuj, le renoi* – terms like these (for people of Arab, Jewish, and African descent) had become, by the 1990s, shorthand for caricatures whose origins needed no explanation. This is how I first learned about empire – a strange displacement for someone whose own country's imperial history often goes unnamed.[27]

As life in the UK has since reinforced for me, the allure of projecting one's own colonial guilt onto another is a powerful storm-like force. Yet, as *A Political History of Immigration in France* shows, these histories are not so easily separated. The transatlantic (and transpacific)[28] slave trades of France, Britain and the United States were not discrete projects, but part of an interconnected system that enriched these nations and forged brutal legacies of gendered, racial hierarchies reverberating across the oceanic South. Adeptly navigating between both the logics of French exceptionalism and colonial convergence, Escafré-Dublet's discussion of the 1685 *Code Noir* reiterates that France's systematization of racial slavery was a cornerstone of its imperial wealth, a history that is often obscured by national myths of *Liberté, Égalité, Fraternité* – a desire to forget that directly informs the politics and policies of immigration in France today. Indeed, the state's policing of immigrants echoes the 'savage-making' detailed in Julian Go's work on the US and British Empires, where colonial techniques of control were later repatriated to manage metropolitan populations.[29]

---

[25]The suburbs and 'the street', slang and back-slang (created by the inversion of syllables of a word).

[26]Reinforcing this impression, students at the school were encouraged to take French V, as this course was titled, instead of university-level Advanced Placement French Language and Culture, if they were either a weak language learner and/or were taking numerous other Advanced Placement courses in other subjects already.

[27]In my Advanced Placement United States History course, I was actively discouraged from writing my final paper about the Philippine-American War because it was 'not American history'. This clearly had consequences.

[28]These practices did not end after emancipation following the American Civil War (1861–1865); for an introduction to 'blackbirding' in the Asia-Pacific region (which superseded slavery in the American South), see Gerald Horne, *The White Pacific: U.S. Imperialism and Black Slavery in the South Seas after the Civil War* (Honolulu: University of Hawai'i Press, 2007).

[29]Julian Go, *Policing Empires: Militarization, Race, and the Imperial Boomerang in Britain and the US* (Oxford: Oxford University Press, 2024).

Similar ideas sourced a wellspring of 'savage' tropes from which Tahimik drew and deployed in *Perfumed Nightmare*. As its protagonist declares at the end of a migrant life lived in Paris, 'the sleeping typhoon must learn to blow again'.[30] Subsequently, Kidlat's butchering of the positivist church motto, written on the side of *La chapelle de l'Humanité* (the Church of Humanity) in the Marais, is a poignant rendition of *komedya* (a historical adaptative Philippine theatre genre), weaponizing classically French assumptions about 'the foreigner' against a phantasmagorical 'colonizer'.[31] In jest, Kidlat learns French, literally, from the streets: 'La-moor poor pran-seep (*L'amour pour principe*), lor-door poor la bahz (*l'ordre pour base*). Lor-droor... lor-door poor la bahz; pro-gress poor boo (*le progrès pour but*). Le pro-gress poor voo – boo'.[32]

(Im)migrant futurism and solidary fusion

'Ten, nine, eight ...'[33] – at a quarter to seven on any given weekday evening between 1965 and 2022, millions of people in France could be found tuning into *Des chiffres et des lettres* (*numbers and letters*).[34] Popular among students, homemakers and the elderly, for more than fifty years, this publicly funded game show connected those often marginalized or excluded from public life to France's nation-building project by testing vocabulary and numeracy skills that its citizens should ostensibly have. As Escafré-Dublet reminds us, however, language and culture are themselves only recent additions to the French lexicon of nationality. State-run media played a key role in their successful entrenchment over the second half of the twentieth century – just as France was being relieved of much of its empire.

When unprecedented numbers of its colonial subjects and settlers began arriving in the metropole, programming like *numbers and letters* was deployed

---

[30]Kidlat in *Perfumed Nightmare*, 01:28:40.

[31]For an introduction to the Spanish *comedia* and Philippine *komedya*, see Vincente L. Rafael, 'The Colonial Uncanny: The Foreign Lodged in the Vernacular', in *The Promise of the Foreign: Nationalism and the Technics of Translation in the Spanish Philippines* (Durham: Duke University Press, 2005), 96–118; especially 'Phantasmagorias of Europe', 106–13.

[32]'Love as a principle, and order as the basis; progress as the goal'; Kidlat in *Perfumed Nightmare*, 01:06:14.

[33]Europ Assistance, 'L'astronaute (The Astronaut)', television advertisement, Antenne 2, 6 July 1981. This commercial was aired shortly before *Des Chiffres et des lettres* (numbers and letters) on that day.

[34]While technically, *Des Chiffres et des lettres* first aired in 1972, its precursor, *Le Mot le plus long* (The Longest Word), began service in 1965. See Barbara Laborde, '*Des Chiffres et des Lettres*: distraction, variations, habitudes', *Mise au point* [Online], 3 (April 2011), http://journals.openedition.org/map/894; and Jérome Bourdon, 'Some Sense of Time: Remembering Television', *History and Memory* 15, no. 2 (2003): 5–35.

to 'assimilate' them. In time, however, it would bear influences from these newcomers, however subtle, forever altering what it means to be 'French'. Against this backdrop of societal transformation, a glimpse into the life of Lola – and the actual egg seller who played her in *Perfumed Nightmare*, Georgette Baudry – offers us a unique lens through which to consider how colonial migration informed experiences, opportunities and shared struggles on the ground in post-war France. From these, we can elicit further insights into the solidarity that developed between her and Kidlat/Tahimik – and how, in turn, such sympathies catalysed various forms of activism that challenged the public expectations of race, class and gender divisions within French civil society, informing the decisions of policymakers, as discussed in this book.

Following the advent of mass television globally in the 1950s and 1960s, not just the shows themselves, but everything around them was orchestrated to promote a certain *je ne sais quoi* that (much like a scent) distinguishes something or someone as quintessentially French. Interspersed among Antenne 2's televised segments were advertisements, often featuring leading symbols of French enterprise. Immediately before a Monday broadcast of *numbers and letters* in July 1981, for example, the network aired a commercial for Europ Assistance, a global French travel insurance company. It features a young, blond and blue-eyed French boy and girl, watching, with their equally archetypal white French parents, the first American Shuttle *Columbia* launch into space. 'Seven, six, five' – the NASA Launch Conductor continues counting down, while the announcer speaks over him: '*Plus le monde va loin, plus Europ Assistance se rapproche de vous. Europ Assistance, c'est maintenant chaque jour avec vous, même chez vous*'.[35] A brief, suspenseful pause transpires. Then, 'ignition!' As the ship blasts off, the children leap to their feet and embrace their parents triumphantly. The advertisement concludes with the voice of the narrator: '*Parce que même chez vous, si quelque chose ne va pas, c'est comme si vous étiez à l'autre bout du monde. Europ Assistance, nouvel abonnement annuel, c'est Europ Assistance même chez vous*'.[36]

This promise of domestic security lands with a particular resonance in the twilight of a series of French colonial conflicts that erupted at the end of the Second World War. 'The other side of the world' was not just a geographic reality, but a state of mind, redolent of the long shadow of decolonization. This was a trauma built on successive shocks: the military humiliation of the Anti-French Resistance War in Indochina (1946–54), the geopolitical embarrassment of the Suez Crisis (1956), and the violent unwinding of the Algerian War (1954–62). With each event, the 'other side of the world' was

---

[35] 'The further the world takes you, the closer Europ Assistance gets. Europ Assistance: now with you every day, even at home'; Europ Assistance, '*L'astronaute*', 6 July 1981.
[36] 'Because if something goes wrong at home, it can feel like you're on the other side of the world. The new annual subscription from Europ Assistance: bringing help to you, even at home'; ibid.

no longer safely *over there*; it had returned to the metropole in the form of immigrants, bringing the empire, in all its socio-economic, ethnic and racial diversity, home to roost. Europ Assistance's vision of a very white, nuclear family, looking forward to a high-tech future, the advertisement suggests, is a balm for this colonial anxiety: the loss of dominance abroad and the perceived threat of the Other at home. It seeks to insure against the phantoms of the lost empire, promising that even if the world feels chaotic, foreign and 'far' (*loin*), the sanctuary of the white French home can be secured.

If, as Europ Assistance insinuates, this is the only kind of family capable of producing the next man or woman in space, then things did not bode well for Kidlat. French media evidently had no words and no place in its programming for the adoptive familial relationship Lola forms with the aspiring astronaut, sealed with seven kisses and double-yoked eggs in the film. Instead, the aerospace-themed advertisement reassures only the 'pure' white family of its place in the future, while pointedly disassociating from the colonial Other, at home in France and *le pays lointains* (the faraway land).

In this echo chamber of mainstream media, it is easy to forget the reach of French media extended then (as it does now) beyond the country's formal borders. While means and access may have shaped immigrant viewership of *numbers and letters* in different ways in metropolitan France itself, the show was broadcast and enjoyed across the Francophone world.[37] As recently as April 2024, The Hon. Stephan Toussaint, a government official from Mauritius, recalled this shared experience during debates on the French-Speaking Union Bill in the National Assembly. '*Combien d'entre nous*', he reminisced, '*étions scotchés devant notre télévision à regarder Des chiffres et des lettres et à essayer de trouver les mots et le compte?*'[38] Out there, in 'outer space', such shows have helped create not just aspiring French citizens, but social cohesion within new, multi-ethnic nations, each with many 'native' languages vying for dominance, much like in the linguistically diverse Philippines. Only that for Kidlat, it was not *numbers and letters*, but the American government-sponsored Voice of America that captured his imagination, enthralling him and his fellow members of the Werner von Braun [*sic*][39] Fan Club in Balian.

Absent too from such state narratives was the Third World's own fascination with space. Recent work by Robin Kelley, Mark Dery, Leslie James and others attest to a rich tradition of Afrofuturism, for example, that used

---

[37]For a thirty-six-year-old woman's recollection of what it was like watching *numbers and letters* in her native Tunis, see Bourdon, 'Some Sense of Time', 30.

[38]'How many of us were glued to our televisions watching *Des chiffres et des lettres*, trying to find the words and the count?' Republic of Mauritius, National Assembly, *Parliamentary Debates (Hansard)*, Seventh National Assembly, First Session, No. 04 of 2024, 23 April 2024, 112.

[39]The misspelling of the German American aerospace engineer, Wernher von Braun's first name was an intentional gesture to Tahimik's cinematic mentor, Werner Herzog.

fantastical 'astronauts, rockets, and space' to process the 'absurd reality' of decolonization.[40] Presented sequentially through a series of postcards, each featuring a postage stamp commemorating space exploration, *Perfumed Nightmare*'s closing credits offer a fitting homage to this neglected chapter in the history of the Global South.[41] Panama, Paraguay, Mongolia, Vietnam, Guinea, Equatorial Guinea, Afghanistan, the United Arab Emirates (Sharjah and Ras al Khaimah)—among the real Cold War-era stamps from this emerging, increasingly 'non-aligned' block,[42] Tahimik slips in his own (double-yoked) easter egg: mock Philippine postage depicting Kidlat, gazing at our home planet from his very own rocket ship, built from a 'super chimney' for burning Parisian rubbish, stolen from the *supermarché*.

On another postcard, for 'KAMERA (spontanius emergencius)' services rendered during filming, Tahimik thanks an anonymous 'immigrant worker from the Pompidou Museum construction' – the very structure that displaced Lola and her real-life counterpart Baudry.[43] With this gesture, Tahimik aligns the plight of the displaced native vendor with that of the foreign worker. Even the smallest of vehicles can bridge the streets of Paris to the shores of *ailleurs* (elsewhere).

We would do well to remember, of course, that Kidlat/Tahimik only knew the version of Lola/Baudry that she wanted him to see. An initial look into the historical record, reveals an archival reality far more complicated, raising questions as to who constitutes a 'native' or a 'migrant' in the first place. To begin with, while Tahimik and the 1911 census agree on a 1907 birth year for the *merchande*,[44] the 1906 census points to a more plausible 1902.[45] Yet, even knowing that the most basic details of her life may never be completely verifiable on paper (and perhaps this is how she preferred it), it is striking how all the Georgette Baudrys I have encountered in my research so far entwine with Kidlat/Tahimik through a shared, although different, experience of migration.

---

[40]Robin Kelley, *Freedom Dreams: The Black Radical Imagination* (Boston: Beacon Press, 2002); Mark Dery, 'Black to the Future: Interviews with Samuel R. Delany, Greg Tate, and Tricia Rose', in *Flame Wars: The Discourse of Cyberculture* (Durham: Duke University Press, 1994), 179–222; and Leslie James, 'The Flying Newspapermen and the Time-Space of Late Colonial Nigeria', *Comparative Studies in Society and History* 60, no. 3 (2018): 569–98.

[41]Tahimik, *Perfumed Nightmare*, 01:31:55-01:34:30.

[42]Paraguay (aligned with the US) and Mongolia (with the Soviet Union) are the only countries featured in *Perfumed Nightmare* that were not full members of the Non-Aligned Movement by 1977.

[43]Coincidentally, this postcard features a stamp from the UAE, the second-largest employer of Filipino nationals in the world.

[44]France, Seine-Saint-Denis, Neuilly-Plaisance, 1906 Recensement de la population, household 20, lines 63–70, entry for Louis Baudry family; database with images, 'Seine-Saint-Denis, France Censuses, 1821–1911', *Ancestry.co.uk* (http://www.ancestry.co.uk: accessed October 2025), citing original data from Archives départementales de la Seine-Saint-Denis, Bobigny.

[45]France, Seine-Saint-Denis, Neuilly-Plaisance, 1911 Recensement de la population, household 8000, lines 1–5, entry for Louis Baudry family; database with images, 'Seine-Saint-Denis, France Censuses, 1821–1911', *Ancestry.co.uk*.

Reconstructing Baudry's life before *Perfumed Nightmare* requires confronting what Marisa Fuentes terms 'the fragmentation of the archive'.[46] Census records do not offer an unassailable biography, but rather what Fuentes terms 'violent abstractions', which reduce Baudry to a shifting status: *'fille'* (daughter) of a Belgian father and French mother, both *journaliers* (day-labourers) and parents to four other children at the time of her birth in the *banlieue* of Neuilly-Plaisance to the east of Paris – and later, *domestique agricole* (agricultural domestic servant) in rural Jalognes.[47] While the archives are silent on what prompted Baudry's move south (then back up to greater Paris), reading against the grain suggests this not to be a simple career choice, but a profound social and geographic displacement – a likely necessity for a young woman from a family such as hers at the time. Leaving us to speculate on the lived experience of this journey, these archival traces themselves punctuate an early chapter in what Fuentes calls a 'dispossessed life', defined by precarity, itineracy and labour.

Baudry's migration story may yet still have deeper roots. In *Perfumed Nightmare*, she tells Kidlat that it was her grandfather who had bred the first chicken to lay her special double-yoked eggs. Regardless of its authenticity, sharing this anecdote was a savvy move, indicative of other veritable truths. Since the great internal migrations from provincial parts of France that reshaped the capital over the nineteenth century, Les Halles had become a patchwork of identifiable regional enclaves: Normans controlled much of the fresh food supply via Gare Saint-Lazare, while Auvergnats dominated roles like the *forts des Halles*, strong porters who carried carcasses and crates in the central marketplace.[48] By presenting herself as a third-generation *marchande des quatres-saisons*, Baudry (registered with the local Seine-Saint-Denis authorities as a Belgian national in 1911) strategically aligned herself with this older provincial diversity, a move that legitimized her business in a trade dominated by *'Normands'*.[49] Her biography can thus be understood as a continuous exercise in adaptation – from *journaliers'*

---

[46]Marisa J. Fuentes, *Dispossessed Lives: Enslaved Women, Violence, and the Archive* (Philadelphia: University of Pennsylvania Press, 2016).

[47]France, Charente-Maritime, Surgères, 1921 Recensement de la population, household 3, line 4, entry for Georgette Baudry; database with images, 'Charente-Maritime, France, Recensements de la population, 1921', *Ancestry.co.uk*.

[48]G. Billen, S. Barles, P. Chatzimpiros, and J. Garnier, 'Grain, Meat and Vegetables to Feed Paris: Where Did and Do They Come from? Localizing Paris Food Supply Areas from the Eighteenth to the Twenty-First Century', *Regional Environmental Change* 12 (2012): 325–35; about the Auvergnats, see Marianne Bröcker, 'A French Minority in Paris', in *Manifold Identites: Studies on Music and Minorities*, ed. Ursula Hemetek, Gerda Lechleitner, Inna Naroditskaya and Anna Czekanowska (Amersham: Cambridge Scholars Press, 2004), 129–61; and Leslie Page Moch, *The Pariahs of Yesterday: Breton Migrants in Paris* (Durham, NC: Duke University Press, 2012).

[49]Granted, 'Baudry' is a quintessentially French name of Germanic origin, common to the country's western regions, which suggests her ancestors came from Normandy, Poitou-Charentes or the Loire Valley.

daughter to the version of herself we see in Tahimik's film – the resilient, lifelong performance of an immigrant navigating the capital.

As Escafré-Dublet stresses, prior to the mid-twentieth-century, French immigration controls never operated in simple binaries of 'native' versus 'foreigner'. They created existential frontier zones, where solidarities between the Kidlat/Tahimiks and Lola/Baudrys of French society could grow and flourish. Historically, the term 'immigrant' primarily denoted labourers and political exiles alike, European or otherwise, as legally distinct from French 'citizens'.[50] The movement of French *imperial subjects* was governed by a different logic altogether, which, strangely enough, did not extend to Rizal and other '*Indios Bravos*' arriving from Europe's other empires.[51] Only with the event of mass decolonization after the Second World War did the French state consciously repurpose its colonial frameworks, creating an 'immigration regime of racial preference' (as Escafré-Dublet puts it) that systematically favoured white European immigrants, deemed more 'desirable' and 'assimilable' than their non-European colonial and postcolonial counterparts arriving in metropolitan France. And yet, humans like Baudry's father, Louis (a French-speaking Belgian, who successfully passed himself off as French for the first nine years of her life) are still finding ways to cross the borders anyway.

Having resided in working-class and immigrant neighbourhoods in and around Paris for most of her life and survived two World Wars (during which metropolitan France relied heavily on its empire), it would likely have been very easy for Baudry to feel a sense of kinship with new arrivals from the colonies, French or otherwise. With Kidlat in particular, she could share in a deep connection to the land of their ancestors, real or imagined – his to the bamboo groves of Balian, and hers the *bocages* (small-hedged fields) of Normandy. The archive has not been forthcoming when she died, but if she had been fortunate enough to live into her nineties, Baudry would have not only witnessed first-hand the protracted 'war' for Les Halles, but also been privy to the one being fought around it, cutting across divides between natives and migrants. Collective strikes over rents and workplace exploitation (in the

---

[50]Leslie Page Moch, *Moving Europeans: Migration in Western Europe Since 1650* (Bloomington: Indiana University Press, 1992).

[51]Although not with a Frenchman, Rizal's friendship with Austrian scholar and educator, Ferdinand Johann Franz Blumentritt, comes to mind; Paul A. Dumol, 'Rizal Contra European Racism: An Autobiography of José Rizal Embedded in Blumentritt's Obituary of Rizal', in *European Studies: Essays by Filipino Scholars*, ed. Vyva Victoria Aguirre (Quezon City: University of the Philippines, 1999) 3–43. See also Filomenita Mongaya Hoegsholm, ed., *In De Olde Worlde: Views of Filipino Migrants in Europe* (Quezon City: Philippine Social Science Council and Philippine Migration Research Network, 2007); Raquel A. G. Reyes, *Love, Passion and Patriotism: Sexuality and the Philippine Propaganda Movement, 1882–1892* (Singapore: NUS Press, 2008); and Benedict Anderson, *Under Three Flags: Anarchism and the Anti-Colonial Imagination* (London: Verso, 2005).

1960s), leftist support for the autonomous immigrant movements (that formed in the 1970s), anti-racism and second-generation mobilization (in the 1980s), and the *Sans-Papiers* (Undocumented Migrants) Movement (in the 1990s) – Escafré-Dublet's discussion of these events is a particular highlight of this book.

Imperial fission and fortress Europe

'Bridges, bridges! Everywhere bridges!'[52] – Kidlat's joyous exclamation upon arrival in France reminds us that not all bridges need to be crossed, just because they are there. Some are better cherished from afar, lest things fall away and the centre falls apart.[53] Upon deplaning at Charles de Gaulle, Kidlat is greeted on the tarmac by a reception. Two French government officials are standing on a white podium, one of whom looks to be giving a speech over the faint, yet stirring sounds of an orchestra, inaugurating his arrival in France. What we see, however, is out of sync with what we hear. The two officials are Valéry Giscard d'Estaing (president of France, 1974–81) and Raymond Barre (prime minister of France, 1974–6), whose administration sought to restrict – not facilitate – migration into the country; the images come from stock newsreel footage of a state ceremony receiving some important-looking dignitary. Instead, the *tsuper* is addressed by the disembodied voice of a ubiquitous customs official, in a language he does not yet understand: *Bienvenue en France. Avez-vous quelque chose à déclarer?*[54]

Tahimik's reimagining of Kidlat's arrival in Europe in *Perfumed Nightmare* echoes many first disembarkations in the Global North by migrants from the South. Immediately for me, it evokes discordant memories of American customs officers rummaging through cardboard balikbayan boxes from a fourteen-hour flight from Manila in search of some pungent, illicit animal product – which makes the tsuper's subsequent joy all the more remarkable. Already alerted to the peculiar vehicle accompanying him, French customs allow both to enter, albeit unseen, offscreen. As 'Ode to Joy', the anthem of the Council of Europe (now European Union), crescendos, he enters the terminal with wide eyes and a heart open to the awaiting cross-cultural encounter. When the music drops, the voice of a pleasant, but again unseen French announcer, instructing travellers in the crowded waiting lounge to 'se présenter' (present themselves) at the gate to board their respective flights, fills the void.

---

[52]Kidlat, *Perfumed Nightmare*, 00:56:05.

[53]Neferti X. M. Tadiar, *Things Fall Away: Philippine Historical Experience and the Makings of Globalization* (Durham, NC: Duke University Press, 2009). Also see Chinua Achebe, *Things Fall Apart* (London: Heinemann, 1958).

[54]'Welcome to France. Do you have anything to declare?'; ibid., 00:54:52.

What captivates him the most, however, is a structural part of the airport itself: the central atrium, whose maze of criss-crossing travelators convey passengers to many levels. Each is protected by its own glass tube to withstand the elements and anything else that would try to harm its precious cargo. Sultry new-age jazz begins to play when Kidlat steps on the moving walkway, gazing up transfixed by the space and sky above, as if riding these bridges to and from the future. Repeatedly, he casts a French banknote onto the belt, delighted each time by its return. 'One, two, three-four, five-six bridges!' he exclaims – 'Bridges!'

But as his airport antics continue, the phantasmagoria begins to crack and Kidlat senses some hostility from the natives. A French policeman visibly takes offence to Kidlat's frivolous travelator testing, an insult to his specie. As the officer walks past, he is caught in the act, on film, of glaring back, as if to say, 'I am watching you'. (This parallels a later incident in which Kidlat 'practises [his] French' – to talk his way out of a ticket issued by another policeman for illegally parking his jeepney.) It does not take long for the atrium to reveal itself as a site of surveillance, and the airport for the controlled border crossing that it is. As the announcer calls out 'Dakar' (in Senegal) and 'Saint-Denis' (Réunion), no one in the hall moves to comply – tingi (sachets) of empire, littered everywhere.

That none of this seems to have concerned the tsuper speaks volumes about Tahimik's chosen artifice. Kidlat's outward naivety becomes Fredric Jameson's 'art naïf' – not mere simplicity, but a canny aesthetic weapon exposing the 'ineradicable gap between figuration and meaning'.[55] It transmutes into what Miguel A. Valerio dubs 'sovereign joy', an anti-colonial defiance performing its own komedya within the very citadels of power it lampoons.[56] The scene's jarring dada-esque soundscape, layering the aspirational strains of 'Ode to Joy' over the unfolding farce, lays bare Tahimik's stratagem: to disarm the panopticon with incredulous delight. His alter ego meets the customs official's unseen query not with apprehension, but with exhilaration. Yet, if Tahimik's oeuvre orbits fundamentally around anti-colonial resistance, what gravity holds his bond with Lola/Baudry? Was their friendship merely incidental, or a deliberate navigation of complex human terrain? Herein lies a tension: Could this very connection fuel Kidlat's awakening from his colonial stupor? The airport's opening vignette, with its gleaming surfaces reflecting watchful eyes, prefigures this interpersonal crux. Their alliance becomes a crucible where French societal categories collide, rendering their friendship as improbable as it is poignant, perhaps ultimately untenable in its pure form.

---

[55] Jameson, '"Art Naïf" and the Admixture of Worlds', 197.
[56] Miguel A. Valerio, *Sovereign Joy: Afro-Mexican Kings and Queens, 1539–1821* (Cambridge: Cambridge University Press, 2022).

As Escafré-Dublet meticulously charts in *A Political History of Immigration in France*, the post-war decades witnessed France convulsed by the unwinding of empire. Decolonization, far from being a distant affair, reverberated within the metropole itself as subjects-turned-immigrants arrived, stirring dormant anxieties about lost prestige and the unsettling presence of the Other. Racism festered in this climate of imperial reflux, finding political expression in concepts like the 'seuil de tolérance' – a sociological term readily weaponized, especially under Giscard d'Estaing, to rationalize exclusion. The official welcome extended, as seemingly to Kidlat, often veiled a harsher reality: a framework favouring 'preferred' origins that sorted newcomers, privileging 'integrable' Europeans, while casting a colder eye on those arriving from the wreckage of the colonial world. Tahimik confronts this shadowed history, this selective national gaze, in Kidlat's seemingly innocuous drive down the Champs-Élysées. The exchanged wave with a farmer on a tractor, framed against the Arc de Triomphe, uncannily mirrors newsreels of Paris' Liberation – a moment notoriously 'whitewashed' by Allied decree, erasing the faces of the African and Caribbean soldiers pivotal to that victory.[57] Kidlat's naïf gesture, suffused with this historical resonance, becomes a quiet, piercing query into the conditions of belonging, the fickleness of national memory and the uncertain future of fraternity forged across the colour line.

Yet, to read this encounter solely through the prism of Third Worldist solidarity is to flatten its contours, ignoring the inconvenient textures of class and gender. Any genuine reckoning with such struggles must be viewed through such lenses, as well as race and racial prejudices against immigrants – even towards those who are social and financial elites. Tahimik (born Eric de Guia) was no subaltern plucked from the margins. Scion of a prominent Philippine family – his mother, Virginia Oteyza de Guia, a pioneering councilwoman and mayor of Baguio City – he moved through Paris not just as a wide-eyed provincial. He honed his French while living and working in Paris as an American Ivy League-educated economist navigating the corridors of the Organization for Economic Co-operation and Development (OECD).[58] This biography diverges sharply from his cinematic avatar, placing him perhaps closer in social orbit to Kassovitz's Jamal, son of affluent African diplomats, in the 1993 film Métisse (Café au lait), than to the labourers whose lives Escafré-Dublet documents. The film's apparent solidarity thus acquires a different valence, nuanced by Tahimik's own privileged passage. Kidlat may lionize

---

[57]Cécile Bishop, 'Photography, Race and Invisibility: The Liberation of Paris, in Black and White', *photographies* 11, nos. 2–3 (2018): 193–213.
[58]Tahimik holds a master's degree in business administration from the Wharton School at the University of Pennsylvania (although he later tore up the physical diploma). He worked at the OECD from 1968 to 1972.

Wernher von Braun (1912–77) as the archetypal immigrant success story – 'Don't you know Werner [*sic*] von Braun? He's that American immigrant who invented the rockets to the moon!' – yet Tahimik's own path mirrors the German scientist's ascent more than Lola's precarious tenacity. His art becomes less a direct testimony of oppression than a complex performance of identity, echoing Russell's description of Benjamin's self-conception as 'a socially constructed identity, one who finds himself in a shifting series of others, in the topography of city streets and in the detail of daily life'.[59]

Further complicating the weave are the spectral presences and glaring absences of women in the critical narrative surrounding Tahimik's work. As Deborah Dixon and Leo Zonn observe, Jameson's influential reading suffers from a gendered myopia,[60] yet their own corrective lens fails to bring Lola into focus. The significant roles played by white European women – Lola/Baudry in Les Halles, and the German woman who gives birth in Kidlat's jeepney on his vacation to von Braun's hometown, played by Tahimik's own wife, the late artist and scholar, Katrin de Guia – remain largely peripheral in scholarly accounts. Does this silence betray a reluctance to untangle the intricate knot of race, gender and power in these cross-cultural intimacies, particularly given the enduring Western trope of the effeminizing of Asian men? E. San Juan Jr's hopeful interpretation – 'when we see the Parisian vendor riding next to Kidlat in his jeep, the "weak link" is seized: an alliance with other oppressed subalterns across race and nationality, across space and generation, is established'[61] – feels incomplete without this gendered dimension. In a letter back home, Kidlat may herald 'the bold decision in the last meeting to accept women members' into his fantastical space club. But his deepest on-screen connections resonate not with women from his homeland (or even the aspirational America), but with these European figures. Their centrality challenges any simple narrative of anti-colonial brotherhood, insisting on a more intricate, perhaps more fraught, map of affiliation within the migrant imaginary.

These intimate dramas play out on a stage increasingly dominated by the architecture of exclusion. The late twentieth century, as Escafré-Dublet chronicles, witnessed the rise of a new 'Fortress Europe'. The term itself, freighted with the grim echo of the Nazi Atlantic Wall, reframes migration not as movement, but invasion; immigrants not as people, but as a tide to be stemmed. Under the aegis of accords like the Dublin Convention and through agencies like Frontex, Europe began to police its perimeter with renewed vigilance, even as internal borders dissolved for its own citizens. This

---

[59]Russell, *Experimental Ethnography*, 295.
[60]Deborah Dixon and Leo Zonn, 'Confronting the Geopolitical Aesthetic: Fredric Jameson, *The Perfumed Nightmare* and the Perilous Place of Third Cinema', *Geopolitics* 10, no. 2 (2005): 290–315.
[61]San Juan Jr, *After Postcolonialism*, 154–5.

project inevitably inscribed a hierarchy onto movement itself. Giscard's France exemplified this contradiction: While the state-funded Des chiffres et des lettres wove a tapestry of national belonging through language and logic for a broad Francophone audience, the specially commissioned Mosaïc, bankrolled entirely by the State Secretary for Immigrant Workers, addressed immigrants as a distinct constituency. As Escafré-Dublet reveals, this targeted programming served a complex agenda: a gesture of cultural acknowledgement functioning as 'compensation' for tightened controls, a tool for managing identities deemed transient, a subtle encouragement towards eventual return (epitomized by the 'Stoleru million' departure incentive), and a channel for state messaging.

Within this fortress, gradations of belonging proliferated, marked by divisions between people from different colonies, as well as former and current overseas territories. Colonial histories cast long, uneven shadows: Spain, invoking laws rooted in its imperial past (Article 22.1 of the Civil Code, built upon the 1889 classification of Filipinos as Spanish subjects) now offers nationals of Ibero-American countries, Andorra, Equatorial Guinea, Portugal and the Philippines an expedited route to EU citizenship with just two years' residency. This 'Via Spagna' has opened doors across Schengen, a privilege starkly contrasting with the labyrinth faced by France's own postcolonial migrants from Africa or Asia, or even, tentatively, citizens from territories like New Caledonia, with its tangled legacy of indigenous displacement and white-settler colonialism. Such incongruities render Fortress Europe's walls permeable, but selectively, sometimes arbitrarily, so.

Migration, Tahimik reminds us, defies the neat linearity of state narratives; it resists the wrong assumption that migration from the global South is a one-way journey, from periphery to metropole. Sometimes we go back, or somewhere else altogether. The glittering bridges of Charles de Gaulle, under this colder light, transform into drawbridges, their mechanisms governed by the capricious logics of history and statecraft. They stand as monuments to a continent constructing its future by carefully curating its past, leaving the fragile solidarities forged in the vanishing marketplaces of Les Halles, the human connections like that between Kidlat and Lola, suspended over the abyss.

Migration history in the multiverse

'I choose my vehicle. I choose my bridge'.[62] A young man interviewed by Escafré-Dublet for this book, named Stéphane, echoed this sentiment, the final iteration of Kidlat's extended metaphor, when he remarked: 'People

---

[62] Kidlat in *Perfumed Nightmare*, 01:29:00.

cannot know that I have foreign origins if I don't tell them'. He, like roughly one in four French citizens under sixty, identifies as having 'foreign origins'. Premised on the one hand, Escafré-Dublet writes, on the undeniable reality of 'stigmatization and discrimination of visible minorities in France', Stéphane's utterance on the other conveys a degree of agency withheld. Within the spectral empires of assumption and appearance, he chooses his vehicle. He chooses his bridge. It is worth foregrounding the subtle power resting in that choice – whether to disclose parts of oneself, and to whom. The rules and regulations controlling who is 'French' and the movements of those deemed 'foreign' will continue to change, as they have for centuries. So, too, will the responses from those subject to them, the lingering sillage of empire overwhelming both trajectories.

In France, museums are said to lead their own lives. We humans merely contribute to them. And yet, our involvement in their storied existences is contingent on our place in the world – or, in the case of the Louvre, as migrant or native. In 2006, the museum invited Nobel Prize-winning author Toni Morrison to curate a series of events. In justifying the choice, director Jean-Marc Terrasse revealed the institution's careful calculus: The idea was 'to find people able to bring something new to the life of the museum', specifically 'somebody who is not an artist or who is not a specialist'.[63] The implication was clear: The institution sought the prestige of an outsider, a Black American, rather than risk the critique of an insider, a French person of migrant descent. Instead, Morrison chose her own vehicle, *The Foreigner's Home*,[64] centred on Théodore Géricault's 1818–19 painting *The Raft of the Medusa*.

She saw in its depiction of a colonial shipwreck not just a historical tragedy, but an allegory for a fragile modernity: a sinking ship where migrants and natives go down together, dying as equals. 'I began to look at wordless forms like painting and choreography', she said, 'as journeying somewhere that I'd never thought of'.[65] It was a tacit rejection of the weight of French society, a nod to the recurring theme of resistance through language – including its absence – and in so doing, bringing a different meaning to the mantra of equality than perhaps intended. This was her own *art naïf* moment. Instead of occupying the safe role of the foreign dignitary, she used her platform to amplify the 'wordless' critiques already present within France, hosting readings, lectures

---

[63] Jean-Marc Terasse as quoted in Rachel Somerstein, 'A Novelist's Approach', *Arttalk*, November 2006, 52.

[64] The process is documented in *The Foreigner's Home*, directed by Rian Brown and Geoff Pingree (USA and France: Lens Pictures, 2017). For the inspiration behind this exhibition, refer to Toni Morrison, 'The Foreigner's Home' (lecture, University of Toronto, Ontario, Canada, May 2002). See also Liedeke Plate, 'Portrait of the Postcolonial Intellectual as a Wise Old Woman: Toni Morrison, Word-Work, and *The Foreigner's Home*', *Transnational Screens* 13, no. 2 (2022): 96–110.

[65] As quoted in Somerstein, 'A Novelist's Approach', 52.

and performances by the very French immigrant and migrant artists the Louvre had ostensibly sidestepped – an act not wholly unlike one performed by Tahimik himself. Upon learning in the 1970s that Baudry had acted in 'about a dozen' silent films in the 1920s,[66] he appealed to pioneering French film archivist Henri Langlois at the Cinémathèque Française, querying why tributes should be reserved only for movie stars: 'Why not make a hommage to Georgette Baudy at the Cinémathèque? Why only hommages to Alain Delon or Marlon Brando?'[67] Forty years later, Tahimik successfully petitioned the Berlinale Forum to screen Raymond Bernard's 1924 silent classic *Le miracle des loups* (*The Miracle of the Wolves*), in which she doubled for Yvonne Sergyl, alongside his own debut – a poignant gesture bridging migrant geographies and generations.

Following Buck-Morss, this Afterword has been a story of immigration in France 'told within a story' of Kidlat/Tahimik's own historical experience, 'with the goal of bringing to life the cognitive and political power' of *Perfumed Nightmare* that 'lies dormant within the layers of historical data of which it is composed'.[68] Kidlat/Tahimik's experiences in France – his observations of the Parisian streets, his interactions with Lola, his witness to the destruction of Les Halles – become emblematic of a larger social reality: the collision of global capitalism with local ways of being, played out in the heart of a former empire. Read from this multi-nodal standpoint, Escafré-Dublet's book provides the macro-political context for the micro-personal experiences Tahimik explores, detailing the state logics that create the very conditions of 'temporal maladjustment' for its colonial and postcolonial subjects. My reading of *A Political History of Immigration in France* is accordingly premised on these confluences.

The emotional intimacy between a young Filipino jeepney driver and an elderly Parisian poulterer might have instinctively seemed like a curious place to start an essay commenting on a *political* history of immigration; however, this conjoining of the macro-political and the micro-personal is precisely the analytic ground Escafré-Dublet's book masterfully navigates. The approach this monograph takes is self-avowedly 'social', centring not just grand narratives but 'the circulation of ideas, how policy makers take decisions', and crucially, 'how politics affect people's lives' – people like Lola, but also Kidlat. Having been bought and imported by an American, the automobile Kidlat drove

---

[66]Hering and Baumgärtel, '"I trust the cosmos"', 167–8.
[67]Introductory note from Henri Langlois, enclosed with a 1977 letter from Kidlat Tahimik to Erika and Ulrich Gregor, as quoted in 'Le miracle des loups (The Miracle of the Wolves)', *Kidlat Tahimik /// the films /// Retrospective 2016*, http://kidlattahimik.de/en/retrospective-2016/films-in-context/.
[68]Buck-Morss, *The Dialects of Seeing*, ix.

around the 1st and 4th arrondissements of Paris did not technically belong to him. But it was his all the same.

Can one, after all, really talk about immigration without the (im)migrant? Escafré-Dublet's work attests to a growing 'thirst' among immigrants and their descendants in France to 'locate one's family history in a larger narrative'. But what, then, does 'family' mean? Is it the nuclear, future-facing ideal of the Europ Assistance advertisements? The outward silence about racial and ethnic representation in aeronautics is equally salient.[69] Or is it something closer to the adoptive bond between a *tsuper* and his *lola*? From my own lived experience, I know family can mean many things and be very multinational. As a historian working mostly on Southeast Asia and the Pacific, whose nuclear family are nationals of several different Asia-Pacific countries, this book leaves me curious to hear the stories of individuals from French Polynesia and the Pacific, or Vietnam in Asia – immigrants from European territories overseas, past and present, whose conceptions of kinship may offer other bridges entirely. Lola also took control of her own migration story, recalling a time when Normans, Auvergnats, and Bretons settled a city teeming with provincial diversity, and where not all the burghers identified as, or even spoke, French. Used then as a foil for *A Political History of Immigration in France*, *Perfumed Nightmare* highlights the volume's contributions to global history. No longer is it a question of can the migrant speak, but how and to what effect? Who even is this 'migrant'?

As embedded in its Tagalog title *Mababangong Bangungot*, there is a fine line between *bango* (sweet fragrance) and *bangungot* (nightmare). It seems fitting, then, to end this chapter as speculatively as it began. Whether Kidlat returns to Balian or becomes the first Filipino to 'fly supersonic' from Paris to New York with his American patron aboard the Concorde is a hotly contested topic. A third possibility is one that supposes the birth of a new bamboo universe. Intent on finding Lola, Kidlat remains in France, eventually tracking her to Rungis. They establish a wildly successful *jeepney* grocery delivery service, extolling the health benefits of Lola's double-yoked eggs against the egg phantoms of the *supermarché*. They buy some land on the French-German border near Strasbourg, where Kidlat builds Lola a *nipa* hut in which to retire. Not long after, emboldened by the opening of European borders in 1985, the German woman who delivered baby Kidlat in his vehicle reconnects with

---

[69]The European Space Agency (f.1975) does not publicly share specific statistics on the racial and ethnic demographics of its workforce. While its official Diversity and Inclusiveness policy states a commitment to equal opportunity and welcomes all qualified candidates 'irrespective of gender, sexual orientation, ethnicity, religious beliefs, age, disability or other characteristics', its published diversity data and targets focus on other areas – namely, nationality, gender, age and disability; European Space Agency, 'Diversity and Inclusiveness', https://www.esa.int/About_Us/Careers_at_ESA/Diversity_and _Inclusiveness.

the *tsuper*, and they fall in love. In the countryside, they have more children and live happily ever after – or at least, until the time comes for them to be documented and passports obtained to cross yet more borders.

To the naysayers, Kidlat would reply (as he does in the film), 'there is another way out of the village. It is a bridge used by my grandfather when he left Balian after ninety-five years of building bamboo huts'. 'I am a jeepney driver', he continues. 'To earn my living, I need both bridges'.

Bibliography

Achi, Raberh. 'La séparation des Eglises et de l'Etat à l'épreuve de la situation coloniale. Les usages de la dérogation dans l'administration du culte musulman en Algérie (1905–1959)'. *Politix. Revue des sciences sociales du politique* 17, no. 66 (2004): 81–106. https://doi.org/10.3406/polix.2004.1017.

Akoka, Karen. 'France: Boat People Brought by Plane'. In *When Boat People Were Resettled, 1975–83: A Comparative History of European and Israeli Responses to the South-East Asian Refugee Crisis*, edited by Becky Taylor, Karen Akoka, Marcel Berlinghoff and Shira Havkin. Cham: Springer, 2021. https://doi.org/10.1007/978-3-030-64224-2_2.

Allport, Gordon. *The Nature of Prejudice*. New York: Addison-Wesley, 1954.

Amiri, L. 'La bataille de France. La guerre d'Algérie en métropole'. Paris: Robert Lafont, 2004.

Aprile, Sylvie, and Delphine Diaz. 'Europe and Its Political Refugees in the nineteenth Century'. *Books & Ideas*, 18 April 2016. https://booksandideas.net/Europe-and-its-Political-Refugees-in-the-19th-Century.

Arnaud, Lionel. *Réinventer la ville: Artistes, minorités ethniques et militants au service des politiques de développement urbain. Une comparaison franco-britannique*. Rennes: University of Rennes Press, 2015.

Asal, Houda. 'Islamophobie: la fabrique d'un nouveau concept. État des lieux de la recherche'. *Sociologie* 5, no. 1 (2014): 13–29. https://doi.org/10.3917/socio.051.0013.

Asal, Houda, and Marwan Mohammed. 'Islamophobie en France: formes, définitions et mesures'. In *Migrations et mutations de la société française*. Paris: La Découverte, 2014. https://doi.org/10.3917/dec.poins.2014.01.0316.

Banton, Michael. *The Idea of Race*. London: Tavistock, 1977.

Barnabà, Enzo. *Mort aux Italiens!: 1893, le massacre d' Aigues-Mortes*. Toulouse: Editalie, 2012.

Barnett, Michael. *Empire of Humanity: A History of Humanitarianism*. Ithaca, NY: Cornell University Press, 2011.

Barros, Françoise de. 'L'état au prisme des municipalités: Une comparaison historique des catégorisations des étrangers en France (1919–1984)'. Doctoral thesis, Paris 1, 2004.

Barthélemy, Martine, and Guy Michelat. 'Dimensions de la laïcité dans la France d'aujourd'hui'. *Revue française de science politique* 57, no. 5 (23 October 2007): 649–98. https://doi.org/10.3917/rfsp.575.0649.

Baubérot, Jean. *Histoire de la laïcité en France*. Paris: Universities of France Press, 2000.

Beaman, Jean. 'France's Ahmeds and Muslim Others: The Entanglement of Racism and Islamophobia'. *French Cultural Studies* 32, no. 3 (1 August 2021): 269–79. https://doi.org/10.1177/09571558211009370.

Beauchemin, Cris, and David Lessault. 'Migration from Sub-Saharan Africa to Europe: Still a Limited Trend'. *Population and Societies*, no. 452 (2009): 4.

Belgacem, Samir Hadj, and Hanane Karimi. 'Politisation du voile et mobilisation des accompagnatrices scolaires contre la circulaire Chatel: Le cas du collectif Sorties scolaires: avec nous!' *Sociétés contemporaines* 127, no. 3 (2022): 95–119. https://doi.org/10.3917/soco.127.0095.

Bereni, Laure. *Le management de la vertu: La diversité en entreprise à New York et à Paris*. Paris: Sciences Po University Press, 2023.

Bereni, Laure, and Alexandre Jaunait. 'Usages de la diversité'. *Raisons politiques* 35, no. 3 (2009): 5–9. https://doi.org/10.3917/rai.035.0005.

Bernardot, Marc. *Loger les immigrés: La Sonacotra 1956–2006*. Bellecombe-en-Bauges: Croquant, 2008.

Berstein, Serge. *Les cultures politiques en France*. Paris: Seuil, 1999.

Bigo, Didier. 'Les attentats de 1986 en France (Partie 2)'. *Cultures & Conflits*, no. 4 (1991). https://doi.org/10.4000/conflits.750.

Blanc-Chaléard, Marie-Claude. *En finir avec les bidonvilles: Immigration et politique du logement dans la France des Trente Glorieuses*. Paris: Sorbonne, 2016.

Blanc-Chaléard, Marie-Claude. *Histoire de l'immigration*. Paris: La Découverte, 2001.

Blanc-Chaléard, Marie-Claude. 'Les Italiens dans l'est Parisien des années 1880 aux années 1960: Une histoire d'intégration'. Doctoral thesis, Paris, Institut d'études politiques, 1995.

Blanc-Chaléard, Marie-Claude, Geneviève Dreyfus-Armand, Nancy L. Green, Gérard Noiriel, Patrick Simon, Vincent Viet, Marie-Christine Volovitch-Tavarès and Patrick Weil. 'Un amalgame inacceptable!', *Le Monde*, 21 May 2007.

Blanchard, Emmanuel. 'Contrôle au faciès: une cérémonie de dégradation'. *Plein droit* 103, no. 4 (2014): 11–15. https://doi.org/10.3917/pld.103.0011.

Blanchard, Emmanuel. *Histoire de l'immigration algérienne en France*. Paris: La Découverte, 2018.

Blanchard, Emmanuel. *La police parisienne et les Algériens*. Paris: Nouveau Monde, 2011.

Blanchard, Pascal, Nicolas Bancel and Sandrine Lemaire. *La fracture coloniale: La société française au prisme de l'héritage colonial*. Paris: La Découverte, 2006.

Bleich, Erik. *Race Politics in Britain and France: Ideas and Policymaking Since the 1960s*. Cambridge University Press, 2003.

Bleich, Erik. 'What Is Islamophobia and How Much Is There? Theorizing and Measuring an Emerging Comparative Concept'. *American Behavioral Scientist* 55, no. 12 (2011): 1581–600. https://doi.org/10.1177/0002764211409387.

Bogart, Leo. 'Leo Bogart Papers, 1912–2010 and Undated'. 62.0 Linear Feet, Archives & Manuscripts. Duke University Libraries, n.d. RL.10146. https://archives.lib.duke.edu/catalog/bogartleo.

Boons, Marie-Claire, and Françoise Collin. 'Le voile et la question de l'identité'. *Les cahiers du GRIF* 43, no. 1 (1990): 197–201. https://doi.org/10.3406/grif.1990.2431.

Borjas, George J., and Anthony Edo. 'Monopsony, Efficiency, and the Regularization of Undocumented Immigrants'. National Bureau of Economic Research, 2023. https://www.nber.org/papers/w31457.

Boucheron, Patrick. *Histoire mondiale de la France*. Média Diffusion, 2017.

Bourdieu, Pierre, Mouloud Mammeri and Yacine Tassadit. 'Du Bon Usage de l'ethnologie | Cairn.Info'. *Actes de La Recherche En Sciences Sociales*, 2003.

Boussaguet, Laurie, and Florence Faucher. 'La construction des discours présidentiels post-attentats à l'épreuve du temps'. *Mots. Les langages du politique*, no. 118 (2018): 95–115, https://doi.org/10.4000/mots.23867.

Brace, Richard, and Joan Brace. 'The Black Community in Paris: 1777–1790', *Centennial Review* 21, no. 4 (1977): 374–81.

Brahim, Rachida. *La Race tue deux fois: Une histoire des crimes racistes en France*. Paris: Syllepse, 2021.

Braudel, Fernand. *L'identité de la France, 3 tomes: Espace et histoire / Les hommes et les choses / Les hommes et les choses, tome 2*. Paris: Arthaud-Flammarion, 1986.

Brinbaum, Yaël, Mirna Safi and Patrick Simon. 'Les discriminations en France: entre perception et expérience'. In Cris Beauchemin, Christelle Hamel and Patrick Simon (eds), *Trajectoires et origines. Enquête sur la diversité des populations en France*. Paris: National Institute for Demographic Studies Press, 2015. https://www.ined.fr/fr/publications/editions/document-travail /discriminations-france-perception-experience/.

Brodiez-Dolino, Axelle. 'The Conjunction of Social and Health Considerations in Policies against Poverty and Vulnerability in Twentieth-Century France'. *Le Mouvement Social* 242, no. 1 (2013): 9–29.

Brouard, Sylvain, Emiliano Grossman and Isabelle Guinaudeau. 'La compétition partisane française au prisme des priorités électorales: Compétition sur enjeux et appropriations thématiques'. *Revue française de science politique* 62, no. 2 (2012): 255–76. https://doi.org/10.3917/rfsp.622.0255.

Brouard, Sylvain, and Vincent Tiberj. *As French as Everyone Else?: A Survey of French Citizens of Maghrebin, African, and Turkish Origin*. Philadelphia: Temple University Press, 2011.

Brun, Solène, and Claire Cosquer. *Sociologie de la race*. Malakoff: Armand Colin, 2022.

Büttner, Olivier, and Bénédicte Héraud. 'L'accueil en gare. Pratiques de l'entre-soi du Comité Lyautey', in Michel Hastings, Bénédicte Héraud and Anne Kerlan (eds), *Le sens pratique de l'hospitalité. Accueillir les étrangers en France, 1965–1983*. Paris: CNRS, 2021.

Camus, Albert, and Arthur Goldhammer. *Algerian Chronicles*. Cambridge, MA: Harvard University Press, 2002. https://doi.org/10.2307/j.ctvjf9xg8.

Chabal, Emile. *France*. Medford, MA: Polity Press, 2020.

Chanet, Jean-François. *L'École républicaine et les petites patries*. Paris: Aubier, 1996.

Charef, Mehdi. *Tea in the Harem*. Main ed. London: Serpent's Tail, 1989.

Chérifi, Hanifa. 'Application de la loi du 15 mars 2004'. *Hommes & migrations* 1258, no. 1 (2005): 33–47. https://doi.org/10.3406/homig.2005.4391.

Choi, Sung-Eun. *Decolonization and the French of Algeria: Bringing the Settler Colony Home*. Houndmills: Palgrave Macmillan, 2015.

Cissé, Madjigène. *Parole de sans-papiers*. Paris: La Dispute, 1999.

Cohen, Muriel. *Des familles invisibles: les Algériens de France entre intégrations et discriminations (1945–1985)*. Paris: Sorbonne University Press, 2020.

Cohen, Muriel. 'Les bidonvilles de Nanterre', in Benjamin Stora and Linda Amiri (eds), *Algériens en France: 1954–1962: La guerre, l'exil, la vie*. Paris: Autrement, 2012.

Colin, Robert. 'Louis Chevalier. Le problème démographique nord-africain'. *Politique étrangère* 13, no. 2 (1948): 197–8.

Coller, Ian, Manuel Covo, Bruno Maillard, Jennifer Palmer, Karine Rance, Éric Saunier and Cécile Vidal. 'Race et Révolution française'. *Annales historiques de la Révolution française* 410, no. 4 (2022): 139–62.

Cooper, Frederick. *Decolonization and African Society: The Labor Question in French and British Africa*. African Studies. Cambridge: Cambridge University Press, 1996.

Davidson, Naomi. *Only Muslim: Embodying Islam in Twentieth-Century France*. Ithaca, NY: Cornell University Press, 2012.

De Gaulle, Charles. 'Le discours du Général De Gaulle devant l'Assemblée consultative'. *Le Monde*, 5 March 1945.

Dedieu, Jean-Philippe. 'L'internationalisme ouvrier à l'épreuve des migrations africaines en France'. *Critique internationale* 50, no. 1 (2011): 145–67. https://doi.org/10.3917/crii.050.0145.

Déloye, Yves. *Ecole et citoyenneté: l'individualisme républicain de Jules Ferry à Vichy: controverses*. Paris: Sciences Po University Press, 1994.

Demangeon, Albert. 'Les étrangers en France'. *Annales de géographie* 41, no. 232 (1932): 408–11.

Denis, Florence. 'Entre mission et développement: Une expérience de laïcat missionnaire, L'association ad lucem 1945–1957'. *Le Mouvement Social*, no. 177 (1996): 29–47. https://doi.org/10.2307/3778951.

Dewitte, Philippe. '1950–2000. Des Cahiers nord-africains à Hommes & Migrations'. *Hommes & migrations* 1257, no. 1 (2005): 62–8.

Diaz, Delphine. *Un asile pour tous les peuples?: Exilés et réfugiés étrangers dans la France au cours du premier XIXe siècle*. Paris: Armand Colin, 2014.

Dornel, Laurent. *Indispensables et indésirables: Les travailleurs coloniaux de la Grande Guerre*. Paris: La Découverte, 2025.

Dornel, Laurent. *La France hostile*. Paris: Hachette Literature, 2004.

Dornel, Laurent. 'L'appel à la main-d'œuvre étrangère et coloniale pendant la Grande Guerre: un tournant dans l'histoire de l'immigration?' *Migrations Société* 156, no. 6 (2014): 51–68.

Dos Santos, Irène, and Sónia Ferreira, *Les Portugais en France: Une immigration invisible: XXe-XXIe siècles*. Paris: Cavalier Bleu, 2024.

Douglas, R. M. *Orderly and Humane: The Expulsion of the Germans after the Second World War*. New Haven, CT: Yale University Press, 2012.

Douniès, Thomas. 'The Time of Origins: The Rise and Fall of a Diversity Policy toward Migrant Pupils in France (1960s–1990s)'. *European Journal of Cultural and Political Sociology* 12, no. 3 (2025): 226–47.

Dreyfus-Armand, Geneviève. *L'exil des républicains espagnols en France. De la guerre civile à la mort de franco*. Paris: Albin Michel, 1999.

Dubedout, Hubert. 'Ensemble, refaire la ville. Rapport au premier ministre'. CNDSQ – Commission nationale pour le développement social des quartiers, 1982.

Escafré-Dublet, Angéline. 'Aid, Activism and the State in Post-War France: AMANA, a Charity Organisation for Colonial Migrants, 1945–1962'. *Journal of*

Modern European History 12, no. 2 (1 May 2014): 247–61. https://doi.org /10.17104/1611-8944_2014_2_247.

Escafré-Dublet, Angéline. 'Art, Power and Protest. Immigrants' Artistic Production and Political Mobilization in France', *New Diversities* 12, no. 1 (2010): 5–19.

Escafré-Dublet, Angéline. *Culture et immigration. De la question sociale à l'enjeu politique, 1958–2007*. Rennes: University of Rennes Press, 2014.

Escafré-Dublet, Angéline. 'Le comité lyautey et l'accueil en gare des migrants (1952–1975)'. *Migrance*, no. 46 (2015): 43–54.

Escafré-Dublet, Angéline. 'Préserver les loyautés nationales. Le rôle des États d'origine dans l'immigration en France, 1962–1975'. *Annales de démographie historique* 124, no. 2 (2012): 141–60. https://doi.org/10.3917/adh.124.0141.

Escafré-Dublet, Angéline. 'The Soundtrack of Immigration: A Look Back at the Exhibition "Paris–Londres: Music Migrations (1962–1989)" at the French National Museum of Immigration History'. *French History*, crad052 (2023). https://doi.org/10.1093/fh/crad052.

Escafré-Dublet, Angéline. 'The Whiteness of Cultural Boundaries in France'. In Meer, Nasar (ed), *Whiteness and Nationalism*. London: Routledge, 2020.

Escafré-Dublet, Angéline, Virginie Guiraudon and Julien Talpin, eds. *Fighting Discrimination in a Hostile Political Environment: The Case of 'Colour-Blind' France*. London: Routledge, 2023. https://doi.org/10.4324/9781003441489.

Escafré-Dublet, Angéline, and Camille Hamidi, 'From Victims to Culprits? The Reshaping of Local Antidiscrimination Policy in France', *Ethnic and Racial Studies* 46, no. 4 (2029): 228–48.

Escafré-Dublet, Angéline, and Lionel Kesztenbaum. 'Measuring Immigrant Inclusion: The Genesis and History of the Girard-Stoetzel Surveys, 1945–1953'. *Geneses* 84, no. 3 (2011): 93–112.

Escafré-Dublet, Angéline, Lionel Kesztenbaum and Patrick Simon. 'La greffe coloniale en métropole. Les Français musulmans dans le recensement de 1954'. *Sociétés contemporaines* 110, no. 2 (2018): 35–59, https://doi.org /10.3917/soco.110.0035.

Escafré-Dublet, Angéline, and Christine Lelévrier. 'Governing Diversity Without Naming It: An Analysis of Neighbourhood Policies in Paris'. *European Urban and Regional Studies* 26, no. 3 (2019): 283–96. https://doi.org/10.1177 /0969776417750439.

Escafré-Dublet, Angéline, and Patrick Simon. '9 Ethnic Statistics in Europe: The Paradox of Colourblindness', in Nasar Meer, Tariq Modood and Anna Triandafyllidou (eds), *European Multiculturalisms: Cultural, Religious and Ethnic Challenges*, 213–38. Edinburgh: Edinburgh University Press, 2011.

'Far Right: Voters Generally Prefer the Original to the Copy'. 24 November 2023. https://www.lemonde.fr/en/opinion/article/2023/11/24/far-right-voters-generally -prefer-the-original-to-the-copy_6285464_23.html.

Fassin, Didier, and Eric Fassin. *De la question sociale à la question raciale?* Paris: La Découverte, 2009.

Fassin, Didier, and Sarah Mazouz. 'Qu'est-ce que devenir français? la naturalisation comme rite d'institution républicain'. *Revue Française de Sociologie* 48, no. 4 (2007): 723–50.

Faure, Sylvia, and Marie-Carmen Garcia. 'Hip-hop et politique de la ville'. *Agora débats/jeunesses* 49, no. 3 (2008): 78–89. https://doi.org/10.3917/agora .049.0078.

Favell, Adrian. *Philosophies of Integration: Immigration and the Idea of Citizenship in France and Britain*. 2nd ed. New York: Palgrave Macmillan, 1998.

Fleming, Crystal Marie. *Resurrecting Slavery: Racial Legacies and White Supremacy in France*. Philadelphia: Temple University Press, 2017.

Freedman, Jane. 'The French "Sans-Papiers" Movement: An Unfinished Struggle'. In W. Pojmann (ed), *Migration and Activism in Europe since 1945*. New York, Palgrave Macmillan, 2008.

Garbaye, Romain. *Getting into Local Power: The Politics of Ethnic Minorities in British and French Cities*. Malden, MA: Wiley-Blackwell, 2005.

Gastaut, Yvan. 'Français et immigrés à l'épreuve de la crise (1973–1995)'. *Vingtième Siècle. Revue d'histoire* 84, no. 4 (2004): 107–18. https://doi.org /10.3917/ving.084.0107.

Gastaut, Yvan. '1973, l'année intense'. *Hommes & migrations. Revue française de référence sur les dynamiques migratoires*, no. 1330 (2020): 9–13. https://doi.org/10.4000/hommesmigrations.11346.

Gauthier, Jérémie, and Fabien Jobard. *Police: questions sensibles*. Paris: University Press of France, 2018.

Geisser, Vincent, and El Yamine Soum. *Discriminer pour mieux régner. Enquête sur la diversité dans les partis politiques*. Ivry-sur-Seine: Atelier, 2008.

Gervereau, Laurent, Pierre Milza and Émile Témime. *Toute la France: histoire de l'immigration en France au xxe siècle*. Paris: Somogy, 1998.

Girard, Alain, and Jean Stoetzel. *Français et immigrés. Nouveaux documents sur l'adaptation. Algériens – Italiens – Polonais. Le Service social d'aide aux émigrants. Travaux et Documents. Institut national d'études démographiques. Cahier no 20*. Paris: University Press of France, 1954.

Gordon, Daniel A. *Immigrants & Intellectuals: May '68 & the Rise of Anti-Racism in France*. Pontypool: Merlin, 2012.

Gordon, Daniel A. 'A Victory for the March for Equality? Immigration, Policy, Protest and the Ten-Year Residency Permit of 1984'. *French History* 37, no. 3 (2023): 294–316. https://doi.org/10.1093/fh/crac073.

Green, Nancy L. 'Filling the Void: Immigration to France, Before World War I', in Dirk Hoerder (ed), *Labor Migration in the Atlantic Economies: The European and North American Working Classes During the Period of Industrialization*, 143–61. Westport, CT: Greenwood Press, 1985.

Green, Nancy L. 'A French Ellis Island? Museums, Memory and History in France and the United States'. *History Workshop Journal* 63, no. 1 (2007): 239–53.

Green, Nancy L. 'La mode en production: La confection et les immigrés, Paris-New York, 1880–1980'. Doctoral thesis, Paris 7, 1996.

Green, Nancy L. 'Le Melting-Pot: Made in America, Produced in France'. *Journal of American History* 86, no. 3 (1999): 1188–208. https://doi.org/10.2307 /2568611.

Guerry, Linda. *Le genre de l'immigration et de la naturalisation. L'exemple de Marseille (1918–1940)*. Lyon: ENS Editions, 2013.

Guiraudon, Virginie. 'Les effets de l'européanisation des politiques d'immigration et d'asile'. *Politique européenne* 31, no. 2 (17 November 2010): 7–32. https://doi.org/10.3917/poeu.031.0007.

Guiraudon, Virginie. 'The Reaffirmation of the Republican Model of Integration: Ten Years of Identity Politics in France'. *French Politics and Society* 14, no. 2 (1996): 47–57.

Gurrey, Béatrice. 'Missak et Mélinée Manouchian entrent au Panthéon à l'issue d'une cérémonie émouvante et engagée', 22 February 2024. https://www .lemonde.fr/politique/article/2024/02/22/missak-et-melinee-manouchian -entrent-au-pantheon-a-l-issue-d-une-ceremonie-emouvante-et-engagee _6217869_823448.html.

Hachimi-Alaoui, Myriam, and Janie Pélabay. 'Contrats d'intégration et "valeurs de la République": un "tournant civique" à la française?' *Revue européenne des migrations internationales* 36, no. 4 (2020): 13–33. https://doi.org/10.4000 /remi.17069.

Hajjat, Abdellali. *La marche pour l'égalité et contre le racisme*. Paris: Amsterdam/ Multitudes, 2013.

Hajjat, Abdellali. 'Le MTA et la "grève générale contre le racisme" de 1973'. *Plein Droit*, no. 67 (2005): 35–40.

Hajjat, Abdellali. *Les frontières de l'"identité nationale": L'injonction à l'assimilation en France métropolitaine et coloniale*. Paris: La Découverte, 2012.

Hajjat, Abdellali. '2. La barrière de la langue. Naissance de la condition d'assimilation linguistique pour la naturalization'. In Fassin, Didier (ed), *Les nouvelles frontières de la société française*, Poche / Sciences humaines et sociales, 53–77. Paris: La Découverte, 2012.

Hajjat, Abdellali, and Marwan Mohammed. *Islamophobie: Comment les élites françaises fabriquent le 'problème musulman'*. Paris: La Découverte, 2013.

Hamidi, Camille. 'Riots and Protest Cycles: Immigrant Mobilisation in France, 1968–2008', in David Waddington, Fabien Jobard and Mike King (eds), *Rioting in the UK and France: A Comparative Analysis*, 135–46. Cullompton: Willan, 2009.

Hammou, Karim, and Howard Saul Becker. *Une histoire du rap en France*. Paris: La Découverte, 2012. https://shs.cairn.info/une-histoire-du-rap-en-france –9782707181985?lang=fr.

Handlin, Oscar. *The Uprooted: The Epic Story of the Great Migrations That Made the American People*. 2nd ed. Philadelphia: University of Pennsylvania Press, 1952.

Hansen, Randall. 'Migration to Europe Since 1945: Its History and Its Lessons'. *Political Quarterly* 74, no. s1 (2003): 25–38.

Hargreaves, Alec G. *Immigration and Identity in Beur Fiction: Voices From the North African Community in France*. Oxford: Berg, 1991.

Heran, François. *Immigration: le grand déni*. Paris: Seuil, 2023.

Hervo, Monique. *Chroniques du bidonville: Nanterre en guerre d'Algérie*. Paris: Seuil, 2001.

Hmed, Choukri. 'Challenging an Institution in the Case of an Unlikely Mobilization: About the "Rent Strikes" in the Sonacotra Hostels in the 1970s'. *Societes contemporaines* 65, no. 1 (2007): 55–81.

Hmed, Choukri. 'Loger les étrangers "isolés" en France: Socio-histoire d'une institution d'État: La Sonacotra (1956–2006)'. Doctoral thesis, Paris 1, 2006.

Horn, Gerd-Rainer. *The Spirit of '68: Rebellion in Western Europe and North America, 1956–1976*. Oxford: Oxford University Press, 2008

Horne, Alistair. *A Savage War of Peace: Algeria 1954–1962*. New York: Viking, 1977.

Humblot, Catherine. 'Divertissement sans politique', *Le Monde*, 12–13 March 1978.

Hurst, Jean-Louis. 'Une bombe à *Mosaïque*', *Libération*, 7–8 June 1980.

Institut national de la statistique et des études économiques France. *Recensement général de la population de mai 1954: population légale (résultats statistiques) population, superficie, densité de population des principales circonscriptions administratives, migrations apparentes, logements et maisons*. Paris: INSEE, 1956.

Jablonka, Ivan. *Enfants en exil: Transfert de pupilles réunionnais en métropole*. Paris: Seuil, 2007.

Jakubyszyn, Christophe. 'Les jeunes des banlieues veulent devenir électeurs'. *Le Monde*, 28 December 2005.

Jobard, Fabien. 'An Overview of French Riots: 1981–2004', in David Waddington, Fabien Jobard and Mike King (eds), *Rioting in the UK and France: A Comparative Analysis*, 27–38. Cullompton: Willan, 2009.

Joutard, Philippe. 'La diaspora des Huguenots'. *Diasporas. Histoire et Sociétés* 1, no. 1 (2002): 115–21.

Juhem, Philippe. 'Entreprendre en politique. De l'extrême gauche au PS: La professionnalisation politique des fondateurs de SOS-Racisme'. *Revue française de science politique* 51, no. 1–2 (2001): 131–53. https://doi.org/10.3917/rfsp.511.0131.

Kastoryano, Riva. *Negotiating Identities: States and Immigrants in France and Germany*. Princeton, NJ: Princeton University Press, 2002.

Khemilat, Fatima. 'La construction des prières de rue comme problème public'. *Confluences Méditerranée* 106, no. 3 (8 October 2018): 81–94. https://doi.org/10.3917/come.106.0081.

Kirszbaum, Thomas. 'Les immigrés dans les politiques de l'habitat. Variations locales sur le thème de la diversité'. *Sociétés Contemporaines* 33, no. 1 (1999): 87–110. https://doi.org/10.3406/socco.1999.1752.

'La colonie rapatriée'. *Politix* 76, no. 4 (2006): 3–7. https://doi.org/10.3917/pox.076.0003.

Lacroix, Thomas. *Les réseaux marocains du développement. Géographie du transnational et politiques du territorial*. Paris: Sciences Po University Press, 2012.

'La Diversité des origines et la mixité des unions progressent au fil des générations – INSEE Première – 1910'. Accessed 21 December 2024. https://www.insee.fr/fr/statistiques/6468640.

'La Halde perd sa tête, avant de disparaître?' 17 November 2010. https://www.lemonde.fr/politique/article/2010/11/17/la-halde-perd-sa-tete-avant-de-disparaitre_1440889_823448.html.

Laurens, Sylvain. 'Le Club de l'horloge et la haute administration: promouvoir l'hostilité à l'immigration dans l'entre-soi mondain', *Agone* 54, no. 2 (2014): 73–94, https://doi.org/10.3917/agone.054.0073.

Laurens, Sylvain. *Une politisation feutrée: Les hauts fonctionnaires et l'immigration en France*. Paris: Belin, 2009.

Laurens, Sylvain, and Choukri Hmed. *L'invention de l'immigration*. Marseille: Agone, 2008.

Le Bars, Stéphanie, 'Des mères d'élèves portant le foulard islamique sont interdites de sorties scolaires dans l'académie de Créteil'. *Le Monde*, 26 March 2007.

'Le contrat publicitaire d'Emmanuelle Béart avec Dior ne sera pas renouvelé'. 3
   April 1997. https://www.lemonde.fr/archives/article/1997/04/03/le-contrat
   -publicitaire-d-emmanuelle-beart-avec-dior-ne-sera-pas-renouvele_3765615
   _1819218.html.
Le Cour Grandmaison, Olivier. *De l'indigénat: Anatomie d'un 'monstre' juridique:
   le droit colonial en Algérie et dans l'Empire français*. Paris: Zones, 2010.
Lebovics, Herman. *Mona Lisa's Escort: Andre Malraux and the Reinvention of
   French Culture*. Ithaca, NY: Cornell University Press, 1999.
'Le défilé des "intouchables"'. 24 October 1989. https://www.lemonde.fr
   /archives/article/1989/10/24/le-defile-des-intouchables_4126812_1819218.html.
Lentin, Alana. *Racism and Anti-Racism in Europe*. London: Pluto, 2004.
Lequin, Yves. *La Mosaïque France: histoire des étrangers et de l'immigration*.
   Paris: Larousse, 1988.
Lequin, Yves. *Les ouvriers de la région lyonnaise (1848–1914)*. Lyon: University of
   Lyon Press, 1977.
Lewis, Mary Dewhurst. *The Boundaries of the Republic: Migrant Rights and
   the Limits of Universalism in France, 1918–1940*. Stanford, CA: Stanford
   University Press, 2007.
Long, Marceau, ed. 'Pour un modèle français d'intégration'. Paris: Haut Conseil à
   l'intégration, 1991.
Loytomaki, Stiina. *Law and the Politics of Memory: Confronting the Past*.
   London: Routledge, 2014.
'Lutte contre le racisme: Il y a quarante ans, la marche des beurs de Marseille à
   Paris'. Accessed 25 August 2024. https://www.sudouest.fr/societe/racisme
   /lutte-contre-le-racisme-il-y-a-quarante-ans-la-marche-des-beurs-de-marseille-a
   -paris-en-images-17639111.php?csnt=191890cf0cf.
Lyons, Amelia H. *The Civilizing Mission in the Metropole: Algerian Families
   and the French Welfare State during Decolonization*. Stanford, CA: Stanford
   University Press, 2013.
Lyons, Amelia H. 'Social Welfare, French Muslims and Decolonization in France:
   The Case of the Fonds d'action sociale'. *Patterns of Prejudice* 43, no. 1: 65–89.
Mabon, Armelle. *Prisonniers de guerre Indigènes: Visages oubliés de la France
   occupée*. Paris: La Découverte, 2010.
Marshall, Thomas Humphrey. *Citizenship and Social Class: And Other Essays*.
   University Press, 1950.
Martigny, Vincent. *Dire la France: Culture(s) et identités nationales 1981–1995*.
   Sciences Po University Press, 2016.
Massenet, Michel. *Contrepoison ou La morale en Algérie*. Paris: Grasset, 1957.
Massicot, Simone. 'Effets sur la nationalité française de l'accession à
   l'indépendance de territoires ayant été sous la souveraineté française'.
   Population (French Edition) 41, no. 3 (1986): 533–46. https://doi.org/10.2307
   /1532807.
Maurice, Edenz, and Raberh Achi. 'Le régime de Vichy face aux sociétés
   coloniales: adaptations et recompositions locales'. *Genèses* 120, no. 3 (2020):
   3–7.
Mayeur, Jean-Marie. *Nouvelle Histoire de la France Contemporaine, Tome 10: Les
   Debuts de la Troisieme Republique 1871–1898*. Paris: Seuil, 1973.
Mazouz, Sarah. *La republique et ses autres. politiques de l'Alterite dans la France*.
   Lyon: Ens Lyon, 2017.

McAdam, Doug, Sidney Tarrow and Charles Tilly. *Dynamics of Contention.*
    Cambridge Studies in Contentious Politics. Cambridge: Cambridge University
    Press, 2001. https://doi.org/10.1017/CBO9780511805431.
Meer, Nasar, Per Mouritsen, Daniel Faas and Nynke de Witte. 'Examining
    'Postmulticultural' and Civic Turns in the Netherlands, Britain, Germany, and
    Denmark'. *American Behavioral Scientist* 59, no. 6 (2015): 702–26, https://doi
    .org/10.1177/0002764214566496.
Meslin, Karine. 'Les réfugiés cambodgiens, des ouvriers dociles? Genèse et
    modes de pérennisation d'un stéréotype en migration'. *Revue européenne
    des migrations internationales* 27, no. 3 (2011): 83–101. https://doi.org/10.4000
    /remi.5646.
Michel, Andrée. *Les travailleurs algériens en France.* Paris: CNRS, 1956.
Mills-Affif, Édouard. *Filmer les immigrés: Les représentations audiovisuelles de
    l'immigration é la télévision française.* Brussels: De Boeck, 2004.
Miot, Claire. 'Le retrait des tirailleurs sénégalais de la Première Armée française
    en 1944. Hérésie stratégique, bricolage politique ou conservatisme colonial?'
    Vingtième Siècle. Revue d'histoire 125, no. 1 (2015): 77–89. https://doi.org
    /10.3917/ving.125.0077.
Moch, Leslie Page. *Moving Europeans: Migration in Western Europe since 1650.*
    2nd ed. Interdisciplinary Studies in History. Bloomington: Indiana University
    Press, 2003.
Modood, Tariq. 'Muslims and the Politics of Difference'. *Political Quarterly* 74, no.
    s1 (2003): 100–15. https://doi.org/10.1111/j.1467-923X.2003.00584.x.
Moindrot, Claude. 'Les vagues d'immigration en Grande-Bretagne'. *Population
    (French Edition)* 20, no. 4 (1965): 633–50. https://doi.org/10.2307/1528584.
Momméja, Adèle. 'Les enfants de l'immigration au Centre Pompidou'. *Hommes
    & migrations* 1313, no. 1 (2016): 97–102. https://doi.org/10.4000
    /hommesmigrations.3569.
Moore, Damian. *Ethnicité et politique de la ville: En France et en Grande-
    Bretagne.* Paris: L'Harmattan, 2002.
Morris, Aldon D. *Origins of the Civil Rights Movements.* New York: Free, 1986.
Mours, Samuel. *Le protestantisme en France du XVIIIe siècle à nos jours.* Paris:
    Librairie protestante, 1972.
Ngai, Mae M. *Impossible Subjects: Illegal Aliens and the Making of Modern
    America – Updated Edition.* Revised ed. Princeton, NJ: Princeton University
    Press, 2014.
Noiriel, Gérard. *The French Melting Pot: Immigration, Citizenship, and National
    Identity.* Contradictions of Modernity, v. 5. Minneapolis: University of
    Minnesota Press, 1996.
Noiriel, Gérard. 'Histoire de l'immigration en France. État des lieux, perspectives
    d'avenir'. *Hommes & migrations* 1255, no. 1 (2005): 38–48.
Noiriel, Gérard. *Le Creuset français: Histoire de l'immigration XIXe-XXe siècle.*
    Paris: Seuil, 1988.
Noiriel, Gérard. *Le Massacre des Italiens.* Paris: Fayard, 2009.
Noiriel, Gérard. *Les origines républicaines de Vichy.* Paris: Hachette, 1999.
Pereira, Victor. *La dictature de Salazar face à l'émigration: L'Etat portugais et ses
    migrants en France.* Paris: Sciences Po University Press, 2012.
Pereira, Victor. 'Une migration favorisée. les représentations et pratiques
    étatiques vis-à-vis de la migration portugaise en France (1945–1974)', in *Marie-*

Claude Blanc-Chaléard, Stéphane Dufoix, Patrick Weil (eds), *L'étranger en questions du moyen âge à l'an 2000. Paris, Le Manuscrit*, 2005.

Perrot, Michelle. 'Les rapports des ouvriers français et des ouvriers étrangers, 1871–1893', *Bulletin de la Société d'Histoire Moderne*, 12, 1960.

Peschanski, Denis. *Des étrangers dans la Résistance*. Paris: L'Atelier, 2013.

Peyroulou, Jean-Pierre, Abderrahmane Bouchène, Ouanassa Siari Tengour, Sylvie Thénault and Gilbert Meynier. *Histoire de l'Algérie à la période coloniale, 1830–1962*. Paris: La Découverte, 2012.

Pitti, Laure. *Algériens au travail, une histoire (post)coloniale: Enquête sur les travailleurs immigrés de l'industrie automobile dans la France des 'Trente Glorieuses'"*. Rennes: Rennes University Press, 2025.

Pitti, Laure. 'Ouvriers algériens à renault-billancourt, de la guerre d'Algérie aux grèves d'OS des années 1970: Contribution à l'histoire sociale et politique des ouvriers étrangers en France'. Doctoral thesis, Paris 8, 2002.

Ponty, Janine. 'Les étrangers et le droit d'association au XXe siècle'. *Matériaux pour l'histoire de notre temps* 69, no. 1 (2003): 24–5. https://doi.org/10.3406 /mat.2003.402433.

Ponty, Janine. *Polonais méconnus: Histoire des travailleurs immigrés en France dans l'entre-deux-guerres. Polonais méconnus: Histoire des travailleurs immigrés en France dans l'entre-deux-guerres*. Internationale. Paris: Sorbonne, 1988.

'Premier rendez-vous entre le collectif Devoirs de mémoires et des jeunes à Clichy-sous-Bois'. 20 December 2005. https://www.lemonde.fr/societe/article /2005/12/20/premier-rendez-vous-public-du-collectif-devoirs-de-memoires-a -clichy-sous-bois_723349_3224.html.

Régent, Frédéric. 'Du préjugé de couleur au préjugé de race, le cas des Antilles françaises'. *Revue d'histoire moderne & contemporaine* 68–3, no. 3 (2021): 64–90. https://doi.org/10.3917/rhmc.683.0066

Régnard, Céline. 'Le meurtre du Bordeaux-Vintimille'. *Hommes & migrations. Revue française de référence sur les dynamiques migratoires*, no. 1313 (2016): 73–9. https://doi.org/10.4000/hommesmigrations.3563.

Rochefort, Florence. 'Foulard, genre et laïcité en 1989'. *Vingtième Siècle. Revue d'histoire* 75, no. 3 (2002): 145–56. https://doi.org/10.3917/ving.075.0145.

Rosenberg, Clifford D. *Policing Paris: The Origins of Modern Immigration Control Between the Wars*. Ithaca, NY: Cornell University Press, 2006.

Rosenthal, Paul-André. *L'Intelligence démographique: Sciences et politiques des populations en France*. Paris: Odile Jacob, 2003.

Rygiel, Philippe. 'Archives et historiographie de l'immigration'. *Migrances*, no. 33 (2009): 50–9.

Rygiel, Philippe. 'Mais où sont les immigrés d'antan?: Trajectoires sociogéographiques des membres des familles issues de l'immigration Européenne implantées dans le cher durant l'entre-deux-guerres'. Doctoral thesis, Besançon, 1996.

Rygiel, Philippe, Michael G. Esch, Jair da Souza Ramos, Nicole Fouché and Collectif. *Le bon grain et l'ivraie: La sélection des migrants en Occident, 1880–1939*. La Courneuve: Aux Lieux d'être, 2006.

Salerni, Paola, and Tito Marci. *Politique de la ville et aspects linguistiques de la France multiculturelle: histoire, évolution, contradictions*. Paris/Alberobello (Italy): L'Harmattan/AGA, 2023.

Sartre, Jean-Paul. *Situations, V Colonialisme et néocolonialisme*. Paris: Gallimard, 1964.

Savarese, Eric. *L'invention des Pieds-Noirs*. Paris: Séguier, 2002.

Savarese, Eric. *L'ordre colonial et sa légitimation en France métropolitaine*. Paris: L'Harmattan, 1998.

Sayad, Abdelmalek, and Pierre Bourdieu. *The Suffering of the Immigrant*. Translated by David Macey. Cambridge: Polity, 2004.

Schaub, Jean-Frédéric, and Silvia Sebastiani. *Race et histoire dans les sociétés occidentales (XV-XVIIIe siècle)*. Paris: Albin Michel, 2021.

Schor, Ralph. *L'opinion française et les étrangers en France, 1919–1939*. Paris: Sorbonne, 1985.

Scioldo-Zürcher, Yann. *Devenir métropolitain: Politique d'intégration et parcours de rapatriés d'Algérie en métropole*. Paris: School of Advanced Studies in Social Science Press, 2010.

Scott, Joan W. 'Symptomatic Politics: The Banning of Islamic Head Scarves in French Public Schools'. *French Politics, Culture & Society* 23, no. 3 (2005): 106–27.

Shepard, Todd. *The Invention of Decolonization: The Algerian War and the Remaking of France*. Ithaca, NY: Cornell University Press, 2008.

Siméant, Johanna. *La cause des sans-papiers*. Sciences Po University Press, 1998.

Simon, Patrick. 'The Choice of Ignorance: The Debate on Ethnic and Racial Statistics in France'. *French Politics, Culture & Society* 26 (2008): 7–31. https://doi.org/10.3167/fpcs.2008.260102.

Simon, Patrick. 'Comment la lutte contre les discriminations est passée à droite'. *Mouvements* 52, no. 4 (2007): 153–63. https://doi.org/10.3917/mouv.052.0153.

Simon, Patrick, and Angéline Escafré-Dublet. 'Représenter la diversité en politique: une reformulation de la dialectique de la différence et de l'égalité par la doxa républicaine'. *Raisons politiques* 35, no. 3 (2009): 125–41, https://doi.org/10.3917/rai.035.0125.

Simon, Patrick, Dominique Meurs and Ariane Pailhé. 'Persistance des inégalités entre générations liées à l'immigration: l'accès à l'emploi des immigrés et de leurs descendants en France'. *Population* 61, no. 5–6 (2006): 763–801. https://doi.org/10.3917/popu.605.0763.

Snow, David, Rens Vliegenthart and Catherine Corrigall-Brown. 'Framing the French Riots: A Comparative Study of Frame Variation'. *Social Forces* 86 (2007): 385–415. https://doi.org/10.1353/sof.2008.0004.

Spire, Alexis. *Etrangers à la carte*. Paris: Grasset, 2005.

Stalker, Peter. 'Migration Trends and Migration Policy in Europe', *International Migration* 40, no. 5 (2002): 151–79, https://doi.org/10.1111/1468-2435.00215.

Stoler, Ann Laura. Frederick Cooper, et Christian Jeanmougin, *Repenser le colonialisme*. Paris: Payot, 2013.

Stora, Benjamin. *La gangrène et l'oubli: La mémoire de la guerre d'Algérie*. Paris: La Découverte, 1992.

Stora, Benjamin, and Linda Amiri. *Algériens en France: 1954–1962: la guerre, l'exil, la vie*. Paris: Autrement, 2012.

Stovall, Tyler. 'Universalisme, différence et invisibilité. Essai sur la notion de race dans l'histoire de la France contemporaine'. Translated by Maurice Genty, *Cahiers d'histoire. Revue d'histoire critique*, n°. 96–7 (2005): 63–90, https://doi.org/10.4000/chrhc.956.

Taguieff, Pierre-Andre. *The Force of Prejudice: On Racism and Its Doubles.* Minneapolis: University of Minnesota Press, 2001.

Tapinos, Georges. *L'immigration étrangère en France: 1946–1973.* Paris: University Press of France, 1971.

Thiesse, Anne-Marie. *The Creation of National Identities: Europe, 18th–20th Centuries.* Leiden: Brill, 2021.

Thomson, Alistair. 'Moving Stories: Oral History and Migration Studies'. *Oral History* 27, no. 1 (1999): 24–37.

Thomson, Mike. 'Paris Liberation Made "Whites Only"', 6 April 2009. http://news.bbc.co.uk/2/hi/europe/7984436.stm.

Tissot, Sylvie. *L'Etat et les quartiers. Genèse d'une catégorie de l'action publique – Sylvie Tissot,* 2007. https://www.decitre.fr/livres/l-etat-et-les-quartiers-9782020914857.html.

Tissot, Sylvie. 'Une "discrimination informelle"?: Usages du concept de mixité sociale dans la gestion des attributions de logements HLM'. *Actes de la recherche en sciences sociales* 159, no. 4 (2005): 54–69. https://doi.org/10.3917/arss.159.0054.

Tribalat, Michèle, Patrick Simon and Benoît Riandey. *De l'immigration à l'assimilation: enquête sur les populations d'origine étrangère en France.* Paris: INED, 1996.

Vermeren, Hugo. *Les Italiens à Bône (1865–1940): Migrations méditerranéennes et colonisations de peuplement en Algérie.* French School of Rome Press, 2022.

Vertovec, Steven. 'Super-Diversity and Its Implications'. *Ethnic and Racial Studies* 30, no. 6 (2007): 1024–54, https://doi.org/10.1080/01419870701599465.

Vidal, Cécile, ed. *Français? La nation en débat entre colonies et métropole, XVIe–XIXe siècle.* Paris: School of Advanced Studies in Social Sciences Press, 2014.

Vidal, Cécile. 'Francité et situation coloniale. Nation, empire et race en Louisiane française (1699–1769)'. *Annales. Histoire, sciences sociales* 64, no. 5 (2009): 1019–50.

Viet, Vincent. *La France immigrée: Construction d'une politique 1914–1997.* Paris: Fayard, 1998.

Waddington, David, Fabien Jobard and Mike King. *Rioting in the UK and France: A Comparative Analysis.* Cullompton: Willan, 2009.

Weber, Eugen. *Peasants into Frenchmen: The Modernization of Rural France, 1870–1914.* Stanford University Press, 1976.

Weil, Patrick. *How to Be French: Nationality in the Making since 1789.* Translated by Catherine Porter. Durham, NC: Duke University Press, 2008.

Weil, Patrick. *La France et ses étrangers: L'aventure d'une politique de l'immigration de 1938 à nos jours.* Paris: Gallimard, 1991.

Weil, Patrick. 'Lifting the Veil'. *French Politics, Culture & Society* 22, no. 3 (2004): 142–9.

Yelles-Chaouche, Hédia. 'Africa Fête, une lutte culturelle des travailleurs immigrés', *Hommes & Migrations* 1330, no. 3 (2020): 73–5.

Index